The Organization of American States as the Advocate and Guardian of Democracy

An Insider's Critical Assessment of Its Role in Promoting and Defending Democracy

Rubén M. Perina

University Press of America,® Inc.
Lanham • Boulder • New York • Toronto • Plymouth, UK

Copyright © 2015 by University Press of America,® Inc.
4501 Forbes Boulevard, Suite 200, Lanham, Maryland 20706
UPA Acquisitions Department (301) 459-3366

Unit A, Whitacre Mews, 26-34 Stannary Street,
London SE11 4AB, United Kingdom

Library of Congress Control Number: 2015945855
ISBN: 978-0-7618-6644-2 (pbk : alk. paper)—ISBN: 978-0-7618-6645-9 (electronic)

∞™ The paper used in this publication meets the minimum requirements of American
National Standard for Information Sciences Permanence of Paper for Printed Library
Materials, ANSI/NISO Z39.48-1992.

Contents

Preface

As democracy has become the preferred system of government in the hemisphere in the past thirty years or so, its promotion and defense have also become the cornerstone and raison d'être of the Organization of American States (OAS)–the central and principal inter-governmental institution in the Western Hemisphere. This book presents a comprehensive, substantive and in-depth analysis of the Organization's new role in promoting and defending democracy in the Americas, as well as the constraints and challenges it faces in performing such a role. The book reflects my strong belief in the value of promoting representative democracy, as well as my conviction that it is indeed the best system of government for the Americas. And I hope it also echoes my unwavering belief in the Organization's usefulness, relevance and potential as the most important hemispheric multilateral organization for the promotion and defense of democracy and human rights.

My intention here is to share the knowledge and experience that I acquired over more than thirty years of working at the OAS (1978–2010) on issues of democracy promotion. Throughout my time at the OAS, until this day, I have studied, thought, written and taught about the inter-American system and hemispheric relations, the OAS work in democracy promotion and democratic politics in Latin America. My ideas and reflections about these subjects have also resulted from countless discussions with OAS colleagues, diplomats, academics, students, young political leaders, legislators and politicians in general throughout the Americas.

Some acknowledgements are in order, however. My interest in the inter-American system and the OAS originated with a course I took on the subject, taught by Professor Henry Wells during my graduate studies at the University of Pennsylvania. Professor Wells was also my thesis advisor and his wisdom, generosity, and patience helped me navigate the intricacies of the

Ph.D. process. I also learned about electoral observations from him, as he was an advisor to the OAS mission to the Dominican Republic in 1966 and later participated in election monitoring in Costa Rica, Bolivia, Honduras, and Nicaragua. So, much gratitude goes to him for introducing me to what turned out to be the main focus of my professional career.

When lecturing about institution building, I always stress to my students that institutions, as organizations, are social, human entities. And that is why I must refer now to those individuals that had a considerable impact on my career at the OAS. In the summer of 1978, Dr. Roberto Etchepareborda, a senior official in the Secretariat for Education, Science and Culture during Alejandro Orfila's administration, and a prominent historian, politician and diplomat from Argentina, asked me to join the Organization to implement a program that he and Henry Raymont had designed to support the development of Latin American and International Studies in Latin American universities—incipient fields of study in those days. Not only did he become my unofficial advisor for my doctoral dissertation on military governments in Argentina, but was also my mentor on the inevitable, but unknown to me then, complex and complicated bureaucratic politics of an international organization like the OAS. I could not have been more fortunate, and to this day I remain thankful to him for the opportunity to start my professional career at the OAS. I also owe a tremendous professional debt to José Lacret, Ambassador Robert Sayre, Ronald Scheman, Raul Allard and Ambassador Hugo de Zela for their guidance, trust, support and friendship. My gratitude also goes to Secretaries General João Clemente Baena Soares and César Gaviria for trusting me with significant assignments as head of electoral observation missions in Paraguay, Guatemala, Colombia, and Venezuela. I would be remiss here not to mention how much I benefited from working closely with such a fine colleagues and friends as Marcelo Álvarez, Jaime Aparicio, Jean M. Arrighi, Anne Marie Blackman, Moisés Benamor, Bill Berenson, Jorge Calderón, Marcelo Elissetche, María de los Milagros Freyre, Steve Griner, Rodrigo Idrovo, Ana M. Katz, Jorge Kaufman, Enrique Lagos, Raúl Lago, Katalina Montaña, Javier Montes, Eduardo Núñez, José Luis Ramírez, Ronny Rodriguez, Elizabeth Spehar, María F. Trigo, Silverio Zebral, Pablo Zúñiga, Ana María Villena and many others in the Unit for the Promotion of Democracy and other OAS offices. Much of my personal, professional and intellectual growth is owed to them and to the experiences I had as an OAS official in the field and at headquarters, and I am proud and honored to have worked with all of them in the service of the Organization and its member states. This book in many ways reflects my discussions and exchanges with them and others outside the organization through the years. But errors, excesses or omissions are only my responsibility.

Last but not least I want to express my appreciation to Professors Cynthia McClintock and Robert Maguire of George Washington University's Latin

American and Hemispheric Studies Program at the Elliot School of International Affairs, and to Arturo Valenzuela, Erick Langer and Eusebio Mujal-León of Georgetown University's Center for Latin American Studies at the Edmund Walsh School of Foreign Service, all of whom have been kind enough to allow me to teach about the OAS and the promotion of democracy. Their graduate and undergraduate students' challenges, questions and discussions have also helped shape and refine my thinking about the subjects of this book. And, of course, my immense gratitude goes to my beloved daughter, Anna Perina, a senior at University of Virginia, who has patiently edited and commented on the first version of every chapter in this book. My appreciation is also due to Anna Chisman, who copyedited the manuscript.

The book is dedicated to Edith Quintrell, my wife and best friend of twenty-five years, and to Anna and Natalia Perina, wonderful and loving daughters.

March 10, 2015

Abbreviations

AECID: Spanish Agency for International Cooperation and Development
ALBA: Bolivarian Alliance of the Americas
CAF: Andean Development Corporation
CDB: Caribbean Development Bank
CELAC: Community of Latin American and Caribbean States
CIDA: Canadian International Development Agency
ECLAC: Economic Commission for Latin America and the Caribbean
EU: European Union
IACHR: Inter-American Commission on Human Rights
IDB: Inter-American Development Bank
IADC: Inter-American Democratic Charter
IFES: International Foundation for Electoral Systems
MERCOSUR: Common Market of the South
NDI: National Democratic Institute
OAS: Organization of American States
SPA/OAS: Secretariat for Political Affairs of the OAS
UNASUR: Union of South American Nations
UNDP: United Nations Development Program
UPD/OAS: OAS Unit for the Promotion of Democracy
USAID: United States Agency for International Development

Chapter One

Introduction

NATURE AND PURPOSE OF THIS BOOK

In the founding Charter of the Organization of American States (OAS) of 1948, the member states stated that "the solidarity of the American States and the high aims which are sought through it require the political organization of those States on the basis of the effective exercise of representative democracy." In 1985, they added that the Organization's main purpose is to "promote and consolidate" democracy. Later, in an unprecedented commitment, they also recognized and agreed in the Inter-American Democratic Charter that representative democracy is "indispensable for the stability, peace and development of the region," and that the "peoples of the Americas have the right to democracy and that their governments have the obligation to promote and defend it."

I believe that the OAS, as the nucleus and principal intergovernmental organization of the inter-American system, can play this new role in a significant and effective way, always provided that its members are united and fully committed. The Organization can be a unifying and useful instrument of cooperation for the promotion and protection of democracy and human rights, and for the security and peace of the hemisphere. It is *par excellence* the principal hemispheric forum where South, Central and North American and Caribbean nation-states come together to dialogue, negotiate and cooperate on those and related issues.

This book examines from the perspective of an insider and practitioner how exactly this multilateral institution promotes and defends democracy among its member states; points out the tensions, weaknesses and shortcomings that constrain its performance, and suggests in the final chapter some ways of strengthening and improving the Organization.

1

This unique perspective offers substantive information, insight, and theoretical and empirical analysis that provides readers with greater knowledge and understanding of the complex workings of the Organization, so that they can adequately and accurately assess, criticize, praise or make recommendations about its performance in fulfilling its mandates and role. This analysis will also enable readers to understand how an international organization functions, particularly in an environment that involves national and local politics, relations among member states and diplomatic and bureaucratic politics within the Permanent Council and the Secretariat. It will also show how exactly the OAS performs the day-to-day work of democracy promotion, ranging from policy formulation of guidelines to the design and implementation of technical/political programs, and illustrate the complexities, constraints and limitations of this line of work. It is intended to shed light on the complicated tasks involved in fostering the strengthening and consolidation of democratic institutions, values, and practices.

This book should be of interest to several audiences, as democracy promotion is becoming an increasingly important field of study related to political science and international relations, as well as a growing professional occupation in international organizations, government agencies and non-governmental organizations. It should also be useful both for classroom analysis and as a reference for further research. In addition, it provides the relevant conceptual and practical tools for diplomats, bureaucrats and practitioners involved in policy making and the design of guidelines and instruments for democracy promotion, as well as in planning and implementing programs in the field.

THE CRITICS: EXTERNAL AND INTERNAL

In recent years, critics of the OAS and its Secretary General, from opposing ideological sides, have shown only limited knowledge and understanding of its complex and nuanced nature. Academics, media commentators, so-called experts from think-tanks, politicians, government officials and even diplomats often criticize the Organization's behavior in democracy promotion without properly grasping its inner institutional arrangements, its history, its contradictory and conflicting principles or the internal political differences among its members. They do not fully or adequately address these factors that limit or condition its performance in this critical and increasingly relevant subject of democracy promotion.

Critics tend to analyze the OAS exclusively from the "outside in" perspective and to concentrate on its "high-politics" level of democracy promotion (policy statements, declarations, resolutions, sanctions), without offering a complementary "inside out", "low politics" (technical assistance) view of democracy promotion. Almost invariably, they treat the Organization as an autonomous, monolithic, and supranational entity. Mostly, they ignore the very relevant and determining fact that it is in fact an intergovernmental organization, dependent on the will of its thirty-five members and the dynamics of their relations, which are asymmetrical in some ways and recurrently tense and conflictive; and that its very institutional structure is divided, frequently producing tension and disappointments. In times of ideological division and lack of consensus amongst its members, either or both can paralyze the Organization. These fundamental realities are generally analyzed, if at all, as an afterthought.

Recently published books fall into the usual superficial analysis and criticism. For example, Legler and Boniface's book, *Protecting Democracy* (2007), a collection of scholarly essays that recount and evaluate the OAS experience in promoting democracy in the Americas, does provide useful analysis and critical assessment of relevant cases and issues, but it is essentially an academic exercise that does not explore in depth the complex inner workings of the Organization in the performance of its role. A more recent book by Monica Herz, *The Organization of American States* (2011), presents a comprehensive survey of the evolution of the inter-American system and of the role played by the OAS in the security and democracy fields. She correctly points to the OAS's contributions to disseminating the norms of democracy and to the construction of a liberal democratic order in the region, as well as its contribution to global and regional governance. She criticizes the Organization for being "ineffective with authoritarian regression," but does not explore in depth the internal and external dynamics that are responsible for its "ineffectiveness," a shortcoming that is all too common in academic works on international organizations and on the OAS in particular. There are, however, books on the OAS that do provide more of an insider's perspective and are useful as historical references, but do not cover most of the significant developments in the field of democracy promotion of the past twenty years or so. Such are the texts by Stoetzer (1987), Scheman (1988), Vaky and Muñoz (1993) and Farer (1996).

Nevertheless, the general lack of understanding in academia of the true nature and functioning of the Organization is shared by the media, the political class, some diplomats (surprisingly) and, more understandably, the public in general. This is not unexpected, since academic studies in International Relations, Latin American Studies, or International Law, or even in Diplomatic Academies throughout the hemisphere, for the most part do not offer a course on the OAS or the inter-American system. The OAS is only mentioned or analyzed briefly in required courses related to international organizations. One rare exception, and an example of a course that could be offered, is the course taught by the writer at George Washington and Georgetown Universities in Washington, D.C.

Most critics usually carelessly assume that the Organization is an autonomous, monolithic organization that can act independently of its thirty-five member states. They fail to understand that decisions by the Organization's collective governing bodies to condemn or sanction a member state for violating OAS norms require multilateral negotiations, compromise and consensus, and that decisions are frequently based on the lowest common denominator. This practice frequently dilutes decisions and renders them anodyne, which in effect may paralyze the institution and make it appear ineffective if not irrelevant, precisely on those issues that are critical to its raison d'être.

This failure to understand the Organization properly also leads to the prevalence of misconceptions and unwarranted assumptions and expectations, as well as negative views and misplaced criticism of the Organization. While some of this criticism does not have conscious political or ideological motivations, and in some cases may even be valid and to the point, it can also be erroneous and marked by intentional distortions uttered for domestic political consumption.

Critics also regularly ignore the fact that the Secretary General (SG/OAS) does not have the autonomy or the authority to act or make policy independently without the approval or permission from the collective bodies or from the member state involved. Misunderstanding this reality leads observers and critics to ask or demand from the OAS and/or its Secretary General decisions and actions that are incompatible with its institutional nature and norms. This complexity and limitation, like that of any inter-governmental multilateral organization, is frequently considered only as an afterthought, rarely analyzed in its true dimension and consequences (Cheema 2005) (Diamond 2008) (Pevehouse 2005) (McCoy 2007) (Boniface 2007) (Mainwaring and Pérez-Liñán 2013) (Herz 2011).[1]

In the OAS, this complex reality generates constant tensions and limitations that constrain if not paralyze its performance in promoting and defending democracy. Nevertheless, as we shall see below, while most of the criticism is misplaced and indicates a partial understanding of the nature of the Organization and its inherent tensions and limitations, others make valid points and are quite useful in understanding those very tensions and limitations (Shifter July 2009) (El-Hage 2010) (Murray September 2014).

Most of the criticism, however, falls in the context of the overarching tension between the new mandate for promoting democracy and the traditional principle of non-intervention. Thus, for some, the Organization interferes too much in the internal affairs of member states, and for others, it does not do enough to fulfill its mandate for promoting and defending democracy wherever and whenever it is threatened and violated. For instance, the so called "right wing" or more "conservative-moderate" critics denounced the OAS suspension of Honduras after the 2009 coup against President Zelaya as an "interventionist" overreaction led by Venezuela and the *chavista* coalition at the OAS,[2] as unnecessary given that elections were to take place as previously scheduled, and as unproductive because it cut off all communication with the new government. But they failed to recognize the strength of the commitment that most members have made to defend democracy, particularly in the face of an outright coup d'état. It would have been more appropriate to criticize the OAS and its Secretary General for not "intervening" before the coup to stop Zelaya's attempt to force a referendum to allow for his reelection in violation of the Honduran Constitution (Latin American Advisor Newsletter 2009) (The Human Rights Foundation, 2010).[3]

The different perspectives on the Venezuelan political situation are another case in point. For the Venezuelan *chavista* government, Secretary Insulza's request to visit Venezuela during the student strikes and protests in 2011 was considered "interventionist" and as responding to "pressures" from the United States and Canada. Similarly, in March 2014, the *chavista* coalition at the OAS prevented Panama's attempt to have a Venezuelan opposition leader, Maria Corina Machado, speak to the Council about the situation in her country in an open session,[4] as it would be considered an "intervention" in Venezuela's internal affairs. Moreover, any attempt by the SG/OAS or any of its members to question the *chavistas'* violations of Venezuela's electoral, constitutional and human rights norms and the principles of the Inter-American Democratic Charter would be branded as "interventionist" and an instrument of U.S. imperialism. But the *chavistas* blatantly ignored and prevented activation of the existing collective commitment to defend and promote democracy.

Bolivia, Ecuador and Venezuela have strongly criticized the reports of the OAS Inter-American Commission on Human Rights (IACHR) on human rights violations (press freedoms in particular), as well as its precautionary measures and decisions on reparations for past violations, as interventionist, excessive and unjustified, and have accused the Commission of responding to U.S. interests and pressures. At the 2012 inaugural session of the OAS General Assembly held in Bolivia, Bolivian President Evo Morales, and Rafael Correa, the President of Ecuador, derided the Organization and accused the IACHR of "being totally influenced by the U.S. government and NGOs financed by capitalist interests." They also advised that it must change to adapt to the new realities of the hemisphere or die.

President Correa in particular has called the OAS obsolete and has requested that the Commission be transferred from its current location in Washington, D.C. to another member state. He has also expressed Ecuador's intention of withdrawing from the Human Rights Convention, following the example of Venezuela, which has in fact denounced it and withdrawn from it.[5] His Foreign Minister, Ricardo Patiño, has also said that "the OAS had come to the end of its useful life."[6]

Similarly, President Chavez of Venezuela publicly attacked the two pillars of the inter-American system of human rights: The Inter-American Court and the Commission. He has not allowed the Commission's visits since 2002 and has branded them "useless and interventionist," mainly because of the Commission's 2010 Report and the Court's decisions against *chavista* court rulings that violate the Convention to the detriment of Venezuelan citizens.[7] Even Brazil has criticized the system as interventionist and biased as a result of the Commission's precautionary order against the construction of the Belo Monte River hydroelectric dam in the Amazon, to the point of having withdrawn its Ambassador to the Organization.

This criticism, however, fails to understand (because of sheer ignorance or intentional distortion) the independent nature of the Commission and fails to differentiate it from the OAS at large. While the Commission is part of the Organization (Art. 106 of the OAS Charter), it is an independent body, which does not receive directives from member states or from the Secretary General, although it must be diplomatically mindful of their opinions and concerns.[8] The attack, blurring the subtle but significant difference between the specific nature of the Commission and that of the OAS as a whole, was indeed a deliberate effort to reduce the Commission's independence and, more generally, to diminish the OAS role in promoting and defending democracy (Gaviria 2013) (Aparicio and Perina 2011).

Finally, the *chavista* critics deliberately ignore, for demagogic reasons and domestic consumption, that these days, the U.S. government does not dominate or manipulate the Organization. In fact, observers and diplomats regularly express dismay at the apparent lack of U.S. interest and very low-profile presence in the Organization.[9] Moreover, criticism of the Secretary General for his supposed "interventionism" in the internal affairs of Venezuela seems unwarranted, as his pronouncements about violations of the opposition's human and political rights have always been timid and unconvincing, in his desire not to offend the *chavistas*.

On the other hand, the Venezuelan political opposition to the *chavista* regime has repeatedly requested (unrealistically perhaps) Insulza's forceful "intervention" and has strongly criticized his lack of appropriate response to the regime's frequent and flagrant violations of human rights, its blatant manipulation of the electoral process in order to remain in power, and its political persecution and jailing of prominent opposition figures—all of which contravene the Inter-American Democratic Charter.[10] Furthermore, many in the pro-democracy "liberal" camp have criticized the Secretary's comment that the "OAS will not intervene in Venezuela," since, according to him (inexplicably), conditions in that country did not warrant the application of the Democratic Charter.[11] They have also condemned his failure to raise the issue of Venezuela's eroding democracy at the Permanent Council as the Democratic Charter allows him to do. However, they ignored the fact that such a move would probably be voted down by the *chavista* coalition, even though it would not be "interventionist" because it is, after all, a collective responsibility agreed to by all member states, including Venezuela, when they signed the Democratic Charter.

On the media front, a 2010 editorial in the *Washington Post*, a newspaper that rarely comments on OAS activities, derided the Organization for being led by "leftist" Latin American governments and its Secretary General, and the "champions" of democracy such as Argentina and Brazil for not saying much about President Ortega's manipulation of the legislative, judicial and electoral branches so that he could stand for reelection, in violation of the Nicaraguan Constitution. The *BBC en Español* followed with an editorial that criticized the Secretary General for neglecting the destruction of democracy in Ecuador, Honduras, Nicaragua and Venezuela and for not enforcing the Democratic Charter or at least demanding that its principles be respected. Moreover, according to Andrés Oppenheimer, a prominent columnist from the *Miami Herald*, the OAS member states and its Secretary General made a bad mistake in Nicaragua (November 2011) by giving Ortega's electoral victory a "seemingly unconditional blessing" for what most observers considered a questionable and unconstitutional electoral process. This media criticism, however, once more, overlooks the complex nature of the Organization. It ignores the fact that the Secretary General has limited actual powers to "intervene" in these cases (even if he were willing to do so), and seems to disregard the members' "ideological" fragmentation and tension around the principle of non-intervention and the collective commitment to promote and defend democracy, which effectively paralyzes it.

However, there occasionally appears some criticism that is to the point, accurate and valid, pointing to the non-autonomous and non-monolithic nature of the Organization and reflecting the frequent tensions that arise between member states and the Secretariat. This criticism usually come from "insiders" or, more accurately, from "outsiders" with information provided from inside the Secretariat. For example, in 2011, the former Panamanian Ambassador to the OAS, Guillermo Cochez, disclosed that the Organization was in a state of "chaos." He pointed out that financial reserves had been depleted; that there was no money to repair buildings, implement technical assistance programs or provide job security for professional staff; that several countries were not paying their quotas and there were even rumors of creating a parallel organization. He went on to say that, as a consequence, there were constant layoffs and ongoing job insecurity, which translated into increasing disillusionment, and uneven professional commitment among staff—the main capital of the Organization (Cochez 2011). He also criticized the Secretary General for contracting political friends as advisors in "trust positions" and as heads of Electoral Observation Missions in violation of existing rules, for administrative and financial mismanagement, and for not properly informing the Permanent Council.

This "insider's" report coincides with Democratic Senators Robert Menéndez and John Kerry and Republican Senators Richard Lugar and Marco Rubio's harsh assessment of the OAS situation in November 2012. Their bipartisan letter points to a "lack of strategic focus" and faults the Secretary General for ineffective management and financial practices "to keep the Organization afloat," and for "hiring high-fee contractors" and "senior level political appointees"—a practice which has demoralized "the Organization's most precious asset, its experienced and talented human capital." The Senators' letter was followed by an unusual Act of the US 113th Congress in July 2013, which proposed, among other things, that the Organization cut the U.S. contribution of US$48 million, which represents 60% of the regular budget, to 49%; reduce its mandates to eight core priority functions, and formally integrate the Summit process into the work of the OAS.[12]

Both congressional actions, however, while revealing tensions between a member state and the Secretary General, ignore the fact that the Secretary General has limited powers to implement what they recommended, and that practically all of their recommendations, if they were to be implemented, would require a consensus and a collective agreement by all the member states. In addition, their recommendations require proper follow up and supervision by the U.S delegation to the Organization—which, given its low profile in the Organization in the past few years, is unlikely to happen. Moreover, it fails to realize that eight priorities are no priority at all, and that priorities like "fostering economic growth" and "facilitating trade" are beyond the Organization's expertise and human and financial resource capabilities, and would be best assigned to the Inter-American Development Bank, the Caribbean Development Bank, the Andean Development Corporation (CAF) or the World Bank.

Thus, most of the criticism of the OAS briefly reviewed above fails to address properly, on the one hand, the declining value and applicability of the traditional all-inclusive, absolute principle of non-intervention—particularly in the face of the growing collective interest in the promotion and defense of democracy—and on the other, it also fails to recognize the limits of the applicability of the new principle of the promotion of democracy. Additionally, in their analysis, they err in not focusing on or assessing adequately the non-autonomous, non-monolithic and fragmented nature of the Organization, as well as the limitations, tensions and even paralysis they generate. However, the "insider" critics do make valid points about the Secretariat's bureaucratic and leadership deficiencies, a source of friction and tension between member states and the Secretary General, which, incidentally, the "outsider" critics rarely examine in depth.

Thus, the following Chapters attempt an instructive, substantive response to the critics; they seek to correct a generalized misunderstanding about the nature of the OAS and its role in promoting democracy; and they try to shed light on the intergovernmental non-autonomous nature of the Organization and its complex internal and contextual dynamics.

SURVIVAL OF DEMOCRACY AND RELEVANCE OF THE OAS

International organizations such as the OAS do matter and have a significant role to play in this increasingly interdependent and globalized world—despite the "neo-realists" view of them as irrelevant because they "merely reflect the interests of States." (Snyder 2002). Of course they reflect their interests: they are tools of their foreign policy. But when States seek cooperation (which is actually quite frequently, for whatever purpose or interest), international organizations offer a forum for negotiation, collaboration, consensus building and agreements on world issues. As such, they are indeed quite relevant and useful in today's world, where most of the problems or challenges confronting nation-states are transnational, whether globally or regionally. These issues, such as democracy, security, energy, development, trade and finance, environment, natural disasters, migration, crime and drugs, disease, and others, are "inter-mestic," that is, they are partly domestic and partly international. Policies and actions to manage them require cooperation and coordination. None can be successfully tackled by unilateral action, no matter how powerful a nation-state may be.

This is precisely why multilateral organizations are relevant if not indispensable: They are the main instruments of and for international cooperation. That is why they exist and why governments create them. Within this general context, this book maintains that the promotion and defense of democracy has become a significant subject of international cooperation because democracy has become a supreme value in the international system, and its exercise is correlated with prosperity and peace, as demonstrated by the "democratic peace" literature. Promotion and protection of democracy has not only become a major foreign policy objective of most democratic states, but it is also a growing field of study and of professional occupation.

In this hemisphere, as member states of the OAS (except Cuba) have resumed democratic governance since the mid-1980s, they have also turned their hemispheric organization into an instrument for the collective promotion and protection of representative democracy. This new role of the Organization in many ways represents a historic achievement for its members. For many of them, democracy and its collective defense has been a historical aspiration that dates back to their origins as independent republics in the early 1800s.

To understand properly today's OAS central role in democracy promotion, it is also imperative to understand also the role that democracy has played in Latin American history and in the evolution of the Organization. Chapter 2 succinctly shows democracy's place and role in Latin American history, and how it has survived historical challenges from *caudillismo* and dictatorships, internal and regional wars, oligarchical regimes, anti-democratic ideologies, such as anarchism, socialism, fascism, Nazism, communism, populism, and Castroite communist guerrillas and repressive military regimes. The new republics were also challenged from abroad by ex-colonial powers attempting to restore their dominions after the collapse of Napoleon, by neo-colonial imperialist powers trying to gain a foothold in the Americas in the midst of anarchy and tyranny, and by U.S. military interventions. Chapter 3, also succinctly, shows the OAS evolutionary process, which included several hemispheric conferences held throughout the Americas in the midst of periods of disagreements and agreements, tension, confrontation and cooperation between the United States and Latin American countries, mainly around fundamental principles and values of international and inter-American relations, such as the sovereignty and juridical equality of states, non-intervention, security, peace, development and democracy.

The OAS is indeed the oldest intergovernmental organization in the world. Although its member states created it officially in 1948 when they approved its founding Charter, in reality, the Charter was only the culmination of a historical process in inter-American relations that began with an inter-American conference in Washington, D.C. in 1889/90 and the establishment of the Pan American Union in 1910 at the Fourth Inter-American Conference, with headquarters on the same site where it is today in the U.S. capital.

Chapter 4 defines what democracy promotion is and explains how it is practiced, namely through "high and low politics" approaches. It examines the origin of democracy's Third Wave and explains the "idealist" and "realist" rationale for democracy promotion, as argued by U.S. academics and government officials. Chapter 4 also identifies the national and international actors that engage in democracy promotion, and reviews some of its critics, the "neo-realists" and the "sequentialists," as well as the emerging challenges from a new wave of authoritarian "alternative models."

Chapter 5 identifies the new multilateral diplomatic/juridical instruments that member states have developed ("high-politics") since 1984–85 to perform this critical new role of promoting and protecting democracy, and examines in detail how those instruments (such as the Cartagena Protocol and General Assembly resolution 1080) were used to restore democracy in Haiti, Peru and Guatemala and to prevent its breakdown in Paraguay, for example. In a historically unprecedented way, member states committed themselves to these instruments in order to collectively promote and defend representative democracy whenever threatened or interrupted in a member state, and even to suspend from the Organization a government that resulted from a non-democratic process, such as a military coup (Washington Protocol of 1992).

By 2001, the governments of the hemisphere agreed to further strengthen and consolidate those instruments by approving the Inter-American Democratic Charter (IADC). The Charter represents significant progress in the collective effort to promote and protect democracy, since for the first time OAS members agreed that the peoples of the Americas have a right to democracy and their governments the obligation to promote and defend it.

Chapter 6 examines the significance of the Inter-American Democratic Charter for democracy in the Americas, and evaluates its strengths and weaknesses, with its successes and shortcomings. It argues that as a result of the prevalence of democracy in the hemisphere since the 1980s, and the development of the instruments mentioned, a new paradigm is evolving, one which is reflected in an inter-American democratic regime or system of regional governance for democracy. Chapter 6 thoroughly reviews its applications in Bolivia, Ecuador, Guatemala, Haiti, Honduras, Nicaragua and Venezuela, and examines in some detail the emergence of neo-authoritarian, populist pseudo-democracies (Bolivia, Ecuador, Nicaragua, Venezuela) that resist and challenge the liberal representative democracy model, violating not only their own democratic constitutions but also their own commitment to the Democratic Charter itself.

Chapter 7 provides an in-depth analysis of technical assistance programs, or "low-politics" instruments designed and implemented to foster the consolidation of democratic institutions, values and practices at the operational, in-country level. From an insider's point of view, the Chapter reveals, with examples of OAS programs on the promotion of democratic values and practices, the training of young political leaders and the strengthening of legislative institutions, the complexity and intricacies of the bureaucratic and political/diplomatic processes involved in their implementation. Chapter 7 includes an innovative approach to conceptualizing democracy that brings theory and practice together to enable well-focused technical assistance programs to be designed and implemented to contribute to the consolidation and strengthening of democracy in collective or individual efforts. This combined theoretical and practical approach has not been studied adequately. We argue that the OAS experience provides a foundation for building a theoretical model that can be useful in analyzing and assessing democracy promotion policies and practices, and can also be used to execute programs to promote the consolidation and strengthening of democratic values, practices and institutions.

Chapter 8 gives special attention to OAS Electoral Observation Missions (EOMs), their nature, objectives and functions. Today, electoral monitoring is one of the most visible and useful instruments in the field of democracy

promotion used by international "promoters." In 1989, member states authorized, albeit reluctantly, the Secretary General to organize electoral observation missions to member states that so requested. Since then, the OAS Secretariat has dispatched close to 250 EOMs to about half of its members. EOMs
have become a permanent feature of their electoral processes. Chapter 8
evaluates their successes and shortcomings, and also shows from an insider's
perspective the complexity and intricacies of the bureaucratic and political/
diplomatic processes involved in their implementation.

Chapter 9 argues that democracy has survived, and that in the late 1980s,
the OAS regained its relevance (if momentarily) as the central inter-
American institution, basically as a result of its new role in the promotion
and protection of democracy. Chapter 9 reflects on the strengths of democracy and points to the obsolescence of coups d'état and military dictatorships,
as well as to the prevalence of elections as the only way to select leaders. It
posits that these developments plus the growing universal respect for human
rights and the international protection thereof present a challenge to the principles of absolute sovereignty and non-intervention, which are becoming
outdated—although with lingering anachronistic rhetorical exceptions. This
Chapter also contends that, while resisted by those who still hold obsolete
Cold War views, the presence of the United States and Canada in the Organization, if somewhat diluted of late, is one of its strengths and value added,
because their presence makes the Organization unique as the only institutionalized forum where all the hemispheric democracies can dialogue, negotiate
and cooperate on issues of democracy, human rights, security and peace. It
concludes that the OAS, somewhat debilitated by an "ideologically" fragmented hemisphere, maintains its relevance as the central and go-to institution of the inter-American system for the promotion and protection of democracy and human rights. It is still the institution to activate and legitimize
multilateral action in cases of threats to or interruption of the democratic
order in a member state.

COMPLEXITIES, TENSIONS AND LIMITATIONS

The OAS, like all multilateral organizations, is not a supranational and
monolithic organization that can act on its own, autonomously and independent of its member states. It is an intergovernmental organization, and as
such, its nature, mandates, roles, policies and actions inevitably depend on
the political will and consent of its thirty-five member states. They created
the Organization, they pay for it and they direct it through their Foreign
Ministries and Permanent Representatives (Ambassadors) to the Organization, who make collective decisions either at the annual General Assembly
(OAS/GA) or at the regular meetings of the Permanent Council (OAS/PC) in

Washington, D.C. [13] These two collective bodies are the principal multilateral policymaking bodies of the Organization. Decisions or mandates are formalized in resolutions—a complex process that at times can be slow, grueling and tense. The General Secretariat, the internal bureaucracy headed by the Secretary General, implements the decisions.

The Secretary General is elected every five years, represents the Organization and is its public face. Although the office does have significant internal administrative powers and responsibilities, its political and diplomatic autonomy is limited, as member states will not cede power and sovereignty to an international civil servant. [14] So, praise or blame for the Organization's performance should be directed to its member states, either to one of them, some, or all of them, and not necessarily or exclusively to the Secretary General.

The complex nature of this intergovernmental organization, as discussed in Chapter 10, is reflected in the internal interaction between the collective governing bodies and the General Secretariat around the tension between institutional dependency and autonomy. This tension limits the scope and possibilities of action by the Organization as a whole and by the Secretary General in particular, in performing their role of promoting and defending democracy. Chapter 10 also assesses the performance of the governing bodies and the Secretary General as well as their interaction on complex issues and realities—including the so-called New Strategic Vision for the Organization, the "undemocratic" and perturbing dominance of the executive branch in OAS affairs, and the current management and leadership deficiencies and shortcomings.

Tension also results from institutional obligations and the failure to comply with them, mainly around the clash between the principle of non-intervention and the collective commitment to democracy (the "democracy principle"). From a "realist" perspective, this Chapter argues that when these principles are violated and democracy is seriously threatened or interrupted, and absent a collective response to defend it or restore it, unilateral action is likely, particularly if regional or hemispheric security and peace is concerned—setting the basis for the emergence of a "Democratic Security Doctrine." The Chapter thus attempts to shed some light on the complex reality of the Organization, and endeavors to contribute to a more accurate and profound understanding of its nature and role in promoting and defending democracy.

Simultaneously, while democracy is alive and there are many hopeful signs for its enduring as the preferred system of government, it still faces significant challenges on the horizon that endanger its consolidation. Elections alone do not make a democracy whole; neither does a modicum of socio-economic progress. Elected governments must also govern democratically. Thus, Chapter 11 briefly reviews the domestic challenges to democracy arising from the lingering remnants of an authoritarian political culture of *caudillo* populism (pseudo-democracies) in various countries (the *chavista* alliance) that resists if not rejects many of the liberal values, practices and institutions of representative democracy—the very system of government all agreed to defend and promote in the Democratic Charter. In turn, these domestic developments have generated a contextual "geopolitical" division among member states that have fractured the cohesiveness of the hemispheric commitment to the OAS and its democracy promotion role. Within this fragmented geopolitical context, the *chavista* alliance has attempted to exclude the Organization from actively and effectively performing its democracy promotion role. The attempt intends to marginalize the United States and Canada from "interfering" in South American affairs, particularly Venezuela. The reasoning is that the OAS has been and is a tool of North American "imperialism"—an anachronistic and inaccurate charge since both countries, despite their declared preference for multilateralism, have not engaged the Organization, as of late, in any substantive and convincing way to further their professed interest in democracy promotion. At any rate, together with the internal tensions, weaknesses and shortcomings, these "geopolitical" developments presently tend to excessively constrain the Organization's effectiveness, particularly in preventing the erosion of democracy in certain member states.

Finally, Chapter 12 offers a series of policy recommendations for strengthening and consolidating the Organization and its instruments for collectively promoting and protecting democracy, but particularly for averting the erosion or collapse of democracy. In significant ways they represent a blueprint for how best to use and reinforce the "high politics" and "low politics" instruments that the member states have developed and applied to promote and defend democracy. The recommendations are intended to fortify the Organization's capacity to continue to be the central inter-American institution for the promotion and protection of democracy.

NOTES

1. Exceptions to this failure are Slater's work (1967) and the Inter-American Dialogue Report on the OAS (Dialogue 2006).

2. The *chavista* coalition, led originally by President Hugo Chávez of Venezuela, generally includes the countries of the Bolivarian Alliance of the Americas (ALBA in Spanish), which includes Bolivia, Cuba, Ecuador and Nicaragua plus Caribbean countries such as Dominica, Grenada, St. Kitts and Nevis, St. Lucia, and St. Vincent and the Grenadines–all beneficiaries of Venezuelan oil "largesse"—and supported if not encouraged by Argentina, Brazil and Uruguay.

3. In today's hemisphere, the "right" or conservative moderate forces constitute those governments, organizations and individuals that promote and defend "liberal" democratic institutions, values and practices crystallized in the Inter-American Democratic Charter. I prefer to call this camp "pro-democracy liberal." Contrariwise, the "left" refers to those who promote

and defend populist "progressive" regimes, which favor "participatory" (plebiscitary, direct) democracy, inclusive (clientelistic) social policies, state-run or state-dominated economies, strong control of press and political freedoms, perpetually reelectable charismatic leaders and anti-imperialistic rhetoric, "illiberal democracies", in short, as exemplified by regimes such as those running Bolivia, Ecuador, Nicaragua and Venezuela.

4. For her attempt to speak from the Panamanian chair, the President of the National Assembly stripped Machado of her Congressional immunity and unconstitutionally expelled her from the chamber on charges (unproven) of treason—a decision quickly ratified by the *chavista* Supreme Court on March 31, 2014. Strangely enough, neither the United States nor the Canadian delegations to the OAS could convince the Caribbean group to vote in favor of the meeting being open to the public and the media, let alone to let the opposition leader speak at the Council (So much for U.S. interventionism and domination of the OAS!).

5. Correa dismisses as nonsense the IACHR request concerning the newspaper *El Universo:* see http://www.infobae.com/2012/02/22/1044881-correa-evalua-anular-condena-contra-el-universo, and http://www.noticias24.com/venezuela/noticia/125439/venezuela-denuncio-a-la-convencion-americana-de-dd-hh-ante-la-oea/.

6. See http://www.infolatam.com/2011/11/23/correa-acusa-a-la-oea-de-ser-instrumento-de-ee-uu-y-espera-que-la-celac-la-reemplace/.

7. See http://www.abc.es/20100226/internacional-iberoamerica/chavez-califica-excremento-puro-201002260046.html.

8. Its seven Commissioners are elected by member states as individuals in their personal capacity and in principle do not represent any single country. Its structure and functions are regulated by its own Statute and Regulations.

9. Secretary General Insulza, himself, recently stated that times have changed and that the regular assumption that the U.S. Government intervenes (*mete las manos*) in the OAS no longer holds true, at least for the last few years. See: http://www.lavanguardia.com/politica/20141025/54417532217/no-es-facil-manejar-una-oea-con-discrepancias-ideologicas-reconoce-insulza.html.

10. For example, the opposition leader strongly criticized Insulza as a useless and inept character, when the Secretary General, disingenuously, said that he could not comment on the questioned elections of April 2014 as the OAS was not invited to observe them. See: http://www.prensalibre.com/internacional/Capriles-llama_inepto-Insulza-Venezuela_0_1000700175.html.

11. See http://www.martinoticias.com/content/segun-insulza-en-venezuela-no-hay-condiciones-para-carta-de-oea/.

12. See the full Act at: http://www.foreign.senate.gov/publications/download/oas-bill-as-pased-by-the-house.

13. Foreign Ministers also occasionally meet in special sessions of the General Assembly on democracy issues, or in Meetings of Consultation on security issues. Within the structure of the OAS, there are other less prominent collective bodies for other issue areas.

14. For detailed description of the purpose, structure and function of the Organization and its organs, see its founding Charter at www.oas.org. This site also describes in detail the programs and activities of the OAS. The role of the Secretariat and its relation with the collective bodies, in the context of the tension and contradiction between the principles of non-intervention and the promotion of democracy, will be discussed in later chapters.

Chapter Two

Democracy in the Americas

The Struggle for Survival

INTRODUCTION

To understand the current OAS role in the defense and promotion of democracy, it is necessary to review briefly the place and significance that democracy has had in Latin American history and in the evolution of the inter-American system and the Organization.

Democracy has profound roots in Latin American history. In many ways its history can be viewed as the struggle for fundamental republican/democratic values, principles and institutions, such as independence from colonial powers, political sovereignty, individual liberty, human rights and dignity, the rule of law, equality and justice, and constitutional republicanism with its limits on the central government. It has been a struggle to institutionalize and practice them, to turn them into a lasting reality.

But on their way to achieving democracy, Latin American republics—since their independence in the early 19th century—have confronted several daunting external, regional and domestic challenges, at different times and in different forms.

The Origins of Democracy: Independence and Republican Constitutions

Even as authoritarian and centralist political values and practices dominated the political culture of Spanish and Portuguese America in the colonial period, by the first half of the 18th century, "liberal" ideas from England and France and their philosophers (Locke, Montesquieu, Rousseau) and from the

17

United States (Jefferson, Madison and other Federalists, and later Thomas Paine with his *The Rights of Man, and Dissertation on the First Principles of Government*) reached Latin America and began to circulate amongst local elites, intellectuals and "*caudillos criollos*", awakening their desire for freedom and stimulating their calls and actions in favor of independence, liberty, republican/democratic institutions, political sovereignty and free trade. These liberalizing republican/democratic ideas from the North American and French revolutions spread quickly throughout Central and South America and the Caribbean in the 1800s and inspired and motivated the leaders of the independence movements that eventually overthrew colonial rule. They helped ignite the revolutionary spirit and the political and military liberalizing effort that spread throughout the Americas.

Following the wars of independence (approximately 1810–1830), most of the new republics adopted new constitutions based on liberal ideas, principles and institutions present in the Declaration of Independence and the Constitution of the United States, as well in the French and Spanish revolutionary movements. They provided substantive and concrete examples of liberal institutions and principles that could be adopted and turned into reality. The short-lived liberal monarchical Constitution of Cadiz (1812–14) also inspired Spanish America's revolutionaries. Its provisions for popular sovereignty, elections and representation, freedom of the press, separation of powers, and other democratic principles were powerfully compelling intellectual forces (Drake 2009, 31-67).

Revolutionary "liberal" leaders, both civilian and military, such as Miranda and Bolívar in the Great Colombia (Venezuela, Colombia, Ecuador and Bolivia), Belgrano, Moreno and Alberdi in Argentina, Artigas in Uruguay, Camilo Hernández in Chile, Rocafuerte in Ecuador and Peru, Martí in Cuba, José C. del Valle in Central America and Joaquin del Amor Divino Caneca in Brazil, among many others, admired and were stimulated by the revolutionary movements in the U.S. and Western Europe. Only a few leaders, however, expressed preference for constitutional monarchies (Soto Cardenas 1979, 18–45).

Most of the new constitutions included republican institutions and basic, fundamentally liberal, republican and democratic ideas. That is, they proclaimed that "all men are created equal" and affirmed their equality before the law; they protected and promoted human rights and fundamental freedoms, as well as the rights and duties of man; they incorporated principles such separation of powers to limit government power and protect individual liberties; and they established limits to centralism and presidential authority with restrictions on reelections, as well as decentralization schemes, including in some cases federalism, to avoid undue concentration of power in one person, institution or city and subsequent tyranny, as in federalist Argentina, Brazil, Colombia (up to 1885), Mexico and Venezuela. Further, these liberal constitutions asserted their nation-states' independence from foreign control and their peoples' sovereignty, and affirmed that a government, to be legitimate, must have the peoples' consent through periodic (if restricted) elections (Soto Cárdenas 1979, 28–122).

Admittedly, however, these constitutions could not actually prevent the emergence and prevalence for many years after independence of what have been called "regal presidencies." These hyper-presidencies were not subject to horizontal or vertical accountability by the legislative or judicial powers or by the provincial or local governments. Based on the tradition of Spanish colonial authoritarianism, they concentrated power in the capital, in the person of a *caudillo*, or strongman, and in the institution of the presidency. Presidents/*caudillos* became the central and most important institutional authority of the new republics. They imposed their own harsh authoritarian centralized rule to maintain order and their nation united (Drake 2009, 71–5).

Most constitutions included republican/democratic institutions. They gave the legislatures powers similar to those of the U.S. political system, with their important role in a system of checks and balances, but their elected legislators generally represented only a select electorate and followed directives from the President/caudillo. They also provided for an independent judicial power, but their courts were not known for challenging or limiting the "regal presidents" or their legislatures (Drake 2009, 37–39, 103). Elections, national and local, the principal source of legitimacy in a democracy, even if imperfect and limited, were also contemplated in the new constitutions and were part of the political scenario of the nascent republics. But the elections were indirect and laws restricted the electorate and the candidates to the propertied or salaried classes, and to literate adult males. Secret voting was not the norm and suffrage was frequently fraudulent and the source of political conflict and instability. Political parties also emerged in this period, first as Conservative and Liberals, and later as reformist parties representing the values and interests of the growing urban middle class (Drake 2009, 48–49, 96–98, 106–124).

Although these early constitutions and republican/democratic institutions were not always rigorously practiced and obeyed, they were useful legal instruments for the establishment of independence and political sovereignty. They also set the foundation and precedent for future democratic development.

Pre-OAS Challenges to Democracy

Domestic Challenges

Democracy evolved from hopeful but uncertain beginnings after the wars of independence, followed by a period of civil war and anarchy, which prevented the consolidation of the democratic and republican aspirations reflected in the founding fathers' declarations of independence and national constitutions.

Early on, the new republics had to endure years of tyranny by President/ *caudillos*, political persecution, centralism and hyper-presidentialism.[1] They were frequently challenged and resisted by the "liberal" elites who sought to establish a republican/democratic (if oligarchical) order that would limit the power of the central authority and would guarantee free trade. The result was long years of "Conservative" vs. "Liberal" forces engaged in civil wars that submerged most of Latin American countries in a vicious circle of tyranny and anarchy, isolation and backwardness (Hamill 1965) (Fagg 1963, 530–586).

By the second half of the nineteenth century, oligarchical regimes made up of competitive elites of "Liberals" and "Conservatives," who derived their power and status from agricultural production, commodity exports and state-related businesses, assumed control of the political and economic order of most of the new republics. Fearful of popular democracy because it could lead to chaos and the tyranny of the dispossessed majority, regimes restricted the electorate and practiced electoral fraud to maintain their control of the State, and became a tyranny of the minority, with the support of the military elite.

Thus, throughout most of the century, the political landscape in most of the new republics fluctuated between "tyranny and anarchy" and "countless dictatorships alternated with collapsing constitutions…and [oligarchical] governments" (Drake 2009, 88–125). (Drake 2009, 126–27, 161–62) (Smith 2005, 27).

At the turn of the new century, novel ideologies such as Socialism, Anarchism, Syndicalism, Marxism, Communism, Corporatism and Fascism reached the Americas, along with large influxes of immigrants—all originating in Western Europe. At different times and in different countries, they threatened republicanism and democracy. They also provided the ideological basis of and the excuse for the emergence of an early type of populist authoritarian regime,[2] which once again undermined and suppressed the already fragile democratic institutions in Latin America. These regimes, of the military or electoral variety, with fascist-nazi-corporatist ideologies and their charismatic leaders, also dismissed, ignored or weakened political parties, legislatures, courts and the independent press. They had no use for democratic principles and representative republican institutions; they preferred direct contact with the masses and sought to mobilize the growing working and middle class majority, either to stage coups d'état or win fraudulent elections to prevent socialist anarchy while terminating oligarchical rule.

In some countries, particularly in South America (e.g., Argentina, Brazil and Chile), these military or civilian charismatic populist leaders, imbued with nationalist, fascist/corporatist tendencies copied from Spain, Italy, Portugal and Germany, despised the "liberal oligarchical regime" but also feared the chaos and instability of unorganized and mobilized masses. They took control of the state, organized the labor movement and nationalist industrialists benefiting from import substitution, and installed populist authoritarian anti-liberal regimes, which would carry out nationalist revolutions under the banner of "order and progress" (Germani 1978, 71–73, 85–88) (Collier 1979, 402) (Malloy 1977, 3–17).

External Challenges and Early Collective Responses

The external challenges to democracy were often associated with non-democratic ideologies (from monarchism to fascism to communism), threats and interventions coming from European powers or from an interventionist U.S. government.

In the early years of the Spanish American republics, after the defeat of Napoleon in 1814, European monarchies intended to re-conquer their lost colonies and reestablish monarchical anti-liberal rule over "heretical" republican and/or liberal revolutions. Additionally they sought to collect debts, secure natural resources, protect their nationals and their investments from nationalization, and re-open trade.[3]

This threat to the very existence of the new republics generated attempts to unify the nations in order to defend their independence collectively. Simón Bolívar envisioned and proposed a loose confederation of the independent republics, to protect their independence and republican institutions from Spain and other conservative European monarchies. He convoked the Congress of Panama in 1826, attended by Colombia (consisting of Colombia, Ecuador and Venezuela), Peru, Mexico and the Central American Federation. The participants approved a Treaty of Union and Perpetual Confederation and another on collective defense against foreign intervention, neither of which was ever ratified (Stoetzer 1993, 4–12) (Gil 1971).[4]

In the years following, three more meetings of a similar nature and with similar participation took place in Lima, Peru (1848), Santiago, Chile (1856) and Lima again (1865). Attendees signed treaties on collective security, mandatory arbitration for international disputes, trade and other issues. Other republics later adhered to these agreements, which also were not ratified (Stoetzer 1993, 9–10). The prevailing anarchy in most of the signatory countries, added to regional political disagreements, and territorial disputes and border wars in Central America, the Andean region and the Southern Cone proved to be insurmountable obstacles to the unification of the Spanish American republics.[5] Additionally, some countries such as Argentina and Chile preferred national autonomy and commercial relations with European countries, while Brazil actually plotted against Spanish America integration schemes.[6]

Nevertheless, the emergence of two new Spanish American doctrines advanced the international normative basis for the new republics' legal protection of their sovereignty and territorial integrity from European and, increasingly, U.S. military intervention: One was the Calvo Doctrine (published in 1863), which postulated that, in cases of disputes over private claims concerning unpaid debts from damages sustained as a result of internal commotions, foreign nationals could not appeal to foreign courts. The other, the Drago Doctrine, stipulated that the "public debt cannot occasion armed intervention nor the occupation of the territory of American nations." Both became the basis for fundamental principles of inter-American and international law and organization, such as the juridical equality and sovereignty of the state, non-intervention and compulsory arbitration for international disputes (Gil 1971, 148) (Holden and Zolov 2011, 69, 84). But as it is often the case with international principles, these doctrines could not prevent several interventions and territorial occupations perpetrated first by Europeans and later by U.S. governments.[7]

Nascent Pan Americanism and U.S. Interventionism

At the end of the nineteenth century, the republics of the Americas started once again to engage with each other at the continental level through a series of inter-American conferences. Some historians have pointed to the first International Conference of the American Republics, held in Washington, D.C. between 1889 and 1890, as the beginning of the inter-American system.[8]

The Conference sought to establish mechanisms of cooperation to increase commerce among the American republics, and create instruments such as compulsory arbitration for the pacific settlement of disputes (commercial or not). It also had the underlying strategic objective of preventing and reducing European influence in the hemisphere. To that effect, significantly, the participants agreed to establish the International Union of American Republics, known as the Pan American Union, with headquarters in Washington D.C., the precursor of the OAS, and to hold periodic conferences. However, the next three International Conferences held in 1902 (Mexico City), in 1906 (Rio de Janeiro) and in 1910 (Buenos Aires) did not accomplish much in terms of fostering a coherent unified continental block. Profound differences around the issue of non-intervention prevented greater cooperation and consensus among the American republics.

U.S. military intervention in Central American and Caribbean had intensified in the first years of the twentieth century under the Roosevelt's Corollary to the Monroe Doctrine, and became a bitter and divisive issue between the U.S. government and most Latin American republics. The Corollary asserted that the U.S. had the obligation and the right to intervene in countries with "chronic political instability" and continuous defaulting on their European debts. Ostensibly, its purpose was to preserve those countries' independence from European powers, ensure their political stability and the safety of American interests (trade, investments, banking), and protect the Panama Canal.[9]

President Woodrow Wilson (1913–22) expanded the Corollary's scope to include intervention in favor of democracy and against tyranny, and was used to justify his own military intervention in Mexico after the overthrow and assassination of President Madero. This was part of his larger effort to "make the world safe for democracy" (Davis and Finen 1967, 14).

After World War I, the American republics met again in 1923, in Santiago, Chile and then in Havana, Cuba in 1928. For Latin American countries, U.S. interventionism and its occupation of some countries had replaced the Europeans' and had become the real and immediate threat to their security, territorial integrity and independence. They pressed the U.S. government to recognize the absolute sovereignty of all States (in accordance with the Calvo/Drago Doctrines), to abandon the use of force and the practice of intervention and occupation, and to accept negotiations and arbitration as the means of resolving disputes (Gil, 148–9). U.S. delegates, on the other hand, preferred that these conferences sidestep "security or non-intervention" issues and concentrate instead on trade, patents, customs tariffs, communications, transportation, political asylum, private international law, maritime neutrality, consular affairs, and others.

World War II on the Horizon and Hemispheric Solidarity

The populist authoritarian wave of the early 20th century was now compounded by a growing external menace to the security of the hemisphere, represented by the rise and military expansion of the Fascist-Nazi alliance in Western Europe. The alliance's ideological and subversive activities in several Latin American countries in the 1930s and early 1940s soon became perceived as a threat to the peace and security of the entire hemisphere. It also had the effect of mobilizing collective efforts to prevent its penetration into the Americas.

Under these circumstances, the U.S. Government sought to reset relations with its southern neighbors. Franklin D. Roosevelt's administration recognized that the U.S. interventions of the previous 30 years or so had only produced indignation, ill will and distancing from Latin America. At the Seventh Conference of the American Republics in Montevideo in 1933, the U.S. delegation announced a dramatic change in U.S. policy towards Latin America. It introduced the *Good Neighbor Policy*, which repudiated the

Roosevelt Corollary interventionism (Bemis 1967, 256–76). As a result, the U.S would agree to an Inter-American Convention on the Rights and Duties of States, which recognized their legal equality and stipulated that "no State has the right to intervene in the internal or external affairs of another." To substantiate this shift, the U.S. withdrew its troops from Nicaragua and Haiti.

By 1936, alarmed at the Nazi and Fascist expansionism in Europe and the hemisphere, the American republics gathered at a special Inter-American Conference in Buenos Aires, where they rejected the anti-democratic ideologies spreading in Europe and the Americas and unanimously proclaimed their commitment to republican institutions and their solidarity with democratic governments of the region (General Secretariat of the Tenth Inter-American Conference, 646).

As Germany became more aggressive and expansionist, the American republics met again in 1938 in Lima, where they agreed to collectively confront the Fascist-Nazi threat to the hemisphere, reaffirmed their commitment to democracy and proposed the creation of the Council for the Promotion of Pan American Democracy. They also approved a declaration on the Defense of Human Rights (García Amador 1981, 515).

To deal with the threat posed by the German and Japanese military aggression in Europe and the Pacific, after the German invasion of Poland, the hemisphere's Foreign Ministers once again gathered in Panama in 1939; then in Havana in 1940, after the invasion of France, and in Rio in 1942, after the Japanese attack on Pearl Harbor. At these summits, they agreed to cooperate and coordinate their efforts to face this imminent international threat to the security of the hemispheric nations and their democratic institutions.

The Communist Threat and Hemispheric Agreements

After the war, a renewed interest in democracy and human rights arose in the Americas, this time associated with the threat of an aggressive and expanding communist ideology propagated by an emerging world power, the Soviet Union.

In this context, the American republics met in Mexico City in 1945 at the Inter-American Conference on the Problems of War and Peace, where they agreed to draft a collective security treaty to be adopted in the next conference to be held in 1947 in Rio de Janeiro.

But the Uruguayan and Guatemalan Foreign Ministries went further and proposed a united front for the collective defense of democracy, which they contended was necessary because of the intrinsic relationship between democracy and peace. The Uruguayan Foreign Minister, Rodriguez Larreta, argued that Fascist, Nazi and Communist dictatorships were expansionist and inherently disrespectful of basic rights and freedoms, and that since democracy guaranteed peace, "the inter-American community should take multilateral action to restore democracy whenever violated." He also argued that this collective action "would not contravene the principle of non-intervention" as this principle "cannot be used to violate other fundamental rights." A majority of the members, however, rejected a proposal for a declaration along those lines. The opponents, led by the delegates from Peronist Argentina, alleged that the proposal would open the way for U.S. interventionism (Acevedo and Grossman 1996, 135) (Slater 1967, 240–41).[10]

In the same vein, the Guatemalan delegate insisted that, in view of the increasing probability that anti-democratic regimes would soon emerge in the continent, the conference should consider approving a Convention for the Defense and Preservation of Democracy in the Americas. The participants agreed to forward the proposal to the Inter-American Juridical Committee for its review and advice (General Secretariat of the Tenth Inter-American Conference, 1956, 50). They reaffirmed their commitment to democracy and human rights with the signing of the American Declaration on the Protection of the Essential Rights of Man (Garcia Amador 1981, 527–9).

Two years later, in Rio de Janeiro, Brazil, the American Republics gathered at the Inter-American Conference for the Maintenance of Continental Peace and Security and signed the Rio Treaty on collective security (the Inter-American Treaty on Reciprocal Assistance, better known by its Spanish acronym, TIAR). The Treaty condemned war, committed its signatories to resolve their controversies peacefully, and agreed that an "armed attack by any State on an American State shall be considered an attack against all, and all must assist in its defense" (Article 3). They also affirmed that their collective commitment to "mutual assistance and common defense" was consistent with the notion that regional peace and security rested on the "effective exercise of democracy" (General Secretariat of the Tenth Inter-American Conference, 1956, 92) (Stoetzer 1993, 379–381).

Finally, in Bogotá, Colombia in 1948, the American Republics approved the OAS Charter at the Ninth International Conference.[11] It included what the American republics had been claiming, debating and negotiating for more than a century. It crystalized agreements on basic values and principles such as peace, security, democracy, human rights, solidarity, cooperation and unity, as well as sovereignty, territorial integrity, juridical equality of States and non-intervention; and it established instruments, mechanisms and procedures for the peaceful resolution of conflicts (good offices, arbitration, consultation, non-aggression and conciliation),[12] as well as for the Pacific Settlement of Disputes between Member States (Pact of Bogotá).[13] All of this, in addition to the Rio Treaty, provided structure and substance to the inter-American system, and constitutes today a remarkable, invaluable and distinctive historical legacy for ordering and institutionalizing inter-American relations.

Specific binding legal instruments on the promotion and protection of democracy and human rights did not obtain a general consensus until a few years later, as we shall see. The Guatemalan delegation once more proposed "withholding recognition from antidemocratic regimes on the grounds that they deny human rights and are a danger to the unity, solidarity, peace and defense of the hemisphere" while Brazil and Uruguay also sought to include a declaration on the rights and duties of man, to be enforced by the International Court of Justice, as well as a statement identifying the fundamental principles of democracy. Those proposals, however, were rejected by the delegates of military regimes of the time, because of their alleged violations of the principle of non-intervention (Slater 1967, 239–45).

Nevertheless, the Charter does include the member states' conviction that democracy is a precondition for the security and peace of the hemisphere, as they agreed that "the solidarity of the American States and the high aims which are sought through it require the political organization of those States on the basis of the effective exercise of representative democracy" (General Secretariat of the Tenth Inter-American Conference, 1956, 125).

The delegations also approved a resolution entitled "Preservation and Defense of Democracy in the Americas," which rejected "hegemonic and totalitarian tactics of international communism; reiterated the members' faith on the ideals of democracy; condemned any kind of interventionism from extra hemispheric powers" and called on members to adopt all necessary measures to impede activities instigated by governments that promote political instability and subvert republican institutions. And finally, they also approved "The American Declaration of the Rights and Duties of Man" (General Secretariat of the Tenth Inter-American Conference, 1956, 203–210).

CONCLUSION

As we have seen in this very succinct survey of Latin American political history and inter-American relations from the beginning of the nineteenth to the middle of the twentieth century, democracy had to overcome various challenges, domestic and international, from diverse quarters and in many forms in different countries. The domestic challenges to democracy often coincided with threats from non-democratic ideologies coming from Europe in many forms. But these challenges and impediments did not completely extinguish democracy's flame. Republican and democratic values and institutions remained latent in Latin America's political culture. They showed significant historical resilience.

The struggle for the survival of democracy included domestic responses (often non-democratic themselves) as well as regional multilateral efforts to protect the republican institutions established in the new independent nations. Politicians, intellectuals and diplomats regularly proposed regional or inter-American (Pan American) alliances or cooperative arrangements that would collectively protect and nourish the development of democracy in the hemisphere. Their efforts over a century and a half successfully culminated in the signing of the collective security mechanism known as the Rio Treaty and the creation of the Organization of the American States (OAS).

NOTES

1. See Fagg's chapter on "The Great Dictators of the Early National Period," including Santa Ana in Mexico (1832–55), Rafael Carrera in Guatemala (1838–65), Jean Pierre Boyer in Haiti and the Dominican Republic (1818–43), Pedro Santana in Dominican Republic (1844–61), José A. Paez in Venezuela (1819–46), Tomas Cipriano de Mosquera (1845–49, 1861–64, 1866–67) in Colombia, Juan José Flores (1830–35, 1843–45) and Gabriel Garcia Moreno (1861–65, 1869–75) in Ecuador, Andrés Santa Cruz (1828–38), José Ballivian, Isidoro Belzu and Mariano Melgarejo (1841–71) in Bolivia, Juan Manuel Rosas (1829–52) in Argentina, José Gaspar Rodriguez de Francia (1814–1840), and Carlos Antonio and Francisco Solano Lopez (1844–70) in Paraguay.

2. For a comprehensive and incisive analysis of populism from the Right and the Left, see Germani (1978).

3. For a detailed description of these interventions in Mexico, the Dominican Republic, Peru and Argentina, see Ronning (1970) and Gil (1971).

4. Argentina, at war with Brazil, and Chile, which was engaged in a civil war, did not participate. The Brazilian monarchy/empire, sympathetic to the Holy Alliance, did not attend either.

5. Examples of these regional conflicts are the war between Argentina and Brazil (the Cisplatine War 1826–28); Chile (and Argentina) versus the Peruvian/Bolivian Confederation (1837–39); the U.S. and Mexico (1846–1848); the Triple Alliance War (Paraguay vs. Brazil, Argentina and Uruguay, 1865–1870) and the Pacific War (Chile vs. Peru and Bolivia, 1879–1884). Central America, after independence (1823), remained fragilely united under Francisco Morazán until 1839, but was engulfed in anarchy as the Catholic Church and the provincial caudillos constantly conspired against his liberal policies and authority. Their confederation broke up in 1839. The region also experienced threats of annexation to the U.S. from the filibustering activities of William Walker in Nicaragua (1855–57). In the Caribbean, Haiti and the Dominican Republic confronted each other over Haitian occupation (1818–84). (Fagg 1963, 525–545) (Atkins 1989, 297–301) (Child 1985), (Gil 1971, 36–42).

6. The early sub regional integration schemes did not last very long: The Central American Federation, modeled after the U.S. federal system, lasted from 1823 to 1840. The Greater Colombia union formed under Bolívar's rule, composed of Colombia, Ecuador, Panama and Venezuela, collapsed in 1831. The Peru-Bolivia confederation lasted only three years (1836–39), and the United Provinces of the Rio de la Plata, a loose confederation of political/ regional units, which included parts of Brazil, Chile, Bolivia, Paraguay and Uruguay, lasted between 1810 and 1831.

7. As Zbigniew Brzezinski has advised, "principle without force is useless, and power without principle is forever threatening and immoral" (Brzezinski 1985).

8. On the evolution of the inter-American system see (Atkins 1989) (Bemis 1967) (Gil 1971) (Garcia Amador 1981) (Holden and Zolov 2011) (Stoetzer 1993), amongst others. Some also see this meeting as the initial stage of Pan Americanism and the Western Hemisphere Idea, according to which the peoples of the Americas have a common identity based on common republican/democratic values, ideals and institutions that unite them, differentiate them from Europe, and make the hemisphere unique (Drake 2009, 56) (Whitaker 1954). In theory, the Western Hemisphere Idea may even include the remote possibility of an integrated federalized hemisphere, with the OAS founding Charter of 1948 as the basis for an inter-American consti-

tution and its multilateral governing structure as the embryonic representative hemispheric institutions.

9. During the first thirty years of the twentieth century, the U.S. intervened and occupied various countries in the greater Caribbean numerous times: Cuba, after the Spanish-American war (1898–1903, 1906–09, and 1917–22); Panama (1903); Nicaragua (1912–25, 1927–32), Haiti (1914–34), the Dominican Republic (1916–24), and Mexico (1914). (Ronning 1970, 29–32) and (Gil 1971, 87–145).

10. This proposal occurred in the context of Uruguay's fears of the Argentine military government and its strong pro-fascist/Nazi stance. The U.S. Ambassador to Argentina, Spruille Braden, accepted the idea gladly, as he openly confronted the military government and Perón over their neutrality in the war. He also opposed Perón's election in 1946 and, inevitably, was accused of interventionism and imperialism, and Perón won the election.

11. General Secretariat of the OAS (1981).

12. General Secretariat of the OAS (1972).

13. The few members (16) that ratified this Pact agreed "to refrain from the threat or the use of force, or from any other means of coercion for the settlement of their controversies, and to have recourse at all times to pacific procedures" and recognized "their obligation to settle international controversies by regional procedures before referring them to the Security Council of the United Nations." http://www.oas.org/juridico/english/treaties/a-42.html.

Chapter Three

Cold War Challenges to Democracy and Early OAS Efforts to Defend It (1948–1985)

THE COMMUNIST/CASTROITE THREAT

Following the end of the Second World War and creation of the OAS in 1948, the inter-American community faced a new and emerging challenge: the expansion of Sino/Soviet communism into the hemisphere through the Cuban revolution (1959) led by Fidel Castro.

From the 1950s to the early 1980s, this new challenge and its variants threatened the political stability of the few standing democracies as well as the existing *caudillo* dictatorships and military governments, but also, more generally, it menaced the peace and security of the entire hemisphere. The Americas became ideologically contested, politically fragmented and a Cold War battleground.

More specifically, this threat to democracy in Latin America came from revolutionary socialist and communist movements, which were encouraged, armed and financed by the Soviet Union, Maoist China and Castro's Cuba. In the context of the Cold War, these movements ostensibly had at least two goals: One, to "liberate" Latin America from U.S. "imperialist and capitalist" domination and its domestic allies, be they the traditional oligarchy, the old caudillo dictatorships, the populist regimes or the "liberal" and "bourgeois" democracy; and the other, to bring about a more egalitarian society marked by greater social justice and economic equality. They rejected "bourgeois elections" and democratic politics and engaged instead in urban and rural guerrilla warfare, following the Cuban example, in futile attempts (except in Nicaragua) to capture control of the state. Throughout Central and South

America, few countries were spared the tragedies of internal war. Politics became a warlike struggle, and guerrilla warfare an instrument of politics (Aguilar 1968) (Kohl 1974).

The Domestic Response

In many countries, the response to the communist and Castroite revolutionary threat turned into harsher anti-communist caudillo dictatorships, populist authoritarian regimes and/or outright conservative repressive military regimes, all with military and political backing from U.S. Governments. Both the threat and the reaction, in most countries, relegated republican/democratic institutions, reformist leaders and political parties to second place once again.

The centrist liberal/reformist pro-democracy forces (e.g., Social Democrats, Christian Democrats and centrist democratic parties) were caught in the middle, between the left's avalanche and the conservative reactionary alliance (landed oligarchy, big business interests and the military). When in government they could not satisfy the left's demand for revolutionary socioeconomic measures, nor could they defeat leftist candidates at the polls. Neither could they provide the security and political and economic stability the conservative forces demanded (Drake 2009, 163–200).

Instead, in some countries, the traditional landed oligarchy (still in control of the agricultural and primary export economy) and its allies, the new industrialists and multinational corporations, supported the traditional *caudillo* dictatorship, which remained in power through fraudulent elections and/or strict personal control of the armed forces. Typical of this model of domination were Trujillo in the Dominican Republic, Batista in Cuba, the Somozas in Nicaragua, Strossner in Paraguay, Pérez Jiménez in Venezuela, Rojas Pinilla in Colombia, Odría in Peru and Castillo Armas in Guatemala.

In the more developed countries, on the other hand, the landed oligarchy joined the industrialists and the multinational corporations, the new businesses and middle class professional sectors, as well as the military to form an anti-communist reactionary alliance, which prevailed in through the 60s and 70s. This alliance emerged as a new regime type in Argentina, Brazil, Chile, Peru and Uruguay, which Guillermo O'Donnell described as "bureaucratic-authoritarianism," and which largely displaced the traditional caudillo-dictator and/or populist "strongman" (D. Collier 1979) (O'Donnell, *El Estado Autoritario Burocrático* 1982) (Putnam 1976) (O'Donnell, *Modernización y Autoritarismo* 1972) (Huntington 1968).

The bureaucratic-authoritarianism regime headed by professional military officers enforced a "neo-liberal" economic model of free markets and trade, together with authoritarian and even repressive political order. Ostensibly, the regime presented itself as "developmentalist" and as representing the middle class sectors of society. It was fiercely anti-communist, mistrusting and dismissive of elections and republican/democratic institutions (Nun 1967) (O'Donnell, *Modernización y Autoritarismo* 1972). It disdained the occasional democratic governments of the period (Frondizi and Illia in Argentina, Kubitscheck and Goulart in Brazil, Rómulo Gallegos in Venezuela, Belaúnde in Peru, Arbenz in Guatemala, and others), and perceived them as weak, vulnerable and incapable of containing the onslaught of the revolutionary left and of providing the necessary security and political stability to ensure socioeconomic development. The reactionary alliance sustaining such a regime would frequently stage or support coups to avert leftists victories, or, if they were elected, to overthrow them.

The ensuing confrontation between military regimes and leftist guerrillas, known in some places as the "dirty war," engulfed many Latin American societies, from Central to South America, in a prolonged and tragic period of internal war, marked by guerrilla warfare and repression, state terrorism and horrendous and widespread violations of human rights, which lasted until the late 70s and early 80s.[1]

The Collective Hemispheric Response

As expected, and as in the past, domestic threats to security and republican/democratic institutions, now coming from communist subversive activities, had implications for inter-American peace and security. They threatened the recently agreed upon fundamental hemispheric values and principles.

The Washington Fourth Meeting of Consultation, 1951

In view of the escalation of the Cold War, with the occupation and "sovietization" of Central and Eastern Europe, and the communist Chinese military incursion in the Korean peninsula, the U.S. Government requested the Fourth Meeting of Consultation of Foreign Affairs Ministers, held in Washington, D.C. in April 1951. The U.S. Government, concerned over the growing "aggression by international communism," sought the cooperation of the hemisphere for the Korean war – principally, strategic commodities and raw material supplies, as well as combat troops for the United Nations Command (Secretaría General de la Décima Conferencia Interamericana [General Secretariat of the Tenth Inter-American Conference] 1956, 223).

Most of the member states (fourteen out of eighteen) at the time were military or semi-democratic regimes and tended to agree with the U.S proposal. However, countries like Mexico, Perón's Argentina and Arbenz' Guatemala expressed doubts about the U.S. claim that the Korean war threatened the security of the hemisphere; they were more concerned about the U.S. using the OAS as an instrument for its anti-communist campaign (Lanus 1984, 87). They argued instead for an urgent inter-American program of economic cooperation and assistance, similar to the Marshall Plan, as a way to reduce poverty and social injustice, which they believed communists were exploiting to their own advantage in their revolutionary appeals. Colombia was the only South American country that pledged and actually contributed combat troops for the United Nations forces in Korea (Slater, 111–15).

Less dramatically, member states agreed to cooperate in the collective protection of the hemisphere and reiterated their commitment not to interfere in the internal affairs of other members (that is, not to question dictatorships), in order to maintain the necessary continental unity to respond "to communist external aggression." Remarkably, considering the fact that the majority of the delegations represented non- or semi-democratic governments, the meeting's resolutions also expressed the members' commitment to representative democracy and the observance of human rights, as the foundation for their solidarity and unity in the face of the international communist threat. But, at the insistence of a group led by Argentina, this commitment to democracy had to be linked to economic development and social justice (Secretaría General de la Décima Conferencia Interamericana [General Secretariat of the Tenth Inter-American Conference], 1956, 231–2).[2]

The meeting also approved a resolution entitled "Strengthening the Effective Exercise of Democracy," which proclaimed that "the solidarity of the American Republics requires the effective exercise of representative democracy and the prevalence of social justice and respect for human rights," and instructed the Inter-American Juridical Committee to prepare a draft inter-American convention on the Preservation and Defense of Democracy in the Americas. (Secretaría General de la Décima Conferencia Interamericana [General Secretariat of the Tenth Inter-American Conference], 1956, 237).

The Washington Declaration, which was the culmination of the meeting, emphasized the determination to remain united for the "common defense against the aggressive activities of international communism…which violates the principle of non-intervention and threaten freedom and democracy," and warned that this danger was aggravated by existing socioeconomic conditions, which "require[d] measures to improve the lives of the peoples of the hemisphere." It also asserted that "the respect for fundamental freedoms and principles of social justice…" are "the basis for democracy."

The Caracas Declaration, 1954

In the context of the nascent Cold War and communist intrusion in the hemisphere, tension escalated in the hemisphere as a result of conflicting or contradictory interests and concerns about security, non-interventionism and democracy. Throughout most of the 50s and 60s, some countries in the Caribbean rim (a sensitive zone because of its proximity to the United States and the Panama Canal) experienced political turbulence within their territories, as well as considerable tension in their relations with one another. Anti-communist dictatorships prevailed in Colombia (Rojas Pinilla 1953–57), Cuba (Batista 1952–59), Dominican Republic (Trujillo 1930–61), Guatemala (Castillo Armas 1954–57), Haiti (Duvalier 1957–71), Nicaragua (Somoza 1967–79), Venezuela (Pérez Jimenez 1953–58), and others. These regimes repressed political and press freedoms, violated human rights and were resolutely anti-communist, while they confronted growing demands for democracy, social justice and better living conditions, which the regimes pretended were instigated by communist agitators.

Anastasio Somoza, Rafael Trujillo and Fulgencio Batista also faced incursions from "freedom fighters," known as the Caribbean Legion, made up of exiles and expatriates from surrounding democratic countries (e.g., Costa Rica and Venezuela and Guatemala), whose governments supported and financed the "legionnaires." In turn, some of these dictators also trained, armed and financed exiles to counter-attack democratic regimes, as Somoza did with Costa Rica and Trujillo with Venezuela (Slater 1967, 71–83).

Thus, at the Tenth Inter-American Conference held in Caracas, Venezuela in March 1954, the U.S. Government sought the approval of the "Declaration of Solidarity for the Preservation of the Political Integrity of the American States against the Interventionism of International Communism," as a collective commitment to "prohibit the establishment of communist regimes in the Western Hemisphere." The proposal warned that "the domination or control of the political institution of any American State by the international Communist movement...would constitute a threat to the sovereignty and political independence of the American States, endangering the peace of America." (Gil 211–2) (Slater, 117–118) (Secretaría General de la Décima Conferencia Interamericana [General Secretariat of the Tenth Inter-American Conference], 1956, 263). The declaration obtained the support of the six dictatorships present and eventually found lukewarm support from the majority of member states, on the condition that it would not be used to justify unilateral action. Skeptical delegates believed that Guatemalan conservatives could use this pronouncement to try to depose President Arbenz or, worse yet, that the U.S. could use it to justify unilateral action in Guatemala and other countries. The Guatemalan Foreign Minister opposed the declaration and accused the U.S. of a reactionary attitude towards needed socioeconomic reforms. Argentina and Mexico abstained (Slater 1967, 117).

On the other hand, and significantly, those democratic member states that mistrusted U.S. intentions and despised dictatorial regimes also obtained the meeting's approval of the Caracas Declaration, which, tellingly, renewed the member states' conviction that "one of the ways to strengthen their democratic institutions is to respect and observe human and social rights." (Secretaría General de la Décima Conferencia Interamericana [General Secretariat of the Tenth Inter-American Conference], 1956, 365). They also secured a general consensus on a resolution entitled "Strengthening the System of Human Rights Protection," which stated that the "effective exercise of democracy and the prevention of totalitarian intervention demand not only military measures but the effective functioning of democratic institutions and the protection of human rights and freedoms." (Secretaría General de la Décima Conferencia Interamericana, 1956, 310) (Garcia Amador, 527–8).

Nevertheless, despite the warnings against U.S. interventionism, the U.S. Central Intelligence Agency (CIA), obsessed with communist penetration in the region, prompted (with military advice and supplies) a small group of "freedom fighters" led by Colonel Castillo Armas with the help of Nicaragua and Honduras to overthrow leftist President Arbenz in June 1954 (Gil 209–11) (Slater 1967, 115–129).

THE ANTI-DICTATORIAL ALLIANCE: THE REFUSAL TO HELP DICTATORS

By the end of the nineteen fifties, Latin American progressive and liberal democrats had come to the conclusion that the main impediment to the prevalence of democracy in the region was the traditional caudillo-led despotic military-backed dictatorships, which governed some of the more impoverished countries of the hemisphere, such as Anastasio Somoza in Nicaragua, Rafael Trujillo in the Dominican Republic, Francoise Duvalier in Haiti and Fulgencio Batista in Cuba. From this perspective, their resistance to social change and democracy was the main reason why reformists and progressive forces turned to communist revolutionary activities and were susceptible to the communist-Castroite propaganda advanced by Fidel Castro. Their socio-economic policies only generated poverty and ignorance; and their repressive tyrannical regimes produced exiles, revolutionary fervor, political unrest and the motivation to organize into military guerrilla forces. In short, they paved the way for communist/Castroite penetration and expansion and were the principal source of instability in the region (Gil 1971, 220).

When democratic exiles ("freedom fighters," supported by the Costa Rican and Venezuelan Governments) attempted to oust Somoza and Trujillo, the dictators, invoking the Rio Treaty (TIAR), requested a meeting of Foreign Ministers. The request did not find sufficient support, as most member states did not wish to protect dictators. Arguably, the refusal to apply the TIAR or provide security assistance for Trujillo, Batista and later Somoza's dictatorships may have eventually contributed to their collapse (Tomasek 1989, 468) (Gil 1971, 220) (Slater 1967, 90–91).

The Fifth Meeting of Consultation and the Declaration of Santiago

The Fifth Meeting of Consultation of Ministers of Foreign Affairs met in Santiago, Chile in August 1959 to discuss the tensions and political unrest in the *circum*-Caribbean region. The discussions centered around three controversial issues of the day: dictatorships as the cause of instability in the region, the importance of exercising democracy and observing human rights, and the collective promotion of democracy versus non-intervention.

Note here that the Cuban delegation, headed by the new Foreign Minister of the recently installed Castro Government, Raúl Roa Garcia, joined forces with the Venezuelan delegation to argue that "the root cause of instability was dictatorial repression, and that to alleviate tensions in the area, it was necessary to use vigorous multilateral action to secure democracy and respect for human rights." In their view, "non-intervention was designed to protect only popular and legitimate states not dictatorships…Absolute sovereignty did not apply" in these cases (Slater 1967, 94–96). As expected at that time, most member states rejected this "interventionist" stance and strongly defended the principle of non-intervention in the affairs of any and all the members. Paradoxically, even the U.S. Government favored its application, as it feared that intervening in favor of democracy would alienate the military governments and divide the hemisphere's anti-communist posture. This impeded the approval of sanctions against dictators.

Nevertheless, the debate led to the approval of the ground breaking "Declaration of Santiago," which condemned dictatorship, non-democratic practices and violations of human rights, while upholding values and principles of democratic governance. The Declaration affirmed the member states' conviction that "the peoples of the Americas wish to live in peace and under the protection of democratic institutions, distanced from interventionism of any type and from totalitarian influences," and that absence of democracy and human rights and fundamental freedoms "is a source of regional instability and political tension amongst member states, while the existence of dictatorial regimes constitute a violation of the foundational principles of the OAS and a danger to the solidarity and peaceful coexistence in the hemisphere." It maintained that governments must be the result of free elections, that their perpetuation in power without limits is incompatible with the exercise of representative democracy, and that they must promote social justice while respecting human rights and individual and press freedoms without political persecution (Gil 1971) (García Amador 1981, 532–4). It also instructed the Organization's Inter-American Peace Committee to study the relationship between "the non-exercise of democracy and the political tensions that affect the peace of the hemisphere."[3]

The Foreign Ministers also directed the Council of the OAS to "draft a convention for the effective exercise of representative democracy." (García

Amador 1981, 531–34).[4] In late 1959, at the OAS Council in Washington, D.C., Argentina, Brazil, Mexico and Peru presented a proposal calling "for collective non-recognition of and exclusion from the OAS of any regime established by the forcible overthrow of a freely elected government or otherwise violating various requirements of democracy." (Slater 1967, 244–45).[5]

Most significantly, the meeting created the autonomous Inter-American Commission on Human Rights (IACHR) with the mandate to promote the respect of human rights in member states. The OAS Council later established its specific functions in 1960, which were expanded in the American Convention on Human Rights of 1969. This substantial accomplishment formalized the fundamental interdependent relationship between democracy and human rights (Inter-American Juridical Committee, 1998, 114–118).

The San José Sixth Meeting of Consultation

Soon after the Santiago meeting, the Dominican dictator, Trujillo, sent a small armed group to Venezuela to assassinate its democratically elected president, Rómulo Betancourt, in June 1960. This aggression led Venezuela to urgently convene the Sixth Meeting of Consultation, which was held in San José, Costa Rica in 1960. The Foreign Ministers condemned Trujillo's aggression and called for the suspension of diplomatic and commercial relations and of military cooperation (Gil, 1971, 221). This unprecedented measure reversed the "non-interventionist" position adopted the year before in Caracas. Dictators were not only violating the fundamental democratic values and practices cherished by all, but were also the source of domestic social unrest and political instability with regional repercussions—a situation which communist movements (with Castro's incitement and support) exploited to advance their penetration of the countries in the region. The sanctions imposed against the dictator this time unmistakably pointed to collective "interventionism."

Democracy and Non-Intervention

After the military coups in Argentina and Peru in 1962, the tension between the collective concern for democracy and non-intervention erupted again in inter-American affairs. The collapse of democracy in those two countries prompted the Governments of Venezuela, the Dominican Republic and Costa Rica to convene a meeting of the OAS Council to attempt to establish a policy of non-recognition of non-democratic governments, since "the exercise of representative democracy and respect for human rights have ceased to be an exclusively internal matter of each state and have become an international obligation."

As expected, Argentina, Haiti, Paraguay and Peru rejected the motion, while the U.S. and others abstained—presumably not to offend anti-communist allies. The "traditional" more democratic countries like Colombia, Costa Rica and Venezuela voted for it, as did Bolivia and the Dominican Republic—"circumstantial" democracies at the time. Still, by 1963, Venezuela and Costa Rica insisted on a proposal for an inter-American conference to consider collective reprisals against military coups and how to preserve and strengthen representative democracy. But as more countries (Brazil, Honduras, Dominican Republic) experienced military coups, the conference never took place. These early initiatives nevertheless set a precedent for what would become a standard collective concern and response vis-à-vis coups beginning in the mid-1980s (Slater 1967, 246–47).

The Anti-Communist Alliance

The advent of Castro Communism at the beginning of the 1960s, with its virulent anti-U.S. rhetoric and efforts to export its communist revolution through internal subversion and guerrilla movements, became the new challenge for the aspiring democrats living in dictatorships and for the established democracies in Latin America, and also challenged continental peace and security. The revolutionary communist regime of Fidel Castro began to infiltrate left-leaning political parties, legislatures, universities, labor unions and the press, and to support the organization of rural and urban guerrilla groups, by providing cash, arms, training and logistics (Slater 1967, 135–182) (Aguilar 1968) (Kohl 1974).

To respond to this threat, the anti-communist alliance replaced the antidictatorial alliance. The anti-communist alliance had various members and approaches. Until the late 1980s, the alliance included social democratic "developmentalist" or reformist governments (*à la* Frondizi and Illia of Argentina; Betancourt, Leoni and Caldera of Venezuela, Lleras Camargo of Colombia, José Figueres of Costa Rica, or Kubitscheck and Goulart in Brazil). It also included military governments, which eventually became more prevalent in the alliance and more repressive as the challenge from guerrilla insurrection grew. The democratic alternative became caught in the middle, paralyzed, between the Castro communist thrust and the reactionary anticommunist military regimes. Nevertheless, the anticommunist alliance (with whatever members it may have had) could always count on the economic, strategic, and military support of U.S. Governments, which provided development aid (the Alliance for Progress) and/or counter-insurgency training and military assistance (Slater 1967, 107–182). The Kennedy administration, of course, tried and failed to oust Castro directly with the Bay of Pigs invasion in April 1961.

[handwritten annotation: → third way / social democracy]

At first, the anti-communist alliance adopted the "social democratic" path or "third way," which rejected both the radical revolutionary leftist solutions to governance and to the challenges of economic development with social justice, as well as the authoritarian and repressive military regimes. Under this approach, effective democratic governance and progressive socioeconomic policies would lift the rural and urban dispossessed masses out of poverty and ignorance, and would limit the effect of communist propaganda and mobilization. The assumption was that poverty and underdevelopment provided fertile ground for communist penetration and subversion, and that socioeconomic development was therefore a prerequisite for security, stability and democracy (the optimistic equation, according to Guillermo O'Donnell). This was the essence of the Alliance for Progress proposed by President Kennedy in Punta del Este, Uruguay in 1961.

The Alliance for Progress

Member states adopted the Alliance for Progress as a means of promoting the strengthening of democratic and state institutions so that they could foster accelerated economic growth coupled with social justice and greater equality. It sought to "achieve maximum levels of well-being, with equal opportunities for all, in democratic societies adapted to their own needs and desires." It entrusted the Inter-American Economic and Social Council and its Secretariat at the OAS with the responsibility of providing technical assistance, in coordination with the United Nations' Economic Commission for Latin America and the Inter-American Development Bank, and of formulating and implementing national socioeconomic development plans (Gil 241–3) (Smith 1991) (Scheman 1988) (Subcommittee on American Republics Affairs of the Committee on Foreign Relations 1969) (Consejo Interamericano Económico y Social [Inter-American Economic and Social Council] 1973).

Further support for this approach was later expressed in 1967 at a Presidential summit in Punta del Este, where the Presidents called for rapid but "balanced development in the region…to raise the living standards of their peoples…[and] to strengthen democratic institutions…" in order to "achieve to the fullest measure the free, just, and democratic order demanded by the peoples of the hemisphere."

The Alliance for Progress did help initiate significant economic reform and modernization in most member states. But the socioeconomic changes resulting from those reforms—industrialization, internal migration, urbanization, improved education—also produced and accelerated greater expectations and multiple demands for social benefits, services and general wellbeing. Yet, the economic growth was not sufficient nor fast enough to adequately or promptly satisfy those demands, generating frustration, social unrest and political and even revolutionary fervor and upheaval, which leftist groups in many Latin American countries exploited to advance their cause with the help of Communist Cuba. Further, these developments were not accompanied by the strengthening of state and democratic institutions. Political parties, legislatures, courts, public administration and elections—the crucial links between society and the state—remained weak and undeveloped. They could not manage the avalanche of demands nor the conflicts and tensions resulting from the changes taking place in society. Neither could they allay the concerns and fears of the military and their middle class and conservative upper classes allies from the agricultural and industrial business sectors and from multinational corporations—the domestic core of the anti-communist alliance (Change and the Alliance for Progress 1971) (Consejo Interamericano Económico y Social 1973) (Gil 1971, 238–250).

The anti-communist alliance saw those revolutionary social demands and the increasing pro-Castro guerrilla subversive activities not only as a direct menace to their socioeconomic interests and status, but also as an imminent threat to national security. Inevitably, U.S. Governments shared, if not encouraged this view. In most cases, the alliance did not trust democratic institutions and dismissed their reformist leaders as corrupt, ineffective and incapable of managing the popular demands and mobilizations or their subversive activities.

Cuba's Aggression and Its Suspension

As soon as Fidel Castro came to power after defeating the Batista dictatorship in 1959, his Government began to encourage and support subversive activities by communist guerrillas in several Latin American countries. At the request of the Colombian Government, which was experiencing subversive activities, the Eighth Meeting of Consultation met in Punta del Este in 1962, and, in a momentous decision, suspended the Government of Cuba from the OAS. This despite the fact that some of the most important Latin American countries (Argentina, Brazil and Mexico) abstained or opposed it, alleging it was contrary to the principle of non-intervention and self-determination (Gil 1971, 234).

Nevertheless, member states still collectively affirmed in various resolutions that "communism is not the way to achieve economic development and the elimination of social injustice in the Americas" and that the most effective way of combatting communism was "greater respect for human rights, improvement in democratic institutions and practices." They also recommended that "states whose structures or acts are incompatible with the exercise of representative democracy hold free elections in their respective countries" (General Secretariat, Organization of American States 1973, 70–74).

As Venezuelan and Cuban guerrillas, armed and trained in Cuba, landed in Venezuela in 1963 to disrupt its elections and begin a guerrilla insurgency,

President Rómulo Betancourt called the Ninth Meeting of Consultation of Foreign Ministers in July 1964. The meeting condemned Castro's aggression and intervention, confirmed Cuba's suspension from the OAS and agreed (except for Mexico) to sever diplomatic relations and to "suspend all their trade" with Cuba (Gil 1971, 236–7) (Garcia Amador 1981, 832).

Ignoring the anti-communist alliance alerts, Castro continued his efforts to export the Cuban revolution by supporting rural and urban guerrilla warfare in Venezuela, Colombia and Bolivia, as well as in Argentina, Uruguay, Chile and Brazil during the 1960s and most of the 1970s (Aguilar 1968) (Kohl 1974). In 1965, his support for a leftist civil-military uprising in the Dominican Republic generated a controversial military intervention. Most member states supported, if reluctantly, the establishment of an Inter-American Peace Force in the Dominican Republic in May 1965 to replace a unilateral intervention by U.S. Marines that had taken place a month earlier—to contain a budding civil war and "another Cuba." The intervention strained U.S.-Latin American relations and raised once again fears about U.S. unilateral intervention and its use of the OAS to intervene in the name of democracy and anti-communism (Gil 1971, 251–56). The OAS intervention, however, did pacify the Dominican Republic, which held elections in June 1966, setting the country onto an uneasy but uninterrupted path to democracy.

The Rise of Military Regimes

The Cuban/communist penetration and interference in Latin American nations had tragic consequences, as it provoked the emergence of military regimes in many of them. In their anti-communist crusade, these military regimes, supported by the United States Government's counter-insurgency assistance (Gil, 237), not only destroyed democratic institutions but also terrorized their populations with gross violations of human rights.

During the 1970s, military governments known as "bureaucratic-authoritarian" regimes (such as in Argentina, Brazil, Chile, Uruguay, Peru and Guatemala) replaced the traditional caudillo-dictators like Batista, Castillo Armas, Pérez Jimenez, Somoza and Trujillo (Strossner lasted until 1989). In several countries, these repressive military regimes unleashed a "dirty" war against the leftist guerrillas, undermining and putting democracy on a hold for most of the Cold War in several important Latin American countries—all in the name of an anti-Castro communist alliance.

These regimes enjoyed the support of the Nixon and Ford administrations (1969–77) and later had the support of President Reagan (1981–89). However, President Carter (1977–81), because of his profound commitment to human rights, denied support to military regimes in Argentina, Chile and Guatemala, and was instrumental in producing the downfall of the Somoza dictatorship in Nicaragua (Pastor 1992).

RENEWED CONCERNS OVER HUMAN RIGHTS AND DEMOCRACY

By the end of the 1970s, the hemisphere began to experience the first indications of a new democratic resurgence. Democrats throughout the continent, outraged at the atrocities committed during the "dirty wars," started to question the domination of politics by the leftist insurgents and the repressive military regimes. They also began to voice their concern over human rights and to express their demands for peace and democratization. The spirit of and aspirations for democracy had remained deep and strong in the hemisphere's consciousness, even if dormant and suppressed at times because of the violence and repression and because of the indiscriminate adherence to the principle of non-intervention.

On the other hand, the pro-human rights and democracy advocates had gained a significant concession from the anti-interventionist forces when member states agreed to relinquish a measure of sovereignty by signing the landmark American Convention on Human Rights of 1969, known also as the Pact of San José, which entered into force in 1978. The Convention ratified the irrevocable interdependence between democracy and human rights, and called for the promotion and protection of fundamental rights and freedoms, with a strong emphasis on civil and political rights. It obligates the Parties to respect the rights and freedoms recognized in the Convention, created the Inter-American Court of Human Rights (I/A Court H.R.) and gives the Commission "interventionist" functions such as the authority to examine the human rights situation in countries where flagrant and continuous violations take place, to prepare reports and to recommend to member states that they redress violations and/or adopt progressive measures in favor of human rights. The 1980 OAS General Assembly strengthened the Commission's role, by providing it with the ability to convene annual hearings to receive allegations by individuals or groups of human rights violations; to perform *in situ* visits to analyze the human rights situation in member states; to dictate precautionary measures when states violate the rights of individuals or groups, and others.

Throughout the 1970s, the Commission presented to the General Assembly devastating reports on human rights violations in Argentina, Chile, Cuba, El Salvador, Haiti, Nicaragua, Panama, Paraguay and Uruguay. As a result, between 1971 and 1981, the General Assembly approved twenty-six resolutions on human rights violations in member states. Implicitly or explicitly, these reports made it clear once more that human rights correspond to essential democratic values and practices and that observance and protection of those rights are best guaranteed by a democratic political system (García Amador, 534–38, 546–559) (Inter-American Human Rights Commission 1992, 4–16) (Inter-American Juridical Committee, 1998, 114–18) (Goldman 2009).

Significantly, the Seventeenth Meeting of Consultation of 1978 requested the IACHR to prepare a report on the political and human rights situation of the worsening conflict in Nicaragua between the repressive Somoza regime and the *Sandinista* insurgents—a conflict which also threatened the stability and security of its neighbors. The Commission's report accused the regime of gross human rights violations, which, to no one's surprise, Somoza rejected and called it "interventionist." However, as the Somoza regime attacked the *Sandinista* rebels (now including Cubans) inside Costa Rica, in June 1979, the OAS condemned the incursion as well as the regime's dictatorial and "inhumane conduct," and called for Somoza's resignation and replacement by a pluralistic representative government elected in free elections. This unprecedented demand, involving collective "interventionism" in favor of human rights, democracy and peace, nevertheless asked member states to refrain from intervening unilaterally, in a veiled warning against a possible U.S. intervention–to no avail, however (Atkins 1989, 231) (Wilson 1989, 480–6) (García Zamora 1981, 558).

The collective spirit to protect human rights continued at the 1981 OAS General Assembly. The Commission submitted reports on gross violations of human rights in Argentina, Bolivia, El Salvador, Guatemala and Nicaragua, now under *Sandinista* rule. Note that this exceptional and increasing collective interest in human rights was significantly encouraged and supported by President Carter's administration (1977–81), which additionally negated assistance or refused to cooperate with military regimes that violated human rights (Pastor 1992). However, the subsequent Reagan administration (1981–89) soon disavowed and reversed this progress in human rights. It chose instead to back, or at least not to alienate, anti-communist military regimes that were fighting communist/Castroite guerrillas, and/or to engage in its own substantive efforts to prop up the anti-*Sandinista* guerrilla forces ("Contras"). Nevertheless, these developments, seemingly contradictory, had the combined effect, as we shall see later on, of unleashing a process that led to a historical regional peace and democracy accord in Central America–a process in which the Contadora Group (Colombia, Mexico, Panama and Venezuela) and the Support Group (Argentina, Brazil, Peru and Uruguay) as well as the OAS played a significant facilitating role (Atkins 1989, 233) (Wilson 1989, 479–86) (Grabendorff, Krumwiede and Todt 1984) (Pastor 1992).

Carter —> Reagan

CONCLUSION

Thus, throughout most of the twentieth century, democracy in the hemisphere had to endure and survive significant challenges and impediments from many fronts, including the anarchists, the traditional conservative oligarchies, the corporatist populists, the Fascist and Nazi European threat, in addition to the traditional dictatorship type, as we saw in the previous chapter. Following its creation in 1948, the OAS had to confront the wave of Marxism and Castro-communism with their guerrilla insurrections; and finally it had to face the threat of an anti-communist but anti-democratic alliance led by repressive and even murderous military regimes—all of which disdained and were dismissive of democracy as a way of governing society.

But democracy's defenders and supporters, both domestic and hemispheric, were resilient and resisted its demise. They condemned coups, dictatorships and violations of human and political rights; they proposed not to recognize dictators or assist them, and sought to impose sanctions on them (Trujillo) or called for their departure from power (Somoza); they repudiated communist-Castroite intervention and subversion as well as absolute non-interventionism or its abuse to protect dictators and repressive regimes; they formed anti-dictatorial alliances as well as anti-communist alliances (sometimes with unworthy or unsavory allies); they persisted in upholding fundamental democratic values, principles and practices and advanced proposals for inter-American treaties or conventions for the preservation and defense of democracy as well the observance and protection of human rights; they pressed for and achieved the establishment of the Inter-American Commission and the Inter-American Court on Human Rights. They never relented and always bounced back to set the ideological precedents and foundations for the return of democracy in the mid-1980s. Towards the close of the twentieth century, the spirit of democracy revived and emerged triumphant. Democracy thus became the predominant political system for governing hemispheric societies, and the OAS member states have committed themselves to promote and defend it collectively.

NOTES

1. The literature on the subject is extensive: see for example: Grabendorff, Krumwiede and Todt (1984), Lowenthal, Armies and Politics in Latin America (1976), Drake (2009), Smith (2005) and (2008), O'Donnell (1982), Collier (1979) and Perina, Los Militares en la Política. Onganía, Levingston y Lanusse (1983).

2. At this time, frequent border clashes occurred in the greater Caribbean between the dictatorships in Trujillo's Dominican Republic and Haiti's Duvalier, and between Costa Rica and Somoza's Nicaragua over the incursions of exiles into each other's territories (Slater 1967, 70, 81).

3. See footnote No. 97 in Slater (1967, 104). The Peace Committee was abolished in 1967 and its functions were incorporated into the amended OAS Charter of 1967 (García Amador 1981, 751–754).

4. See resolutions of the meeting in http://www.oas.org/consejo/sp/rc/Actas/ Acta%205.pdf.

5. This proposal was not adopted but it can certainly be considered a precursor of the clause adopted thirty-six years later (1995) as the Washington Protocol and incorporated into the current OAS Charter.

Chapter Four

The International Promotion
of Democracy

ORIGINS AND RATIONALE

The OAS role in promoting and defending democracy must be placed and understood in the wider world of contemporary political/diplomatic and technical efforts to promote and protect democracy, which emerged following the global resurgence of democracy during the 1970s and 1980s. This "third wave" of democracy started with the Portuguese military coup that overthrew the Caetano dictatorship in April 1974. Its demonstration effect was felt in Spain, Greece, Latin America, and later on, with the end of the Cold War (1989) and the collapse of the communist Soviet Union, in Eastern Europe. It also had repercussions in Asia and Africa, and it could even be argued that the Arab Spring of 2012 is a continuation of this process (Huntington 1991) (Diamond 1992).

Western mainstream political/diplomatic, media and academic narratives interpreted these developments with considerable satisfaction and enthusiasm, and perceived these events as auspicious for the resurgence and dissemination of liberal representative democracy. Francis Fukuyama went as far as to maintain that the collapse of the Soviet Union and the surge of the Third Wave at the turn of the century (1989–2007) signaled a final victory of liberal democracy over absolutist monarchy, fascism, communism and other forms of authoritarian and anti-democratic governance. He dubbed this new wave of democracy the "end of history" (Fukuyama 1995 and 1989).

Within Western circles of academia, the assumption has always been that liberal representative democracy is "good" in and of itself, because it embodies and expresses fundamental human values, rights and freedoms aspired to by all individuals in every society. In this view, democracy "guarantees" the preeminence of the authentically democratic values and practices the West cherishes most: individual rights and freedoms, equality, justice, tolerance, mutual respect and trust, pluralism, rule of law, separation of power, limited government, majority rule with minority rights, consent of the governed, and more. For many it also has strategic significance in its relation/association to the concepts of free markets and trade, cooperation, prosperity, and peace and security. Democracies tend to not harbor terrorists and do not go to war with each other (Oneal 1997) (Ray 1997) (Mansfield 1995). From this point of view, it is therefore morally right and "realist" to promote and protect democratic principles.

Several prominent scholars have expressed this worldview in favor of democracy in one way or another. According to Thomas Carothers, the international community of democracies strongly believes that "democracy is a universal aspiration and a universal good." For Samuel Huntington, "democracy is good in itself and it has positive consequences for individual freedom, domestic stability, international peace and the United States of America." Robert Dahl posits that democracy is desirable and preferable to any other form of government because of its inherent virtues and its linkage with prosperity (T. Carothers 2004, 12) (Huntington 1991, xv, 28–29, 30–34, 59–60) (Dahl 1987, 44–61).

While some suggest that democracy should be a universal right, others recommend that once a people "choose democracy as their preferred form of government, other democracies have both the right and the duty to help maintain their democracy when it is threatened." (Frank 1994) (Munoz 1995) (Council on Foreign Relations' Independent Task Force 2003) (Mansfield 1995) (Kagan 2008). And most significantly for our purposes, in 2001 the governments of the Americas have affirmed in the OAS Inter-American Democratic Charter that "democracy is indispensable for stability, peace and development" in the Americas and its people "have a right to democracy" while "their governments have an obligation to promote and defend it."[1]

Democracy is thus no longer perceived as an ideology but as a universal "good" that legitimizes a political regime. As Guillermo O'Donnell said in his acceptance speech at the International Political Science Association's Lifetime Achievement Award, "...there have never been so many rulers who claim that their regimes are democratic... Across most of the globe today, the ultimate claim of a political regime to be legitimate –or at least acceptable— rests on the kind of popular consent that purportedly finds expression in the act of free voting... Today, as never before, we see authoritarian rulers making sometimes amazing contortions to persuade the world (if not their own people) that their right to rule flows from the holding of free elections." (O'Donnell 2007) (Huntington 1991: 47–50) (Fukuyama 1995: 33–11). Nobel Prize winner in economics, Amartya Sen, in a lecture at the World Bank, maintained: "there is strong evidence that economic and political freedoms reinforce each other" and that, "conversely, political repression could produce economic un-freedom." (Sen 1999, xii, 3–11) (Sen, "Democracy as a Universal Value" 1999).

These conceptual and practical policy considerations are consistent with Nobel prizewinner Douglas North's contention that economic development depends on the quality and strength of governmental institutions. In his view, state institutions not only must be efficient and effective but also limited in power, transparent, accountable, responsive to the needs of society and protective of the rule of law and of individual freedoms and rights. In short, they must be credible and legitimate, to provide the stable and predictable political environment that is a necessary condition for savings and investment, and for reducing the risks and the transaction costs of doing business—the conditions required for economic development and prosperity to take place (North 1990, 3–10) (Feng 2003).

In the same vein, one study concludes that in the long run "democratic institutions are instrumental in creating and deepening economic freedom, thus promoting economic development" because "democracy enhances growth by establishing and enforcing rules that protect property rights, promote general education, allow accumulation of private capital, reduce income inequality." (Feng 2003, 295- 299, 301–308) (Huntington 1991, 59–72).

For the past thirty years or so, the revival of democracy, in practice, and as an ideal form of government aspired to by many, has motivated and provided academics and leaders of western democracies and international organizations with the impetus and rationale to justify and engage in policies and actions to defend, preserve and promote democracy as the preferred system of governance for modern societies.

THE DEMOCRACY PROMOTERS

The United States and the European democracies, both individually and collectively, along with some multilateral organizations are the principal and most active defenders and promoters of democracy around the world.

For the United States, promoting and protecting democracy has become a major component of its foreign policy in every administration since President Carter's. George W. Bush, particularly after September 11, 2001, viewed promoting democracy as a "critical mission," of crucial strategic value in the struggle against religious fanaticism, tyranny, and terrorism, the new principal threats to U.S. security.[2] Democracy around the world became an imperative for the United States, largely due to the belief that democratic governments generally do not harbor or protect terrorists and thus are critical to guaranteeing worldwide cooperation, security, peace, and prosperity (Dobrinksy 2004, 73–79). Along with the claim (false as it turned out) that Saddam Hussein possessed chemical weapons of mass destruction, "installing" democracy (regime change at all costs) was the basic reasoning behind the controversial, extensive, and costly military intervention and occupation in Iraq.

According to Professor John Lewis Gaddis, the George W. Bush administration considered it no longer sufficient to follow the Clinton strategy of "engaging" in the "irreversible" process of "enlarging" world democratization. Because of the Bush administration's view that democracy "guarantees" security, it had to be "spread"; the world had to be "made safe for democracy" by any means, even if that meant by way of force, military intervention and occupation (Gaddis 2004, 76–77, 90–91, 106–107).

In his 2007 State of the Union address, President Bush asserted that the "war in Iraq is more than a clash of arms. It is a decisive ideological struggle, and the security of our nation is in the balance. So we advance our own security interests by helping moderates, reformers and brave voices for democracy. Free people are not drawn to violent and malignant ideologies...The great question of our day is whether America will help men and women in the Middle East to build free societies and share in the rights of all humanity. And I say, for the sake of our own security: We must."

He left no doubt as to the perceived threat: "The Shia and Sunni extremists are different faces of the same totalitarian threat. But whatever slogans they chant, when they slaughter the innocent, they have the same wicked purposes: They want to kill Americans, kill democracy in the Middle East and gain the weapons to kill on an even more horrific scale." (*The Washington Post*, 2007).

Nevertheless, for Thomas Carothers, a prominent expert on democracy promotion, Bush's actions in the Middle East damaged the policy of democracy promotion because of their "association with the war in Iraq and with forcible regime change more generally," and have been widely perceived as the cause of the decline of "America's reputation as a symbol of democracy and human rights." (Carothers 2012) (Carothers, "An Unwanted League", 2008).

The Obama administration, after attempting to distance itself from the previous administration's policies, returned to a policy of democracy promotion, but this time by emphasizing a multilateral approach, which involves working with international organizations, with traditional allies ("leading from behind"), supporting pro-democracy local reformers or revolutionaries (Tunisia, Lybia, Egypt), or encouraging emerging democracies that are "dictator-tolerant" (e.g., Brazil, India, South Africa, Turkey) to include democracy promotion as part of their foreign policy. Unlike that of his predecessor, this approach does not concentrate on a single "overarching foreign policy narrative" intent on remaking the world in the image of the United States. In

Afghanistan, for example, most pointedly, the U.S.'s main concern is not with democracy but only with the destruction of Al Qaeda and its security (Hiatt 2010).

As played out in the "Arab Spring" of 2011, however, according to Carothers, Obama's policy combines seemingly contradictory values and interests. In essence, it supports liberalization and democratization where "it appears to be occurring" with concerns and caution (if not paralysis) where security and economic interests appear to be threatened by radical Islam or political instability (T. Carothers 2012). This approach does not use public diplomacy to criticize or push too hard for democratization and human rights observance in countries such as China, Russia, Saudi Arabia, Cuba or Venezuela. Others have characterized it as being marked by a moral imperative combined with practical necessity (Hiatt 2010) (Nye 2011).

Obama's approach is consistent with Carothers' point that U. S. democracy promotion, at least since G.H.W. Bush' presidency (1988–2002), has been a bipartisan "semi-realist policy": strongly promoting democracy where it coincides with U.S. security and economic interests as in Latin America and Central and East Europe; and down-playing it where it collides with those interests, or may produce unintended consequences such as political and economic instability and insecurity and/or the election of anti-American candidates as in Egypt, Pakistan, Saudi Arabia, China and Indonesia. For others, however, this "semi-realist" approach essentially means that "security and economic interests trump democracy." (Carothers 2004, 7–8; 40–41) and (Huntington 1991, 91–100).

In terms of Latin America, the U.S. has, of course, been a key player in the historical process of continental relations that culminated in the creation of the OAS in 1948, as we have seen in previous chapters. That period of inter-American relations was marked by U.S. military interventions and occupations (the Monroe Doctrine, the Roosevelt Corollary, and the so-called Gun Boat and Dollar diplomacy) to protect its security and economic interests from European threats in the *circum* Caribbean, including the Panama Canal. Its dominant and intrusive role in Latin America and within the OAS continued through the second half of the twentieth century. Driven by its Cold War obsessive security concerns over communist (Soviet-Cuban) penetration of the continent, successive U.S. Governments carried out overt and covert interventions, e.g., against leftist Governments in Guatemala (1954), Cuba (1960s), Dominican Republic (1965), Chile (1973), Grenada 1983, and against the *Sandinistas* in Nicaragua and leftists guerrillas in Central America (1980s).

However, the Carter administration's (1977–1981) emphasis on human rights and democracy signaled the beginning of a significant change in U.S. foreign policy towards Latin America. This change was reflected in the OAS 1978 resolution condemning the Somoza dictatorship in Nicaragua and demanding his resignation, and in the OAS Human Rights Commission's visits and reports on gruesome human rights violation in Argentina in the late 1970s, perpetrated by its repressive military government during the so-called dirty war. The Reagan's administration staunch support of anti-communist military governments in South America and Central America, and its backing of the anti-*Sandinista* guerrilla forces in Nicaragua (the Contras), also morphed into a more democracy-friendly stance by the second half of the 1980s, as most Latin American countries returned to democracy and as the Cold War ended. In Central America it supported and even facilitated, unilaterally or multilaterally through the OAS, negotiations that ended in peace agreements, reconciliation, disarmament, guerrillas' reinsertion in society and the process of the democratization through elections.[3] By the late 1980s and the beginning of the 1990s, U.S. governments decidedly supported (led from behind?) a pro-democracy coalition within the OAS (along with Argentina, Canada, Chile, Costa Rica, Brazil, Colombia, Uruguay and Venezuela, among others) that actively participated in the development and application of its democracy norms and instruments, both at the "high and low politics" level, as analyzed throughout this book.

On the other hand, for the European powers, individually and/or collectively through the European Union (EU) or the Organization for Security and Cooperation in Europe (OSCE), democracy has become their raison d'être and its defense and promotion one of their main objectives. Since the early 1990s the EU Commission has played a very influential role in making democracy and human rights concerns and promotion an integral part of its relations with the developing world and with former communist countries in Eastern Europe that were seeking entry into the European Union (Piccone 2005, 116–118) (Santiso 2002) (Levitsky and Way 2005).

The EU nations tend to regard democracy and human rights not only as universal values but also as fundamental to the process of European integration. Democracy is a political criterion that conditions cooperation with and admission to the European Union. Their European Security Strategy calls for "stability of institutions guaranteeing democracy, the rule of law, human rights, and respect for the protection of minorities" and affirms that "the best protection for our security is a world of well-governed democratic states." Democracy promotion is today a "more explicit and central component of [the] external relations" of the EU and of many member states, although it puts greater emphasis on human rights than on political institutions and concentrates mainly on Sub-Saharan Africa. Democracy promotion, which it still requires better coordination and implementation, is nevertheless one of the most important considerations and objectives of European foreign relations, as expressed in the Lisbon Treaty (Youngs 2008) (Cardwell 2011).[4]

Simultaneously, the Organization for Security and Cooperation in Europe (OSCE) has a democracy requirement for membership and a mandate, executed through the Office for Democratic Institutions and Human Rights, to promote democracy by observing elections and providing assistance for the strengthening of democratic institution to the former communist states of eastern and central Europe. The North Atlantic Treaty Organization (NATO) is yet another multilateral organization that has recently acquired the mandate to protect and defend democracy (McMahon 2006, 60–71; 73–90).

Furthermore, some fast emerging democracies, like Brazil, India, Indonesia, Poland, South Africa, South Korea and Turkey, have transformed from once being on the receiving end of assistance for building or strengthening their democratic institutions, to becoming active international actors involved in promoting and defending democracy, through bilateral and multilateral channels. They perform this international function with different intensity, constancy, and commitment. Their rhetorical commitment to democracy is guaranteed and they will always denounce violations of human rights, condemn coups d'état or persecution of opposition politicians, and will even participate in multilateral sanctions against violators. But they are often reluctant or timid to publicly criticize governments that slowly but persistently erode (a coup in slow motion) democratic institutions, particularly if this happens in a neighboring state or in a significant economic/trade partner. [5]

In Latin America, despite the collective commitment to democracy, the hesitancy of a government to call attention to undemocratic governance or violations of human and political rights in another state of the region is based on a couple of considerations. One would be that the "accused" government would perceive such a stance as an interventionist affront to its sovereignty and would probably react with breaking economic/trade ties and possibly diplomatic relations as well. Another would be the likely negative repercussion of such a situation on the accuser's domestic business and economic interests. And finally it is highly probable that the democracy promoter's government may be charged with being a lackey of the imperialist powers (the West and U.S.). This explains why, for example, countries like Argentina, Brazil, Chile or Colombia do not speak up publicly about the erosion of democracy in Venezuela under the *chavista* regime and its increasing tendency to become an electoral autocracy. No one is about to "upset" the regime and forfeit his largesse with oil, petro dollars and his domestic market that imports almost everything it consumes. In this case, economic interests do trump democracy. Even U.S. governments have been reluctant (until recently) to criticize the regime, as Venezuela is one of its major oil suppliers.

Moreover, a multitude of national and international inter-governmental, semi-governmental and nongovernmental organizations also engage in the business of the democracy promotion. For example, even the United Nations, whose member states include non-democracies and does not have an explicit mandate to promote democracy, does carry out, indirectly, programs and activities to advance democratic values and practices. Remarkably, in 2001, its General Assembly passed a Resolution that "calls upon States to promote and consolidate democracy," and in 2005 the community of democracies created a U.N. Democracy Fund (UNDEF) to provide assistance to strengthen democracy (Cheema 2005) (United Nations 2006). Despite its lack of an explicit mandate, the U.N. also promotes democracy "surreptitiously" and indirectly through the United Nations Development Program (UNDP) and its Democratic Governance global programs that support member states in strengthening democratic values and practices and institutions. These programs foster participation, accountability, transparency and probity in governmental affairs as well as access to the justice system; they also support the strengthening of electoral and legislative institutions as well as public administration systems to increase governmental effectiveness and responsiveness in delivering basic services for the poor and fostering socioeconomic development.[6]

Likewise, while the World Bank's mission is to promote development and reduce poverty, its loans, programs and activities now emphasize the importance of fighting corruption and promoting individual rights and freedoms, citizen participation, the rule of law, transparency and accountability in state institutions, as essential components of "good governance." The new development vision includes the Bank's concern, if implicit, for the promotion of democratic values and practices, which are now considered to be "crucial for successful development and poverty reduction." The vision recognizes (finally) that economics is not isolated from politics (democratic or not) and that political institutions do matter: They condition, facilitate or hinder the nature and direction of economic public policy.

In the Western Hemisphere, OAS member states, in a momentous collective decisions changed their constituent Charter in 1985 to establish that one of the Organization's main purposes was "to promote and consolidate representative democracy." As we shall see in future chapters, in 1991 they committed themselves to collectively defend and restore democracy wherever it was interrupted in the hemisphere, and in 1992 they confirmed that democracy be a precondition for OAS membership. Later on, in 2001, they signed the Inter-American Democratic Charter (IADC), consolidating and expanding a collective commitment to promote and defend democracy.

Similarly, the Inter-American Development Bank (IDB), following the lead of the World Bank and of its democratic stakeholders, by the late 1980s also adopted a state modernization strategy, as an instrument to support "state reform for the consolidation of democratic governance," within its overall mission to provide financial and technical assistance for sustainable socioeconomic development and poverty reduction.[7] Additionally, regional subgroupings such MERCOSUR, a trade and political grouping which includes Argentina, Brazil, Paraguay and Uruguay and Venezuela;[8] the Union of South American Nations (UNASUR), the Andean Community, and the

Central American Integration System (SICA) and the Community of Latin American and Caribbean States (CELAC) all have a "democracy clause" as a condition for membership.[9]

Finally, there are numerous international cooperation agencies from individual countries involved in democracy promotion: for example, the United States Agency of International Development (USAID), the Canadian International Development Agency (CIDA), Spanish Agency for International Cooperation and Development (AECID), the Swedish International Development Agency (SIDA), the Westminster Foundation for Democracy (WFD), the Norwegian Center for Democracy (NCD); and political parties foundations such as the U.S. National Democratic Institute (NDI) and the International Republic Institute (IRI), the Konrad Adenauer, Friedrich Naumann and Friedrich Ebert Foundations of Germany, the Olaf Palme International Center of Sweden, and the Netherlands Institute for Multiparty Democracy (NIMD), among others. The Institute for Democracy and Electoral Assistance (IDEA) in Sweden, and the Soros Foundation Open Society Institute also contribute to the effort of promoting democracy (Carothers 2006) (Pevehouse 2006) (Herman and Piccone 2002) (Youngs 2008) (von Meijenfeld 2012).

DEMOCRACY PROMOTION: HIGH AND LOW POLITICS

The "promoters" identified in the previous section have used a variety of approaches and instruments to promote democracy. In general, democracy promotion may include any national or multilateral policy pronouncement, action and activity designed and executed to foster, support, strengthen, protect or defend a democratic regime. Analytically, however, one can discern at least two levels at which nation-states or intergovernmental organizations approach democracy promotion and protection.

One is the "high politics" level, which refers to policy pronouncements, decisions and actions carried out at the highest levels of national governments and/or intergovernmental organizations to protect and promote democracy. It may comprise a combination of declarations, resolutions, international conventions and treaty obligations to promote, exercise and defend democracy (as happens through the OAS, MERCOSUR or the EU). More specifically, democracy promotion at this level may involve high level diplomatic cooperation, consultation, political observation missions, negotiation and mediation or good offices efforts to manage crises, support and sustain or restore democratic processes and institutions. It may also include condemnation, warnings, censure and threat of sanctions; political pressures to prevent a breakdown or a further interruption of democratic institutions; economic embargoes, political/diplomatic sanctions (through non-recognition, exclusion or suspension from an international organization, or severance of diplomatic relations), and/or military intervention and occupation to restore democracy. It could also consist of "positive incentives" such as promises of economic and financial cooperation and admission to the European Union if democracy is observed. [10]

The other level, "low politics," refers to policies, decisions and actions carried out by governmental, intergovernmental and nongovernmental agencies through technical assistance programs and projects designed to implement the policies or guidelines decided at the "high politics" level. This assistance includes a variety of possible approaches and instruments. One approach is through straightforward financial assistance (loans and grants by international banks for general or specific state modernization programs, for example). Another consists of technical assistance, which may involve support for a) research to develop new knowledge on democratic governance or institution building, b) workshops/seminars to exchange experiences and best practices, c) training programs for democratic leadership and d) advisory technical missions on specific topics related to democratic governance. The objective here is the promotion of democratic values and practices (e.g., transparency, probity, accountability in governance) and the strengthening (capacity or institution building) of political and state institutions, like legislatures, political parties, local governments, and electoral bodies. Low politics efforts may also include electoral observations and technical/political missions to support or facilitate in-country political negotiations/dialogue in conflict situations and others. As modest and limited as these instruments appear to be, they are, nevertheless, the last link in the long chain in the process of promoting democracy. Moreover, they represent the whole gamut of instruments of technical assistance provided by international donors/promoters such as USAID, CIDA, the World Bank, the IDB, the OAS and others.

In this vein, Cheema (2005, 245) mentions "workshops, and policy seminars, expert consultancies on institutional design, equipment donations, infrastructure improvement, small grants, skills training courses, study tours" as modalities of intervention or types of technical assistance provided by international actors. On the other hand, Azpuru, Finkel, Pérez-Liñán and Selligson (2008) suggest "empowering civil society and domestic actors" as an approach to promote, consolidate and defend democratic governance. Fukuyama also speaks of the importance of "local ownership" ("Stateness' First" 2006). However, none of these works provides details of how exactly the proposed activities promote democracy. And this indeed is a major query that the literature on democracy promotion has had a hard time addressing. Later chapters in this book will attempt to answer or shed some light on the theoretical and practical aspects of this crucial question.

CHALLENGING DEMOCRACY PROMOTION: THE CRITICS

Democracy promotion certainly has its critics. The challenges come from several quarters.

In the United States, in the context of a political polarization that emerged as a result of G. W. Bush's foreign policy, a group of "neo-realists" emerged to question U.S. democracy promotion in the Arab world and in Iraq particularly. The neo-realists rejected the notion that democracy can be imposed, that it can "flourish" in diverse circumstances once dictators are removed, that it is a universal positive good, and that its absence is dangerous for U.S. security. They argued that the President's neo-conservative or "neo-idealist" indiscriminate push of democracy, in regime change mode, was counterproductive and dangerous for U.S. interests and security–the main concern of the "neo-realist." They believe that G. W. Bush administration's democracy promotion in the Middle East was insensitive to cultural and historical specificities and differences and that it generated resentment, resistance, and anti-Americanism—because it essentially represented a fundamental threat to socioeconomic, cultural and political patterns of power relations in the Muslim world—which are not compatible with democratic values and practices. Moreover, it had the unintended effect of inflaming Islamic opinion and strengthening radical Islamic and anti-U.S. and terrorist forces (Clarke 2005, 245–87).[11]

Essentially, the above argument coincides with Professor Gaddis' questioning of the premise that terrorism originates in non-democratic states, and with his suggestion that its origin might be found "in more complex and less definable [cultural] causes." (Gaddis 2004, 103–104). Furthermore, Fukuyama (2006, 12) argues: "modernization and democracy are a good thing in their own right, but in the Muslim world they are likely to increase rather than dampen the terrorist problem in the short run." Thus, in a region where there are supreme economic and security interests for the U.S., the "neo-realists" would argue then that it is best to concentrate on securing stability and peace, and avoid the volatility, antipathy, and antagonism generated by efforts to foster democratization. For them, regime change and democracy building is not essential for maintaining U.S. security, its survival or its superpower status. Military intervention and occupation, as in Iraq and Afghanistan, may in fact generate regional opposition and international discredit, weaken the country and distract its energy from the real threat to its security: Islamic terrorism and the rise and challenge from China and revisionist Russia (Mearsheimer and Walt 2003) (Zakaria, The Post-American World 2008) (Betts 2014) (Haass 2014) (McFaul, Sestanovich and Mearsheimer 2014) (Kissinger 2014, 224–5).

There are also "preconditionists" or "sequentialists," who believe that democracy promotion, to be effective and viable, requires certain preconditions in the country where democracy is to be promoted, such as compatible values, the existence of the rule of law, stability and a minimum of socio-economic development. In their view, states that do not meet these criteria are failed states that cannot sustain democracy. They require state building first, as Fukuyama would argue ("Stateness' First" 2006). For this group, encouraging and imposing elections is no guarantee that a liberal representative democracy will emerge. In societies that are not "ready," it is likely that elections will not be "free and fair," that winners will not be necessarily democratic and pro-U.S., that they will use elections as a means to justify the imposition of their illiberal values and practices, and that they would likely be anti-American—all of which ultimately threaten US interests and security (Carothers 2007, 12–14) (Berman 2007, 28–29) (Zakaria 1997).

Some others, of course, argue that democracy promotion is "imperialistic" and self-serving, masking intentions aimed at controlling the supply of oil from the Middle East; while others assert that economic and security interests always trump democracy (Elshtain 2007) (Herman and Piccone 2002).

At the operational and practitioners' level, Santiso maintains that the process of democracy assistance in the European Union is too bureaucratic, technocratic, organizationally fragmented, and lacking in conceptual/strategic clarity, integration and coordination. Its objectives and activities are dispersed, which limits the capacity of the European Commission, in charge of international cooperation, to provide democracy assistance effectively; and it places too much emphasis on "improving the management dimension of the technical and financial assistance" instead of focusing more on "political and strategic considerations." Others concur that while democracy promotion in the European Union is a prominent component of its external relations, it is not yet a very coherent and coordinated enterprise (Santiso 2002, 12–14; 27–28) (European Democracy Foundation 2006, 3–12) (Azpuru, et al. 2008).

For Thomas Carothers, one of the most knowledgeable U.S. writers on democracy promotion, practitioners are frequently "guided by fads and overstate their accomplishments" and assume that "the definition of democracy is self-evident and that therefore the goals of democracy assistance organizations do not require intensive elaboration." He also expresses concern that there is "very little rigorous systematic knowledge" about the complexities of democracy promotion and how to accomplish it, and "that the academic world is not up to it." For him, the subject is "remarkably understudied" and "there has been very little research on the impact of democracy promotion." (T. Carothers 2004, 2–35) (Barkan 2012).

More specifically and fundamentally, from this book's perspective, there is a dearth of knowledge and understanding of the technical assistance instruments employed in democracy promotion; that is, how exactly democracy is promoted at the low politics, ground level. The literature on the subject mostly ignores this crucial question, the last link in the democracy assistance process, and does not, inexplicably, focus on its central role and impact on the promotion and/or strengthening of democratic values, practices and institutions.

Similarly, even though Finkel et al. found in their study a "consistent and clear positive impact of foreign assistance on democratization, and that USAID Democracy and Governance programs' funding have a significant positive impact on democracy," they recognize that it is difficult to "measure" impact when there is no consensus on the meaning of democracy (the dependent variable that democracy promotion efforts seek to impact), and that the "broader its definition, the more complex is the task." This essentially pinpoints what is missing: an operational definition of democracy.

There are still some perceptive analysts, like Carothers and others, that point out that most high officials in the democracy promotion business expect too much of external or international institutions and their "experts"— their attitudes, approaches and instruments—show insufficient confidence in local institutions and their human resources. They fail to recognize the outsiders' limitations and assume that democratic values and practices are desired by all and will be easily accepted and adopted everywhere; they frequently "overestimate the power of elections and underestimate the influence of under-development and poverty, cultural heterogeneity and lack of experience with political pluralism" (Carothers 2004, 22–24). Moreover, these analysts warn that democracy promotion now faces a new troubling world, which includes an emerging alternative model (e.g., Chinese "authoritarian capitalism") that resists and challenges democracy assistance and questions its legitimacy, as well as the value and preeminence of liberal democracy. In Carothers' view, this new development presents a "daunting new challenge" for democracy promoters, which requires reflection and new thinking (Carothers 2007, 114–115) (Gershman 2006).

In a similar track, Robert Kagan argues that liberal democracy is neither irreversible nor inevitable and that it faces serious challenges from advancing "great autocratic powers" and "reactionary forces of Islamic radicalism," and that the world's democracies must come together and constitute a "concert of democracies" to defend it and promote it (Kagan 2008, 97–105).

Finally, Larry Diamond suggests that democracy promotion must focus on fixing certain elements of political culture that are dysfunctional to good democratic governance, such as corruption, patronage and abuse of power, which he emphasizes are not flaws "that can be corrected with a technical fix or a political push" from one day to the other. In a most relevant and prescient comment, he proposes that reducing the negative effects of those dysfunctional elements on a democratic political culture "requires revolutionary change in institutions (Diamond, 2006, 114–115 and 119–120). And it must be added, as we shall see later on, that promoting democracy also requires promoting change in the political culture—from the predominance of anti-democratic values and practices to the prevalence of democratic ones.

A CAVEAT ON THE COMPLEXITY AND LIMITS OF DEMOCRACY PROMOTION

As we shall see, democracy promotion at the technical assistance level is not always or strictly or exclusively a "technical" endeavor; hence the notion of the "low politics" level. It is both technical and political. In fact, democracy promotion at the technical "low politics" level is an unpredictable, politically sensitive, difficult and complex undertaking, because it involves attempts to effect changes in political values, attitudes, behavior and institutions. It is the necessary complement of "high politics" democracy promotion. Those involved in technical activities of democracy promotion need political skills and political support from international, national and local leaders to facilitate the implementation of their programs. Likewise, political leaders intent on introducing political changes related to democracy promotion need the support of those with technical/substantive knowledge to have credibility for their proposals for political change.

Furthermore, democracy promotion from external actors is an international cooperation activity, which involves complex and complicated "donor-client" or "promoter-recipient" relations. At a minimum, it requires coordinating many interactions (sometimes conflictive) amongst several international, national and local agencies, their interests, mandates and capabilities. It involves harmonizing the funding requirements of recipient countries and the funding capacity or interest and preference of the international donor or promoter community (e.g., intergovernmental organizations, foundations, international development agencies, international development banks).

International organizations and development agencies, for example, have to follow certain principles (e.g., of non-intervention), mandates and bureaucratic/administrative procedures (frequently cumbersome), and have to address and satisfy diplomats of recipient member states, national governmental officials (from foreign or economy ministries, political party or congressional official/authority), plus the executing agency (government institution or a nongovernmental organization) and their national experts who work on the program or project being implemented. Additionally, the national counterparts have their own regulations and interests, and usually face issues or challenges such as lack of institutional or organizational capacity (human and material resources) to design, receive and implement international aid for democracy. Even good intentioned efforts aimed at "local ownership" have to contend with these internal factors.

Thus, international institutions and organizations involved in democracy promotion need qualified and dedicated democracy practitioners and adequate organizational resources. Institutions, practitioners and programs must not only be strategic but also politically sensitive to different political cultures and changing circumstances, and must have sufficient flexibility and agility to adapt to them. The promoters must not be impatient with the pace of results, must avoid seeking short-term gratification, and must be mindful that changes in political culture are complex and take a long time. Those involved must have a solid understanding of the nature of democracy, as well as political/diplomatic skills to negotiate and build consensus across cultural frontiers. Individuals from the donor community must be knowledgeable about the region they assist and must have the ability to fund raise, lead, coordinate and execute relevant international cooperation programs/projects with transparency, efficiency and effectiveness. Democracy promotion requires prudence, humility and realism about the limitations and difficulties of the task.

Additionally, performance indicators designed to evaluate democracy promotion programs must absolutely take this complexity into consideration; they must recognize the fact that the real changes in institutions, values and practices that are sought will only be perceived indirectly, in the long run, when and if democratic political institutions are no longer dismissed by citizens as ineffective or irrelevant, but are accepted and valued as fundamental for the sustainability of democracy.

Moreover, the complex promoter-recipient relationship that characterizes international cooperation for the promotion of democracy requires not only clarity of purpose, well-focused assistance programs, relevance and effectiveness, but also leadership and organizational-managerial capacity at both ends; and because democracy promotion is a gradual, long-term task, it also requires sustained external and internal institutional commitments. This is what makes democracy promotion respected and valued and what eventually confers its due legitimacy.

As we shall see in future chapters, this book develops a useful theory of democracy promotion (i.e., how to do it effectively). This theory is based on an understanding of democracy in terms of a democratic political culture, leadership and institutions (the dependent variables or "the target" of the promotion effort), and is based on more than twenty years of field experience to promote democracy in Latin America using technical assistance instruments developed at the OAS.

But before we enter that complex but exciting field, one needs to understand how the OAS acquired its present prominent role of promoting and defending democracy in the hemisphere, and how it became the central and most important multilateral institution in the Americas for democracy promotion.

NOTES

1. See http://www.oas.org/OASpage/eng/Documents/Democractic_Charter.htm.

2. President Woodrow Wilson, at the beginning of the 20th century, had a foreign policy of "making the world safe for democracy."

3. The U.S. Government was a major source of voluntary funding for the OAS International-al Commission of Support and Verification (CIAV in Spanish), which was in charge of verifying and supporting the implementation of those agreements (Comisión Internacional de Apoyo y Verificación 1998). In addition the U.S. and Canada have been major financial contributors to the work of the OAS in democracy and human rights promotion and protection.

4. See Art. 21 of the Lisbon Treaty (2009), http://europa.eu/lisbon_treaty/faq/

5. For an extended discussion on various democracy promoters, see articles in the *Journal of Democracy* (2011) on the question of whether or not "new democracies support democracy," and particularly Piccone's article (2011). On Poland and other eastern European countries' efforts to promote democracy in their neighborhood, see Petrova (2012).

6. See United Nations GA/RES/55/96, "Promoting and Consolidating Democracy" (December 2000), which reaffirms and goes beyond the principles of Universal Declaration of Human Rights of 1948, and the International Pact on Civil and Political Rights of 1966. (United Nations Development Program 2002) (United Nations 2006). See also http://www.undp.org/content/undp/en/home/ourwork/democraticgovernance/overview.html.

7. See http://www.iadb.org/aboutus/III/strategies. See also Inter-American Development Bank (IDB 2003).

8. See *Protocolo de Ushuaia sobre Compromiso Democrático en el Mercosur, la República de Chile y de Bolivia* (MERCOSUR July, 1998). Argentina, Brazil, Paraguay and Uruguay are full members; Bolivia and Chile are associate members. A controversial decision, while Paraguay was suspended, incorporated Venezuela as a full member in 2012. In 2006, its members created the Democracy Observatory, which has not been fully operative.

9. CELAC, however, is an odd and incongruous anti-U.S. block that includes Cuba, whose dictatorial government recently held its pro-tempore presidency.

10. Pevehouse (2006, 1–14, 15–45) correctly inserts the issue of democracy promotion in the broader context of international relations and its impact on domestic politics. See also Council on Foreign Relations' Independent Task Force (2003), Herman and Piccone (2002), Cheema (2005), and as we shall see in later chapters, the OAS "high politics" efforts in defending democracy in some of its member states.

11. For Huntington, Confucianism and Islam are "peculiarly hostile to" democracy (Huntington 1991, 300).

Chapter Five

The New Diplomatic and Legal Instruments for the Collective Promotion and Defense of Democracy

THE NEW GLOBAL AND HEMISPHERIC REALITIES

The new, drastically changed international and hemispheric order that emerged at the end of the Cold War in the late 1980s provided the context within which the new OAS role in the defense and promotion of democracy evolved.

With the end of the Cold War, the "third democratic wave" grew with the spread of liberal democracy into the formerly Soviet bloc, while simultaneously ushering in a process of liberalization of world markets and commerce. The emergence of this new international order was characterized by the preeminence of democracy and free market economies, and by a process of growing global interdependence that extends to virtually every aspect of society, culture, economics and politics. Falling prices in communications, information, technology and transportation facilitated and fueled this process. Issues and challenges related to drug trafficking, terrorism, security, democracy, the environment, trade, human rights, and health, among others, have become more and more interdependent, and have also linked governments and societies in an increasingly complex and widespread interdependent global network. These challenges are *"inter-mestic"*: that is, part international and part domestic, requiring increased solidarity, collaboration, and international and regional cooperation. They cannot be handled or resolved unilaterally or only within the borders of any single country, no matter how powerful an individual nation-state may be.

In the Western Hemisphere, by the mid-1980s most member states of the OAS had returned to democratic governance. This new continental reality stood in stark contrast to the first thirty some years of the Organization (1948 to early 1980s) when dictatorial, military, authoritarian, semi-democratic, and democratic governments co-existed in the hemisphere. That lack of regime congruence, however, did not prevent member states, through the OAS or unilaterally, largely for reasons related to the Cold War, from taking action to defend democracy against dictators such as Francois Duvalier, Rafael Trujillo, and Anastasio Somoza, or against the Fidel Castro Communist regime. But, precisely because of the regime differences, those actions did not lead to specific permanent instruments for the defense and promotion of democracy.

Thus, the post-Cold War changes at the global level plus the new democratic regime congruence in the region produced a general consensus on the need to defend and promote democracy in the hemisphere. This new reality eventually led the OAS member states to commit themselves to collaborate to strengthen and consolidate the democratic order in each country, and through their hemispheric organization, to develop new diplomatic, legal and bureaucratic (operational) norms and instruments to collectively promote and defend democracy. The interruption of democracy in one member state thus became a threat to every democracy in the hemisphere. Moreover, hemispheric peace and security came to depend on the security, stability, and continuity of each democracy in the region–conforming to the Kantian notion of "democratic peace," whereby democratic freedoms and institutional checks and balances tend to favor peaceful solutions to international disputes and conflicts.[1]

The development of this new role, however, has not been linear, automatic or easy. It required a tortuous, in-depth debate to overcome the tension arising between this new collective commitment to defend and promote democracy, and the long-held principles enshrined in the inter-American system, including the legal equality of states, their absolute sovereignty and non-intervention. Despite the long-standing hemispheric aspiration and concern for democracy, and despite the fact that as early as 1948, the OAS Charter had required that member states be organized "on the basis of the effective exercise of representative democracy," some countries' reluctance to forgo those principles presented a formidable obstacle to the adoption of the OAS norms and instruments for the defense and promotion of democracy in the Americas—at least until the mid-1980s. Secretary General Baena Soares reveals, for example, a heated discussion among delegates from the member states as to whether or not electoral observation would violate the principle of non-intervention (Baena Soares 1994, 142–145).

Another example of the unwillingness to relinquish the non-intervention principle is the Mexican declaration expressing its disagreement with the adoption in 1995 of the "Washington Protocol," now Article 9 of the OAS Charter, which allows for the suspension from the Organization of a *de facto* government. The statement emphasized that democracy cannot be imposed from the outside and that "it is unacceptable for a regional organization to be given supranational authority and tools to intervene in the internal affairs of our states." (Inter-American Juridical Committee 1998, 87).

THE NEW LEGAL/DIPLOMATIC INSTRUMENTS AND THEIR APPLICATION

However, since the mid-1980s, the collective commitment to democracy materialized in the approval and application of a series of legal and diplomatic instruments.[2]

1985 Charter Amendments

The first set of instruments came about through a series of amendments to the OAS constituent Charter itself. With the modifications made in 1985, the promotion and consolidation of representative democracy explicitly became one of the main purposes of the Organization, with the caveat that it had to be carried out with due respect for the principle of non-intervention. Another amendment to the Charter (Article 110) also conferred new "powers" on the Secretary General, authorizing him to bring to the attention of the Permanent Council or the General Assembly of the OAS "any matter which in his opinion might threaten the peace and security of the hemisphere."

These changes in the Charter opened the way for the OAS and its Secretary General to participate in and influence the peace and democratization process in Central America in the late 1980s. The subregion had long been engulfed in low-intensity warfare between the leftist guerrillas (pro-Castro and pro-Soviet Union) and the militarized Governments of El Salvador, Guatemala and Nicaragua—the latter until 1979 when the *Sandinista* guerrillas took over from the Somoza dictatorship (Child, 1986) (LeoGrande, 2000). With the *Sandinistas* in power, the conflict in Nicaragua changed in nature and greatly intensified, as the anti-Sandinistas turned into a rebel guerrilla force known as the "Contras" (financed by the U.S. Government and operating out of Honduras and Costa Rica) bent on overthrowing the pro-Cuban and pro-Soviet Union *Sandinistas*.

Concerned over the worsening conflict in Central America, in November 1986, the Secretaries General of the OAS, Baena Soares, and of the United Nations, the Peruvian Pérez de Cuellar, in an unprecedented effort at coordination among the two organizations, offered their support and cooperation to

the Central American countries and to the Contadora Group (Mexico, Colombia, Venezuela and Panama) and the Support Group (Argentina, Brazil,
Peru and Uruguay). Their objective was to sustain and consolidate the ongoing but fragile peace process in the region. The OAS and the U.N. offered
assistance focused on monitoring, encouraging and facilitating the negotiation process as well as compliance with the "peace and democracy" agreements that were eventually signed in Esquipulas (Guatemala), Sapoa, (Nicaragua) and Tela (Honduras).

A few years before, the OAS had played a significant role in delegitimiz-
ing the Somoza government, when the Seventeenth Meeting of Consultation
of Ministers of Foreign Affairs acting as the Organ of Consultation in 1979
recommended that the Somoza regime be replaced immediately and a democratic government installed. This OAS involvement in Nicaragua against the
Somoza dictatorship represented perhaps the beginning of a new era of acti-
vism by the Organization on behalf of democracy, which later crystallized in
the political and diplomatic instruments discussed here. On that occasion, as
on others before and after the conflicts in Central America and the Caribbean, a cause and effect relationship was established between the struggle
against dictatorship and in favor of democracy, on the one hand, and the
threats to the peace and security of the region, on the other (Wilson 1989,
480) (Seventeenth Meeting of Consultation of Ministers of Foreign Affairs,
1979).

The Foreign Ministers of both groups swiftly accepted the OAS-U.N.
offer of cooperation and assistance, and invited the two Secretaries General
to participate in a fact-finding mission to review and give a new impetus to
the peace effort. The Ministers and the Secretaries General traveled to Central America and held a meeting in Mexico City (January 1987) at which
both officials were requested to continue their support of the peace process
(Caminos & Lavalle, 1989) (Baena Soares 1994, 183–203).

Following a proposal by the President of Costa Rica, Oscar Arias, entitled
"Procedures to Establish a Solid and Lasting Peace in Central America," the
Presidents of Central America signed the Esquipulas II agreement in August
1987, which created the International Verification and Monitoring Commis-
sion (IVMC). This Commission was made up of the Foreign Ministers of
Central America, the Contadora Group, the Support Group, and the two
Secretaries General. The Commission's principal function was to monitor the
peace process and verify that parties were upholding their commitments. [3]

Subsequently, the OAS Secretary General participated as an observer, and
on some occasions as an informal mediator and facilitator of the negotiation
process between the Nicaraguan Government and the rebel guerrilla army,
the "*Resistencia Nicaragüense*," or the "Contras," which culminated in the
Sapoa Accord of March 1988. The accord called for the cessation of military
operations, the beginning of negotiations, a general amnesty, guarantees of

free press and free elections, and the establishment of a specific Verification Commission for Nicaragua, composed of Cardinal Miguel Obando and the OAS Secretary General. As a result, the *Sandinista* government requested the OAS to send an observer mission for its national elections in February 1990, in accordance with the 1989 OAS General Assembly resolution on "Human Rights, Democracy and Electoral Observations," which instructed the Secretary General to organize electoral observations at the request of a member state.

The Presidents of Central America, at a summit meeting in Tela, Honduras, in August 1989, made further progress toward peace and democracy in the region by creating the International Support and Verification Commission (CIAV-OAS), and assigned to it the responsibility of developing a humanitarian program for the demobilization, repatriation, and voluntary relocation of former irregular combatants (Contras) and their families, and requested the Secretaries General of the OAS and the U.N. to establish the Commission immediately (International Support and Verification Commission, 1996). The OAS became responsible for guaranteeing the Tela Agreement and facilitating its compliance as far as Nicaragua was concerned. The agreement included a cease-fire, disarmament, demobilization, repatriation and resettlement of the Nicaraguan Resistance, as well as the provision of social services, socioeconomic assistance, and guarantees of no reprisals. The U.N. became responsible for demobilizing the Contras in Honduras. By March 1990, in the Tocontín (Honduras) Agreement, the new Nicaraguan Government of Violeta Chamorro (elected in February) ratified all the components of the peace plan and the leaders of the Nicaraguan Resistance agreed to disarm and demobilize. [4]

In short, the 1985 Charter amendment establishing the new OAS role of promoting democracy in the hemisphere made it possible for the Organization to have an active and critical participation in the Central American peace and democratization process.

Resolution 1080

The 1991 OAS General Assembly resolution 1080, "Representative Democracy," approved in Santiago, Chile, became the second diplomatic instrument for the collective defense and promotion of democracy. Resolution 1080 reiterates the member states' commitment to promote democracy but further establishes a mutual commitment to take joint and immediate action to protect or restore democracy when threatened or breached in a member state. The resolution also invests the Secretary General with new powers—specifically, the authority to convene a meeting of the Permanent Council of the Organization when there is "a sudden or irregular interruption of the democratic political institutional process or of the legitimate exercise of power by a democratically elected government" in a member state. The Permanent Council, in turn, may convene an ad hoc Meeting of Ministers of Foreign Affairs or a special meeting of the General Assembly, to decide on the specific measures to be adopted by the OAS.

APPLICATIONS OF RESOLUTION 1080

Resolution 1080 was applied in four specific cases: Haiti in 1991, Peru in 1992, Guatemala in 1993, and Paraguay in 1996. It was not invoked in the political crisis of Venezuela in 1992 or in Ecuador in 1997.

Haiti's Military Coup

On September 29, 1991, General Raoul Cédras staged a military coup, which deposed the constitutionally and democratically elected Government of President Jean-Bertrand Aristide. Immediately after the overthrow, Secretary General Baena Soares invoked Resolution 1080 and convened a meeting of the Permanent Council. The Council condemned the coup d'état and called an ad hoc Meeting of Ministers of Foreign Affairs. The Foreign Ministers also condemned the coup, and decided, inter alia, not to recognize the illegal military government; to recommend the suspension of financial, commercial and diplomatic relations; to suspend cooperation and financial and military assistance; and to send a mission headed by the Secretary General to express to the new authorities the OAS's condemnation of the action taken against the constitutional government. These were unprecedented and ground breaking "interventionist" measures by an organization whose member states had always invoked the principle of non-intervention to prevent any collective action which might be considered interference in the affairs of one of its members.[5]

Over the next three years, the Foreign Ministers met five times within the framework of the OAS to analyze the situation in Haiti. In between their meetings, the Permanent Council also met periodically, monitoring closely, together with the Secretary General, the events taking place in Haiti. Both reiterated their condemnation of the coup d'état, and gradually increased pressure on the *de facto* Government. At these meetings, member states agreed to several measures: to send a civilian mission to observe whether human rights were being violated and to facilitate the restoration of democracy; to impose a trade embargo, with humanitarian exceptions; and to recommend new sanctions that included the freezing of assets in international banks, and the suspension of credit, international assistance and commercial flights. They also agreed to seek the cooperation of the United Nations and the Inter-American Development Bank in applying these punitive measures.

By February 1992, the OAS Secretary General had facilitated, through his good offices at the OAS headquarters, the so-called Washington Agreements between the *de facto* President's (General Cédras) Presidential Commission and the representatives of the Haitian Parliament. All parties recognized the urgent need to find a negotiated solution to the crisis, to fully restore democratic institutions, and to reestablish constitutional guarantees and freedoms. They also called for the return of President Aristide, a general amnesty, separation between the armed forces and the police, and the presence of an OAS Civilian Mission to guarantee compliance with the accords (Baena Soares 1994, 95–97).

After much foot-dragging by the *de facto* government, the OAS sent a small civilian mission (eighteen members), known as OAS-DEMOC, to Haiti. The mission arrived in September 1992, and began observing and promoting respect for human rights, helping to reduce the level of violence and verifying and promoting compliance with the Washington Agreements. The OAS requested U.N. assistance, and a group of observers from the world organization joined the OAS mission. Together, as of February 1993, they formed the International Civilian Mission in Haiti (MICIVIH), which at one time had as many as two hundred members. As a result of this, a close and fruitful collaborative relationship began to develop between the OAS and the U.N. through their respective Secretaries General. Also, the governing bodies of both organizations (the OAS Meeting of Foreign Affairs Ministers and its Permanent Council, and the U.N. General Assembly and its Security Council) explicitly provided mutual support for their respective actions to end the crisis.[6]

The crisis came to a dramatic and unsatisfactory end about a year after the signing of the Governors Island Agreement (July 1993), which had stipulated a number of steps for the return of President Aristide prior to October 30 of that year (Forsyte, 1996).[7] The *de facto* government had failed to comply with the aforementioned agreement by blocking progress in the dialogue between the Presidential Commission and representatives of the Haitian Parliament. There had also been no movement on reforming the judicial system or the police force, or with the appointment of new military authorities or the early retirement of the Commander of the Armed Forces. In October 1993, the *de facto* Government prevented the landing of American and Canadian troops sent to the country within the framework of Security Council Resolution 867 to facilitate the implementation of Article 5 of the Governors Island Agreement. To make matters worse, the military government expelled the MICIVIH, and the human rights situation deteriorated dramatically, while the flow of refugees to the United States increased considerably.

Against that backdrop, the U.N. Security Council, by means of Resolution 940 of July 31, 1994, within the framework of Chapter VII of its Charter, authorized "member States to join a multilateral force…to use all means necessary to facilitate the departure from Haiti of the military leaders in accordance with the Governors Island Agreement, the prompt return of the legitimately elected President, and the reestablishment of the legitimate authorities of the Government of Haiti." This decision of the highest multilateral entity, the U.N., permitted the Government of the United States to begin exerting diplomatic and military pressure that culminated in the removal of the *de facto* government and the return of Aristide as President of Haiti in October 1994.[8]

Although the crisis in Haiti took about three years to resolve and ended in a rather unsatisfactory manner, the member states did comply with their new commitment to democracy and, in an unprecedented collective action, for the first time used the new instruments of the OAS to restore democracy where it had been breached by a military coup.

Venezuela's Attempted Coup

The young Venezuelan military officers, Colonels Hugo Chávez and Francisco Arias Cárdenas, who led the violent but unsuccessful military uprising on February 4, 1992 against the constitutional if corrupt and inept government of President Andrés Pérez, evidently did not learn from the Haitian case nor were they concerned with the possible application of Resolution 1080. However, perhaps because the revolt never actually interrupted "the legitimate exercise of power by the democratically elected government," the Pérez Government did not formally invoke it. Nevertheless, in view of the tragic events (fourteen deaths and threats to the President's life), the Secretary General convoked an immediate meeting of the Permanent Council.

At the meeting of the Council, the member states reiterated their recent commitment to democracy and the principle of democratic solidarity, and adopted a resolution entitled "Support for the Democratic Government of the Republic of Venezuela," which "forcefully condemned the armed uprising against the democratic Government of President Carlos Andrés Pérez as well as the criminal attempt on his life"; denounced those who "have used force to usurp popular sovereignty and the democratic will of the Venezuelan people"; expressed their "resolve and unconditional support for that Head of State" and, significantly, reaffirmed "that there is no room in the hemisphere for regimes established by force." The Chairman of the Permanent Council and the Secretary General traveled to Caracas and publicly delivered the resolution to President Pérez (Coppedge, 1994) (Jimenez, 1996) (Baena Soares 1994, 130–33).[9]

In short, even though the Colonels' revolt did not succeed and collective action was not necessary to restore democracy in Venezuela, once again member states were determined to use the new OAS instruments to reject attempts to overthrow democratic governments.

Peru's Auto-Coup

Shortly after the Venezuelan crisis, to the surprise of many, the Organization faced another interruption of the democratic order in a member state: on April 5, 1992, President Alberto Fujimori dissolved the Legislature, and took over the Judiciary, the Office of the Public Prosecutor, and the Court of Constitutional Guarantees. Secretary General Baena Soares, invoking Resolution 1080, convened the Permanent Council of the OAS, which held an emergency meeting. In view of the "serious events that had occurred in Peru, [which] had led to an interruption of the democratic political institutional process in that country," the Permanent Council unanimously condemned the events, urged the Peruvian authorities to facilitate, immediately, the full functioning of democratic institutions, and decided to convene an ad hoc Meeting of Ministers of Foreign Affairs, pursuant to Resolution 1080 (Permanent Council of the Organization of American States, April 6, 1992).

The ad hoc meeting took place on April 13, 1992, and the member states once again condemned the interruption of democracy and urged the Peruvian authorities to release the detained legislators, political leaders, and trade union leaders. They also called on member states to reassess their relations with Peru, and to ask the President of the ad hoc meeting to organize a diplomatic mission to go to Peru in order to promote a dialogue between the Peruvian authorities and the political forces represented in the legislature (Meeting of Foreign Affairs Ministers, April 13, 1992).

The OAS mission, headed by the then Foreign Minister of Uruguay, Hector Gross Espiell, and Secretary General Baena Soares, visited Peru three times and met several times with government representatives and various opposition groups. Both sides explained their positions: Fujimori's representatives proposed holding a plebiscite on the actions taken, while the opposition was seeking his resignation and prosecution, and the immediate calling of general elections. Eventually, the OAS mission facilitated a sort of a compromise agreement, which stipulated that elections for a Constituent Assembly would be called (Baena Soares 1994, 41–44). This agreement was ratified at the second Foreign Ministers Meeting of May 18, 1992, held in the Bahamas, during which President Fujimori formally committed himself to hold elections with OAS monitoring (Meeting of Foreign Affairs Ministers, May 18, 1992). The elections were held in November of that year and Fujimori's party won a sizeable majority, which allowed him to dominate the Assembly and achieve the constitutional changes he sought. The new Constitution eliminated the bicameral Congress and established a unicameral national legislature. It also approved the reelection of the President. National elections were called for April 1995 and President Fujimori won reelection with 60% of the votes.

Thus, the immediate and automatic application of OAS Resolution 1080 contributed significantly to the restoration of the democratic order in Peru, but it was not the only factor. The international community, including the United States, Japan, Spain, the European Union, the Rio Group, and the Inter-American Development Bank, also played a significant role. They exerted bilateral pressure and suspended assistance to Peru. Within Peru, despite the popularity of President Fujimori's action, the independent media, the traditional political parties and the intellectual community also strenuously pressured for the return to the constitutional order (Novak 2000).

The OAS continued monitoring the political process and was invited to observe the April 2000 election. The Electoral Observation Mission (EOM), however, refused to endorse Fujimori's election due to serious irregularities identified in the electoral process, which undermined the validity of the results and the Government's legitimacy. The EOM presented its report to the OAS General Assembly held in Windsor, Canada, which, after a heated debate, decided to send a high level politico-diplomatic mission presided by Secretary General Gaviria and Lloyd Axworthy, Canadian Foreign Minister.[10]

With Fujimori's acquiescence, the high level mission explored with all concerned the options that might contribute to the strengthening of democracy in Peru. At the end of its visit in June 2000, the mission proposed an agenda for negotiations on political reforms that was accepted by most of the political actors. In order to monitor the negotiations and implementation of them *in situ*, the Secretary General established a political observation mission, headed by the former Foreign Minister of the Dominican Republic, Eduardo Latorre. Throughout its presence in Lima, this political mission frequently facilitated and mediated the negotiations between the Government and opposition leaders.

Although Fujimori began his second term in July, his regime collapsed not long afterwards, as revelations of widespread corruption and bribery schemes within his inner circle became publicly known. In September 2000, Fujimori fired his principal advisor, Vladimir Montesinos, and proposed constitutional reforms that would allow for early elections and no further reelection. Surprising everyone, however, he resigned abruptly in November 2000 and went into exile in Japan. Fair elections were held in April and June 2001 (Smith 2005, 130–131) (Cooper & Legler, 2001).

For some, this OAS response to Fujimori's coup was timid or insufficient, but it must be understood in its proper context: the OAS is an intergovernmental organization and its decisions reflect and are the result of its members' long and arduous negotiations and compromises, its traditional method of decision-making. The OAS response at Windsor was consistent with that tradition. It was a compromise between some Foreign Ministers who wanted a more activist position in favor of democracy and fair elections, and those who preferred a less "interventionist" posture.

Guatemala, Another Auto-Coup

On May 25, 1993, President Jorge Serrano Elías suspended the Constitution; dissolved Congress, the Supreme Court and the Constitutional Court; removed the Attorney General; ordered the detention of the Human Rights Ombudsman, and suspended electoral law and political parties. Just like the Venezuelan military officers, Serrano ignored the lessons from the inter-American community's reaction to the Haitian and Peruvian coups, and even to the Venezuelan failed coup, and miscalculated the reaction of the Guatemalan people and the nations of the hemisphere to his reckless takeover.

In light of these events, the OAS Secretary General, invoking Resolution 1080, immediately convened a meeting of the Permanent Council. The Council condemned these events and urged the Guatemalan authorities to reestablish "immediately the complete functioning of democratic institutions." It also called for an ad hoc Meeting of Ministers of Foreign Affairs, and called on the Secretary General to head a fact-finding mission to examine the situation in Guatemala and report its findings to the Foreign Ministers Meeting. The Secretary General's mission, which included the Foreign Ministers of Barbados, Nicaragua and Uruguay, met with officials of the institutions affected by Serrano's action, the leaders of political parties and the armed forces, and with representatives of pertinent sectors of Guatemalan society (Baena Soares 1994, 53–68) (Permanent Council of the OAS, May 25, 1993).

In the meantime, the international community and a number of member states also rejected the auto-coup and started to assess their relationship with the Guatemalan Government. For example, Argentina withdrew its Ambassador. Chile withdrew its military cooperation. The U.S. ambassador to the OAS announced the suspension of trade preferences for Guatemala. The Presidents of Central America and the President of Mexico issued an appeal to their Guatemalan counterpart. In addition, the vast majority of the Guatemalan media and people widely and vehemently resisted the coup. The Constitutional Court itself did not recognize alteration of the democratic order, and declared the decree issued by President Serrano to be unconstitutional. Additionally, the Supreme Electoral Tribunal refused to accept Serrano's call for a referendum (Baena Soares 1994, 53–68) (Villagrán, 1993).

The Foreign Ministers Meeting on the situation in Guatemala convened on June 3, 1993 in Washington, D.C. It took note of the Secretary General's fact-finding mission, condemned once again the events that had occurred, and urged the Government to reestablish democratic institutions. In addition, it called on member states to evaluate their relations and cooperation with

Guatemala, and asked the Secretary General to return to the country to continue providing support for "the efforts of the Guatemalan people to reestablish constitutional order through dialogue and cooperation." The Foreign Ministers also approved and applauded the Guatemalan people's rejection of the auto-coup and their strong support for the peaceful efforts "to find a democratic solution." (Second Ad Hoc Meeing of Foreign Ministers, 1993) (Villagrán, 1993).

The crisis came to an end during the Secretary General's second visit. In the face of the unrelenting domestic and international opposition to his unconstitutional actions, Serrano had resigned on June 1, 1993 and left the country. Since Vice President Gustavo Espina Salguero was considered to bear joint responsibility for the events, the Constitutional Court called on the Congress of the Republic to elect a new President for the remainder of the constitutional term. On June 6, the Congress appointed Ramiro de Léon Carpio, the Human Rights Ombudsman, to the Presidency (Baena Soares 1994, 53–68).

Once again, the member states used the OAS instruments they created for the defense of democracy and contributed to the restoration of democracy in Guatemala. It must be borne in mind, however, that the restoration of democracy could not have happened without the active rejection of the auto-coup by the Guatemalan people and its democratic institutions.

Paraguay, Almost a Coup

The political crisis that almost led to a coup in Paraguay began when President Juan Carlos Wasmosy (constitutionally also the Commander in Chief of the armed forces) sought the resignation of General Lino Oviedo, head of the Army, on April 22, 1996. In view of upcoming internal elections within the Colorado party, as well as the presidential elections, Oviedo had been distancing himself from the Government and increasing his participation and political influence within the Colorado party. Wasmosy not only considered this to be inappropriate and illegal conduct on the part of a military officer, but also a challenge to his authority and presidency. The General's refusal to comply with the presidential order propelled the country into an institutional crisis. His insubordination and failure to recognize presidential authority was perceived an ill-disguised attempt to carry out a coup d'état. The attempt included a call for Wasmosy's resignation, as well as military, political and personal threats and pressures. Strictly speaking, these events cannot be classified as an "institutional rupture," but they did create an ambiguous and murky situation that led to uncertainty about institutional continuity. For the national media and the political class, as well as for the international community, the situation posed an imminent threat to the interruption of the "legitimate exercise of power by a democratically elected government" as stipulated in Resolution 1080.

In that context, and at the request of Secretary General César Gaviria, the Permanent Council's Chairman, Panama's Permanent Representative, Ambassador Lawrence Chewning Fábrega, convened the Council on April 23 to assess the situation.[11] The Council condemned the attempted coup, and expressed its decisive support for the constitutional Government of President Wasmosy, calling for the Constitution and the legally established government to be respected. It also convoked an ad hoc Meeting of Ministers of Foreign Affairs without setting a date–a meeting that in fact did not take place because the crisis ended quickly (Permanent Council of the OAS, 1996).

On that same day, Secretary General Gaviria, together with the Bolivian Deputy Foreign Minister, Jaime Aparicio (Bolivia was serving as Secretary pro tempore of the Rio Group), went to Asunción to express the support of both organizations for President Wasmosy and Paraguayan democracy. The Argentine Foreign Minister, the Uruguayan Foreign Minister, and the Brazilian deputy Foreign Minister also went to Asunción for the same purpose. In the meantime, the Ambassadors of the United States, Argentina and Brazil worked intensely, both publicly and privately, to support President Wasmosy and to explicitly reject the actions taken by General Oviedo. The Argentine, Uruguayan and Brazilian Ambassadors also expressed their support for Wasmosy on behalf of MERCOSUR, whose "democratic clause" conditions membership in the group. In addition, the head of the Brazilian Army called on Oviedo to stop his efforts to overthrow Wasmosy.[12]

The crisis ended with the formal resignation of General Oviedo from his position as Army Chief on April 24, in a public ceremony that was attended by Secretary General Gaviria and President Wasmosy. This resignation resulted from an agreement between Wasmosy and Oviedo, according to which the General would give up his position and insubordination in exchange for his appointment as Minister of Defense. However, as many people perceived the agreement as a betrayal of democratic principles and of the support that they had given to Wasmosy during the crisis, and as thousands demonstrated in front of government headquarters against it, the President decided not to appoint Oviedo after all. In his speech on April 25, he announced that he was acting "on a mandate of the people." (Valenzuela, 1997) (Costa and Ayala-Bogarin, 1996).

Once more, the immediate application of Resolution 1080 and widespread support of OAS member states and the international community for President Wasmosy and Paraguayan democracy contributed significantly to the successful management of the crisis. However, what sustained the democratic process and determined the course of events was the support for democracy and the constitutional government emanating from the political parties in Congress, the media, and from the youth demonstrations as well as from the Paraguayan Air Force and Navy, which resisted Oviedo's demands (Costa and Ayala-Bogarin, 1996) (Unidad para la Promoción de la Democracia, 1996).

Ecuador, a Congressional Coup

The Ecuadorian National Congress deposed President Abdalá Bucarám on February 6, 1997, through an irregular, questionable, if not in unconstitutional legislative procedure. The National Congress declared Bucarám incompetent and mentally incapacitated to exercise his presidency, and voted him out of office by a simple majority, without a political trial or proper analysis of the charges leveled against him. His removal, however, was extremely popular. It followed a national strike, violent street demonstrations calling for the President's ouster, and the withdrawal of the Armed Forces' support for the President—all of which precipitated a political/institutional crisis marked by a confrontation between the President and the National Congress. The congressional majority that deposed Bucarám subsequently appointed the President of the National Congress, Fabián Alarcón, as interim President of the Republic. However, in a brief and confusing period, Vice President Rosalía Arteaga also assumed the office of President, as the Ecuadorian Constitution did not provide for any clear procedure for presidential succession. The crisis was finally resolved by another congressional decision confirming Alarcón as interim President.

But because the process of toppling the President maintained a constitutional façade, albeit confusing and obscure, neither the Secretary General nor the Representative of Ecuador to the OAS invoked Resolution 1080 or convoked a formal meeting of the Permanent Council to address the crisis. The Council did not discuss the topic at its regular weekly meeting, even though the United States Ambassador to the OAS, Harriet Babbitt, informally sought consensus for a Permanent Council resolution supporting Ecuadorian democracy. The Ecuadorian Ambassador to the OAS, on the other hand, "provided assurances that all action would take place within constitutional channels and that there was no possibility whatsoever of a coup d'état in his country." (Aznaréz, 1997) (Oppenheimer, 1997) (Schemo, 1997).

Nevertheless, in the spirit of the new paradigm of the defense and promotion of democracy, several OAS member states expressed their concern over the crisis and their interest in resolving it promptly by constitutional and democratic means. Specifically, the Governments of Argentina, Panama, El Salvador, Costa Rica and Nicaragua condemned Bucarám's ouster as they considered that the procedures used were in violation of democratic and constitutional principles. Simultaneously, Secretary General Gaviria, at the request of Bucarám, flew to Quito on February 5th. But as opposition and congressional leaders diapproved of his visit and criticized it as "interference" in Ecuador's internal affairs, Gaviria hurried to declare that "the purpose of his visit was simply to express the concern of the OAS over the complex situation existing in Ecuador," and that he had "profound respect for the capacity of Ecuadorians to resolve their internal disputes on their own."[13]

In short, the member states successfully applied Resolution 1080 to help restore democracy in Haiti, Peru and Guatemala and help prevent a coup in Paraguay. In all of these situations, the popular sentiment and/or the political institutional opposition overwhelmingly rejected the coups or the attempted coups.

THE WASHINGTON PROTOCOL

Member states made further progress in their collective efforts to protect and promote representative democracy in the hemisphere by adopting the 1992 Washington Protocol. The 1992 OAS General Assembly approved this third instrument for the defense of democracy as an amendment to the OAS Charter, and following ratification by the majority of member states, it became Article 9 of the Charter. This legal/diplomatic instrument, in essence, provides for the possibility of suspending from the activities of the Organization any government of a member state that has not resulted from a democratic process.[14] Since Article 9 entered into force, it has been applied only once, in the case of the coup carried out in Honduras in 2009, as we shall see later on.

CONCLUSION: THE EMERGING PATTERN

The foregoing discussion of the new diplomatic instruments for the collective promotion and defense of democracy shows the emergence of a pattern in response to an attempted coup d'état or irregular interruption of the democratic process in an OAS member state. That is, in all cases, members reacted immediately and took collective action through the Organization, through other collective entities (such as the Rio Group or MERCOSUR), or even unilaterally to stop a serious and imminent threat to the democratic order, preventing a coup, or to revert a democratic interruption by an auto-coup or a military takeover.

Whatever action was taken almost always involved the invocation of Resolution 1080, followed by an emergency convocation of the Permanent Council, which in turn called for a special Meeting of Foreign Affairs Ministers or the General Assembly. After deliberations and negotiations, in both instances, the member states would produce a consensus-based resolution that would inevitably condemn the coup and call for immediate restoration of the democratic order and the deposed President. It would also instruct the

Secretary General to organize and lead a diplomatic mission which would investigate the events surrounding the coup or attempted coup and/or provide "good offices" to promote and facilitate dialogue and negotiations amongst the principal actors, in an attempt to help restore the democratic order.

If these short-term collective actions did not lead to the immediate restoration of democracy, as was the case in Haiti, Peru or Guatemala, then members would engage in complex diplomatic negotiations, both domestically and internationally, and would employ diplomatic pressure involving all sorts of instruments and sanctions, such as the breaking of diplomatic, economic and commercial relations, freezing assets, suspending economic, financial and military assistance, cancelling and denying travel visas, threatening military intervention, and finally suspending the illegal government from the Organization, all of which could lead to costly if not devastating isolation.

In the most extreme cases, such as Haiti, member states not only condemned the illegal regime, but also recommended sanctions such as the freezing of bank accounts and assets, the suspension of loans and assistance, the breaking of diplomatic relations, the imposition of embargoes, and eventually the threat of military intervention. In the case of Peru, the application of 1080 even had consequences beyond the scope of the OAS and the hemisphere, drawing complementary responses from the international community. The suspension of Peru's participation in the Rio Group and the threats by pertinent actors of the international community to suspend international cooperation, international investments, and economic and trade relations certainly played a significant role in the decision of the Peruvian Government to return to the more traditional democratic fold. However, when the illegal government resigned (Guatemala, Haiti) or when the transgressor decided to call elections (after negotiations and OAS mediation, as in Peru), the OAS engaged in electoral observation.

In the cases of Venezuela and Ecuador, the instruments were not used or applied. But nevertheless, in the spirit of Resolution 1080, collectively or individually, member states and the Secretary General reacted swiftly to condemn the events. In Venezuela, the attempted coup collapsed very quickly and the OAS Permanent Council had only to state its condemnation of the attempt, without needing to invoke Resolution 1080. In Ecuador, however, Gaviria's attempt to protect the unpopular President failed to stop his dismissal and Gaviria's visit elicited strong rejection and accusations of interference by the congressional authorities that removed the President. Nevertheless, several member states condemned the coup, even though the instruments could not be invoked or activated because the ouster was carried out very quickly and under a constitutional disguise. In addition, the unpopularity of the President plus the popular support for his removal made it very difficult for member states to insist on applying the new instruments and risk being accused of interventionism by the new authorities. And not even Bucarám´s Ambassador in the Permanent Council wished to call a meeting of the Permanent Council on the basis of Resolution 1080. In the end, however, the new authorities suffered no major diplomatic consequences for their illegal actions.

In essence, whether by design or not, these instruments to promote and defend democracy turned out to have a preventive function—a sort of red light against violations of the democratic order or process. The red light gave a warning that there would be an immediate reaction in the face of an attempted coup (Paraguay), and consequences or sanctions if trespassed. Further, if the red light failed to prevent violations, the instruments became reactive-restoration mechanisms that were triggered immediately after the interruption had taken place (Guatemala, Haiti, Peru). That is, members employ them in efforts to restore democracy where it has been interrupted.

In short, the development and application of the new OAS instruments left it very clear that the inter-American community of democracies would no longer accept the interruption of the democratic order in a member state. Although the decisions of the OAS in the cases described took the form of recommendations, making their application voluntary and non-binding (unlike the U.N. Security Council's decisions), they signaled a collective commitment to the defense of democracy, as well as a standard of legitimacy that transcends the formal contours of the Organization.

Recognition of this new reality and of the new role of the OAS in the hemisphere became evident during the second ad hoc Meeting of Consultation of Ministers of Foreign Affairs that was studying the crisis in Guatemala. The Secretary of Foreign Relations of Mexico (a country with a long tradition of invoking/defending the principle of non-intervention) described the OAS as having acted in "a timely and effective manner," thereby showing the "potential of our Organization to provide assistance by means of the promotion of political dialogue to settle disputes." Similarly, the Assistant Secretary for Foreign Affairs of Chile stated that the "rapid and firm action of the OAS should be recognized," adding that "the days of an OAS that is silent in the face of a coup d'état or indifferent to the violation of the will of the people are over." He also saw the emergence of an Organization that is "flexible and actively committed to the best values of representative democracy" (Second Ad Hoc Meeting of Ministers of Foreign Affairs, June 7, 1993).

NOTES

1. In theory, the principle that democratic states do not declare war on one another is sensible and persuasive. Empirically speaking, however, a small number of studies have found

exceptions and have maintained that the correlation is not always linear (Mansfield and Snyder 1995) (Gaubatz 1996) (Ray 1997) (Senese 1999) (Oneal and Russett 1997).

2. On the role played by international juridical norms in the building of international systems as well as in political change, see Martha Finnemore and Kathryn Sikkink (1998).

3. This agreement essentially called for setting up national reconciliation commissions to oversee amnesties, cease-fires, democratization, elections, dialogue with the opposition in El Salvador and Nicaragua, and repatriation of refugees. It also called for countries of the region not to be used as bases by rebel forces with external support, as well as for the end of external support to irregular forces (e.g., United States' support to the Contras in Honduras).

4. By July 1990, the CIAV/OAS had already demobilized some 22,500 combatants and had relocated another 18,000 Nicaraguans returning from Costa Rica and Honduras. CIAV/ OAS also set up a program to help reintegrate former combatants and displaced persons, which provided food, medical assistance, vocational training and support for projects in agriculture, livestock and fishing (Baena Soares 1994, 199–200). In addition to these demobilization and reintegration tasks, the CIAV/OAS provided support for socioeconomic and institutional development in former conflict zones, and collaborated with the National Institute for Municipal Development in training mayors of the conflict zones in municipal legislation and administration. It also undertook surveillance and verification for the observance of human rights, and served as a facilitator for managing and resolving local conflicts. The mandate of the CIAV came to an end formally in December 1996 (International Support and Verification Commmission 1996).

5. See the resolution passed by the Ad Hoc Meeting of Foreign Ministers: "Support for the Democratic Government of Haiti" (Ad Hoc Meeting of Foreign Ministers October 3, 1991).

6. The important contributions of the MICIVIH to the defense and promotion of human rights and democratic institutions have been widely recognized both by the national authorities and by the international community. After seven years of operations, the mandate of the MICIVIH ended in March 2000 at the request of the Government of Haiti.

7. The agreement was the result of the initiatives and negotiations spearheaded by the OAS-U.N. Envoy, Dante Caputo, former Foreign Minister of Argentina.

8. The authorization by the Security Council (SC/RES/841, June 16, 1993) of a comprehensive and mandatory commercial embargo, in accordance with the OAS recommendation, was based on the argument that the humanitarian crisis in Haiti posed a threat to security and peace in the region. The same argument was used for U.N. Resolution 940. The United States Government sent a mission composed of former President Jimmy Carter, Senator Sam Nunn, and General Colin Powell mainly to warn the Government of General Cédras of the imminent arrival of U.S. troops to restore the Government of President Aristide.

9. See Permanent Council resolution CP/RES. 576 (887/92) and General Assembly resolution AG/RES. 1189 (XXII-0/92).

10. See the EOM's report (Unit for the Promotion of Democracy, General Secretariat of the OAS, 2002).

11. On that day, Secretary General Gaviria was on official mission to Bolivia, and in a 2 a.m. telephone call, asked the Chairman of the Council to convene the meeting. See statement by Ambassador Lawrence Chewing Fábrega, who was Chairman of the Permanent Council during the crisis (OAS Unit for the Promotion of Democracy 1996, 14).

12. On the night of the 22nd and during the early hours of the morning of April 23, the Ambassadors of the United States, Robert Service, and Brazil, Oliveira Días, and the Assistant Secretary of State for Latin America, Jeffrey Davidow, and Secretary General Gaviria managed to discourage President Wasmosy from his intention to resign. Wasmosy was convinced that Oviedo would carry out his military threats and that his resignation would avoid a bloodbath. On the morning of April 23, Wasmosy received calls of encouragement from the Presidents of Argentina, Brazil, the United States, Spain, and others (Costa and Ayala-Bogarin 1996) (Valenzuela 1997).

13. See news dispatches of the Spanish news agency EFE, and AFP of February 5, 6, and 7 in OAS *News Bulletin* of February 6, 7, and 10.

14. The article is somewhat elliptical and reads as follows: a "member of the Organization whose democratically constituted government has been overthrown by force may be suspended

from the exercise of the right to participate in the sessions of the General Assembly, Meetings of Consultation, and the Councils of the Organization."

Chapter Six

The Inter-American Democratic Charter

INTRODUCTION

In an effort to improve the scope and effectiveness of the new OAS role of promoting and protecting democracy, member states embarked on a diplomatic process to strengthen the preventive and restorative functions of the existing instruments. The process concluded with the adoption of the Inter-American Democratic Charter (IADC) at the special session of the OAS General Assembly held in Lima, Peru on September 11, 2001. The IADC, which incorporates and expands on those instruments, has become the single most important juridical/diplomatic instrument that member states have at their disposal for the collective promotion and defense of representative democracy in the Western Hemisphere.

The signing of the Charter was the culmination of a process that started with a proposal by the transitional Peruvian President Valentín Paniagua and his Foreign Minister, Javier Pérez de Cuellar (November 2000-July 2001). The initiative was motivated by the trauma of Fujimori's corrupt and discredited authoritarian regime, which ended dramatically with his resignation and exile to Japan in November 2000. The new Peruvian Government sought to develop a new instrument, beyond Resolution 1080 and the Washington Protocol, that would require a stronger hemispheric commitment to the collective promotion and defense of representative democracy. The proposal became the center of discussion at the Quebec Summit of the Americas held in April of 2001, where the Presidents instructed their Foreign Ministers to prepare a Charter that would "enhance our ability to respond" to the many threats to democracy and "reinforce OAS instruments for the active defense of representative democracy" (Office of Summit Follow Up, General Secretariat of the OAS 2002, 314).

Peruvian Deputy Foreign Minister, Manuel Rodríguez Cuadros, headed a working group to that effect and presented its first draft at the thirty-first regular session of the General Assembly in San José, Costa Rica on June 5, 2001. The Foreign Ministers reviewed it and sent it for further strengthening to the Permanent Council (Consejo Permanente de la OEA 2003, 52), where a working group, led by Colombian Permanent Representative, Ambassador Humberto de la Calle, debated it for about three months, revised it and had its final version approved on September 6, 2001. The Lima Special General Assembly received it and approved it without further discussion or debate on September 11.

It must be noted, however, that the adoption of the IADC resulted from an intense, complex, difficult and tortuous process of diplomatic proposals, deliberations, consultations (via Internet) and negotiations, which involved Ambassadors and Foreign Ministry officials from member states, experts in democracy and international law (such as the Inter-American Juridical Committee) and nongovernmental organizations. The lengthy and frank debates focused on the role of the Organization in promoting and defending democracy within the limits of its founding Charter, particularly as they relate to traditional principles like state sovereignty and non-intervention, so cherished in Latin America, as well as its juridical significance or reach as a binding international instrument. The discussions also examined the nature of democracy (representative vs. participatory), its scope (beyond just elections), its components and political culture, its relation to development, human rights, education, poverty, and inequality, as well as the nature of the individual and collective obligations to exercise and defend democracy.[1] The process also included deliberations about the threats to democracy, as represented mainly by traditional coups and auto-coups, military and/or civilian, but also, most controversially, about cases of "grave alterations" to the democratic institutional order. For the Peruvian Foreign Minister, Diego Garcia Sayán (who had in mind Peru's experience with President Fujimori's auto-coup), the latter concept included, in principle, "governments that have usurped legitimate power or, having attained power through free and fair elections, proceed to erode the democratic institutional order by exercising power arbitrarily." (Consejo Permanente de la OEA 2003, 11).

The negotiators also debated measures of appropriate collective action (either preventive or restorative), particularly examining the nature, necessity, sequence and consequences of certain responses and procedures, such as, for example, the convocation of the Permanent Council, the sending of diplomatic missions, the imposition of sanctions such as suspension from the Organization, and the implementation of programs and activities to strengthen democratic institutions and promote a democratic political culture.

The IADC actually represents the final product of a historical effort that gained traction, as we have seen, in the early eighties, when the great majority of member states returned to democratic governance and were determined to work together to consolidate and protect it. In essence, it incorporates all the instruments examined previously, and it is supposed to function, first, as a preventive mechanism, that is, as a red light against auto or military coups, and then, if that fails to stop transgressors, as a reactive or restorative mechanism.

As the commitment to exercise and protect representative democracy appears to have been declining in several Latin American states in the past few years, it is thus a timely occasion to assess the strengths and weaknesses of the Charter.

THE CHARTER'S STRENGTHS

The approval of the Democratic Charter represented a significant movement forward in terms of the member states' consensus and commitment to promote democracy, to prevent its collapse, and to restore it when it has been interrupted.

Most importantly, in signing the Charter, member states established that the "peoples of the Americas have a right to democracy, and their governments have the obligation to promote and defend it." (Art. 1). Significantly also, members chose representative democracy as the preferred form of government, and reached consensus on what constitutes its essential elements, including, inter alia, respect for the rule of law, human rights and fundamental freedoms; periodic, free and fair elections; and a pluralistic system of political parties and the separation and independence of the branches of government (Art. 3). They also identified essential democratic values and practices such as probity and transparency in government activities; respect for diversity, citizen participation, and others (Arts. 4–6). With these pronouncements, member states asserted that democracy entails more than just elections, but is a way of life and a way of governing that respects and treasures democratic institutions, values and practices.

The IADC also strengthens Resolution 1080's "restoration function" in case of "an unconstitutional *interruption* of the democratic order", or of "an unconstitutional *alteration* of the constitutional regime that seriously impairs the democratic order in a member state (Arts. 19–21). In any of these cases, the Charter now makes it possible for any member state or the Secretary General, and not just the government of the state affected, to request an immediate meeting of the OAS Permanent Council, in order to assess the situation collectively and if necessary, and accepted by the government involved, to "undertake diplomatic initiatives" to attempt to restore democracy

(Art. 20). This improves the mechanism that triggers the Organization's engagement in response to the interruption of the democratic order in one of its members. Before this provision existed, it was impossible to activate immediately an OAS reaction without the consent of the government affected. Furthermore, the Permanent Council would respond to a coup with an immediate condemnation of it, a call for a return to the status quo ante and the sending of a diplomatic mission to try to convince the coup makers to restore the democratic order. If this fails, then a special session of OAS/GA is convened to adopt decisions, which "may include new diplomatic initiatives and eventually the suspension of the member from the OAS." (Art. 21).

The Democratic Charter now also allows OAS "intervention" not just in cases of unconstitutional "interruption" but also in cases of unconstitutional "alterations." (Arts. 19 and 20). Note here, however, a subtle and fundamental distinction in what constitutes a threat to, or a break in the democratic order: while the term "unconstitutional interruption" clearly refers to a traditional military coup and/or auto-coup (easily detectable and condemnable events), the concept of "unconstitutional alteration" connotes a different type or form of interruption of the democratic order. This presumably includes, among others, (a) rigged elections, or (b) an illegal challenge by the legislative or judicial branch, or the military against the government's "legitimate exercise of power." These two "alterations" are relatively easy to detect, agree upon and condemn collectively, particularly if it is the executive branch which feels threatened and requests the OAS solidarity and support.

However, a more controversial "alteration" may involve a process in which the executive branch usurps and monopolizes power—after having won democratic elections—in the name of participatory democracy, socialism and anti-imperialism, slowly undermining the democratic order. This process commonly erodes and suppresses essential democratic institutions, values, and practices such as checks and balances, respect for political opposition, the rule of law and fundamental freedoms. More specifically, it could involve authoritarian behavior like removing judges not politically aligned with the government, or disobeying courts' rulings or legislation passed by a legislature controlled by the opposition, manipulating and abusing government institutions to persecute and even arrest political opponents and controlling and intimidating the media, amongst others. The process consolidates a type of regime that may be characterized as an "altered or pseudo-democracy," and because it employs a democratic façade to cover its undemocratic and despotic nature, a majority of member states cannot agree to condemn its practices, thus hindering collective actions in defense of democracy.[2]

The Democratic Charter also reinforces the role of the OAS in preventing the interruption of a democratic order. Article 17 now allows the government of a member state "to request assistance from the Secretary General or the Permanent Council" for the "strengthening and preservation of its democratic system" when it "considers that its democratic institutional process or its legitimate exercise of power is at risk." Additionally, when the democratic system and the legitimate exercise of power is threatened in a member state, "the Secretary General or the Permanent Council, may, with the prior approval of the government concerned, arrange for visits or other actions to analyze the situation." (Art. 18). Notice here, however, that the assistance can be provided only at the request of the executive branch of a state, and that without its consent, no collective support can take place to strengthen the democratic order or prevent its collapse. Nevertheless, this preventive assistance has the potential, in theory, to be activated immediately in case of an imminent threat and deteriorating democratic order. Furthermore, the Democratic Charter also provides for the possibility of supporting member states in their effort to strengthen or modernize their democratic institutions and promote the consolidation of their democratic political culture, which in effect is the most effective long-term way of preventing the collapse of the democratic order (Arts. 26–27).

Finally, the Charter solidifies a collective hemispheric commitment to never again accept a military coup and the government that results from it as part of the inter-American democratic community. In cases of a coup or an attempted coup, the Charter will be used to condemn it, to seek sanctions against the transgressors and even their suspension from the Organization, in an effort to protect or restore the democratic order. Member states actually made this pledge in a 1992 Permanent Council resolution that repudiated the attempted coup by Colonel Hugo Chávez against President Pérez of Venezuela, and they ratified the commitment when they reacted swiftly against the military coups in Venezuela in 2002 and in Honduras in 2009. But the fact that coups will not be accepted does not mean they will not happen again; they probably will, as coup makers are usually not versed in history, are likely not to have read the Charter, or simply do not care about the consequences. But governments that emerge from them (or even civilian coups) will not be recognized, even if they have wide support from the population, as with Fujimori in Peru in 1991, or from the legislative or judiciary branch, as in Honduras.

THE CHARTER'S WEAKNESSES

Despite the significant progress the Charter makes in terms of the collective promotion and defense of democracy, it displays weaknesses that limit or constrain its applications and usefulness to effectively accomplish its mission or purpose.

For example, the Charter does not allow for the possibility of having the legislative or the judicial branch invoke the Charter and ask the Permanent

Council to convoke a meeting to denounce, for example, threats to their independence or their very existence, or even to discuss the political situation/crisis that may be threatening the democratic order in their countries. In theory, this should be possible, given that all member states are democracies that supposedly embrace principles such as the independence, equality and separation of powers. The principle unfortunately seems to be valid only for domestic affairs, and has not been extrapolated to an international organization, no matter how democratic its members are. The executive branch is the exclusive voice of the nation-state in such organizations, at least since the Westphalia Treaty in the 1640s.

The executive branch, through its Ministry of Foreign Affairs, monopolizes the conduct of international relations and the representation of the state in intergovernmental organizations. At the OAS, no other branch of government is permitted to invite the Secretary General to observe the political situation in its country, nor can the Secretary General or a member state invite another branch of government to speak in the Permanent Council, without the consent of the executive branch. That would be denounced as intervention in its internal affairs. Yet if the executive branch requests OAS assistance when it feels threatened in a political crisis, member states will never consider it "interventionist."[3] It seems odd, if not outright undemocratic and anachronistic, that the executive should be the only branch that can speak in defense of democracy, when many a time it is the executive that undermines or threatens the very existence of democracy by abusing power, persecuting political opponents or rigging elections.

As discussed previously, in the event of an unconstitutional alteration, any member state may request a meeting of the Permanent Council "to undertake a collective assessment of the situation and to take such decisions as it deems appropriate." (Art. 20). The problem, however, is that there is no consensus among member states as to what exactly is an "unconstitutional alteration," beyond the obvious military or auto-coup. For example, it is unclear whether the concept also includes an attempted coup, rigged elections, or a rising autocracy, with an increasing monopoly and abuse of power by the executive branch—eroding and suppressing democratic institutions, values and practices like checks and balances, respect for minorities, the opposition, the rule of law, freedom of expression and association, human rights and others; or an illegal challenge "to the legitimate exercise of power" by another branch of government or the military. This lack of clarity and precision weakens the Charter and undermines collective action.

Thus, since member states have not been able to agree on a definition of an unconstitutional alteration, they and the Secretary General have been reluctant to condemn or even to call attention to a situation in a member state whose regime, despite having emerged from democratic elections, shows clear signs of increasing authoritarianism and undemocratic governance, violating the democratic institutions, values and practices enshrined in the Charter. This type of alteration by erosion of the democratic order does not provoke automatic agreement or collective condemnation by member states. For those who support governments that generate these "alterations", they represent democratic, constitutional and legitimate political changes in favor of the previously excluded majority. For others, those alterations constitute an unwelcome imposition, albeit by democratic means, of an authoritarian and intolerant regime that unquestionably violates not only the Charter but often their own constitutions as well.

Another weakness is the limitations the Charter poses on the possibility of proactive "interventions" by the Secretary General or a member state, beyond the mere convocation of the Permanent Council to assess a situation threatening a democracy (theoretically allowed in Art. 20).[4] That is, the Charter does not permit even a visit by the Secretary General to analyze the situation without a request or prior consent from the executive branch (Art.18). Nor can the Secretary General send an electoral observation mission without the request or permission from the executive branch (Art. 24).

A final weakness relates to the fact that the Charter is not a treaty. That is, it is not a legally binding document; it is only a General Assembly resolution, which has moral and political leverage rather than legal force. Nevertheless, the Charter resulted from a formal institutional and legally binding procedure such as a General Assembly resolution, and its status has not impeded member states from using it to react swiftly and forcefully to condemn interruptions of the democratic order or to support the government of a member state when its constitutional order is threatened, as we have seen above. This may be a reason why the Charter is not well known among policy makers, the military, the media or even the academia, which in turn undermines its effectiveness as a red light against possible transgressors. Possible ways to strengthen the Charter will be suggested in the concluding chapter of this book.[5] The next chapter provides a critical assessment of the application of the Charter.

The Inter-American Democratic Regime (IADR)

The development and institutionalization of inter-American principles, norms, mechanisms and procedures developed by the member states for the collective promotion and protection of democracy at the OAS, now incorporated into the Democratic Charter, plus the regimes' congruence in the Americas, suggests that a democratic paradigm is beginning to take root if not predominate in the political culture of the hemisphere.[6] Parallel to this, or perhaps as a result of it—sustaining and giving substance to it—one can observe the emergence of what may be called an Inter-American Democratic Regime (IADR). Such a regime is understood as "an explicit or implicit set

of principles, norms, regulations, and procedures [which guide] the expectations [and actions] of the actors in a given area of international relations"
(e.g., democracy). Regimes' norms and expectations facilitate cooperation
and agreements beyond the pursuit of short-term self-interests (Krasner
1989, p. 2).[7] It is within this framework that we see in the Western Hemisphere an evolving community of nation-states that shares a commitment to
democratic institutions, values and practices, and cooperates around them to
promote and defend them.

This democratic regime emerged out of a historic political and diplomatic
congruence and commitment by hemispheric states to representative democracy and to the revival of the OAS, with its new norms and instruments for
the promotion and defense of democracy.[8] The OAS is indeed the central
institution of this incipient regime; it is the focal point and the institution
around which the regime has developed. Its principles, norms, resolutions,
instruments and actions in defense and promotion of democracy and human
rights are the substantive and most formal components of the regime. They
provide the reference point and the framework that gives legitimacy to the
collective and/or individual measures taken by its members.

But it is not the only or exclusive one. There are also regional groupings,
multilateral institutions, international NGOs and individual member or observer states that are active, directly or indirectly, in supplementing and
supporting efforts to promote and protect democracy and human rights, and
whose policies and behavior have enhanced the performance and strength of
the democratic regime. Such are, for example, MERCOSUR and UNASUR
in South America; SICA in Central America, CELAC for the whole of Latin
America and the Caribbean, and multilateral institutions like UNDP, the
World Bank and the Inter-American Development Bank,[9] as well as individual countries like Canada, Spain, Sweden and the United States, to mention a
few, and nongovernmental organizations such as Human Rights Watch and
the Human Rights Foundation (see the "promoters" in Chapter 4).

The OAS member states also reaffirmed their commitment to democracy
through the Summits of the Americas in Miami (1994), Santiago (1998) and
Quebec (2001), which were an important source of mandates and decisive
support for the development of the Inter-American Democratic Charter and
role of the OAS in defending and promoting democracy. The Summits themselves are guided by a "democracy clause," which excludes from participation in them any member that is not a democracy, and they have become a
force for the promotion of democracy and the observance of human rights,
and for inter-American cooperation.

Two additional non-traditional actors have the potential to contribute to
the strengthening of the IADR. One is the involvement of nongovernmental
organizations (NGOs) in promoting and defending democracy and human
rights at both the national and inter-American levels (Sikkink 1996).[10] The

other, and perhaps more significant, is the participation of national legislatures of member states in OAS activities (see Chapter 7). It should be noted that in 1999, the General Assembly approved a meeting of representatives from the national legislatures, which concluded with the creation of the Inter-Parliamentary Forum of the Americas (FIPA), now morphed into ParlAmericas. In 2005, a General Assembly resolution also approved a formal meeting between the Permanent Council and congressional leaders of the member states. This adds a parliamentary dimension that has been lacking to date in the emerging IADR (General Assembly of the Organization of American States June 2005).

In the final analysis, however, the effectiveness of the IADR will depend on the strength of democracy in the member states and their cohesiveness in their dedication and willingness to collectively promote and protect democracy as well as to apply and respect the OAS norms and instruments created to that effect.

THE APPLICATIONS OF THE IADC: A MIXED RECORD

In terms of its preventive function, the Democratic Charter has been applied on several occasions at the request of a government that perceived a threat to its constitutional and legitimate exercise of power (Art. 18). Thus, following appeals from the Governments of Nicaragua (2005), Bolivia (2005 and 2008), Ecuador (2005, 2010), and Guatemala (2009), the Permanent Council acted diligently and effectively, approving resolutions and sending political missions that successfully contained a political crisis from rupturing the democratic order (Legler and Boniface, Promoting Democracy in the Americas 2007) (Secretary General of the OAS, May 2010).[11]

However, in terms of preventing the erosion of democracy or stopping the slow but clear alteration of the democratic order in some of the member states, the Charter has not been used as intended. In a few cases the Charter, performing as a warning sign, has not deterred transgressors or coup makers, and neither has it been invoked by any member state or by successive Secretaries General to prevent the institutional breakdown or the alteration of the democratic order. Both have failed to use it even to call for a collective assessment in cases of a clear deterioration of democratic governance in a member state.

In terms of its restorative functions, however, in the cases of Honduras (2009) and Venezuela (2002), the collective body reacted quickly once the interruption had taken place, and used the Charter to denounce and reject the coup. In the case of Honduras, members even proceeded to implement sanctions that would eventually lead to the restoration of democracy. Thus, the Charter proved to be a useful instrument for collectively reacting to the actual interruption of democracy in a member state, and for collectively proceeding to restore it; but, as we shall see below, they did not invoke it to prevent its erosion or interruption in certain crucial cases.

Bolivia's Polarized and Controversial Democracy

In May 2008, invoking Article 17 of the IADC, the Bolivian Foreign Minister requested in the Permanent Council OAS assistance to facilitate a process of dialogue and negotiation over the content and approval of the new Political Constitution of the Plurinational State of Bolivia.[12] Controversy and even violence over approval of the Constitution had been brewing between opposition legislators and Prefects (Governors) of important and relatively autonomous Eastern departments (states) and President Evo Morales, ever since his solid election victory in 2005. Morales intended, *à la* Chávez, to have his new Constitution approved by the Constituent Assembly elected for that purpose in December 2007. But as his party (MAS) did not have the two-thirds majority required to approve the new Constituon, it used an obscure procedure on controversial issues to approve the draft and send it to Congress for review and called for a referendum for final approval. This move only confirmed the opposition's fears of an increasingly radical and authoritarian Morales administration, and generated more polarization and violence (Lehoucq 2008, 118–9).

In light of the lack of progress in the approval of the new Constitution and the increasingly violent opposition to Morales and the Assembly, in May 2008 the Bolivian Government asked the OAS for assistance once again. The Permanent Council subsequently passed a resolution entitled "Support for the Process of Dialogue and Peace and for Democratic Institutions in Bolivia," which instructed the Secretary General to use his good offices to promote dialogue and build consensus in order to assure the continuity of the democratic order (OAS Permanent Council, May 3, 2008). To that effect, the Secretary General sent a Special Mission which monitored closely the political situation, opening channels of communication amongst political opponents, encouraging them to use the established republican democratic institutions to manage and resolve their differences, and facilitating dialogue, negotiations and consensus building (Secretariat for Political Affairs, General Secretariat of the OAS 2011, 30).

In addition, the Secretary General sent an OAS Electoral Observation Mission (OAS/EOM) to observe a recall referendum against Morales in August 2008. Morales successfully defeated it, although the opposition claimed that "massive fraud" had been committed through multiple voting supposedly enabled by inaccuracies in the electoral register. The referendum did not subside the tension and polarization between the two sides over the issue of autonomy for the Departments. In October, the two sides, with prompting and facilitation by the OAS Special Mission, agreed to reestablish negotiations in Cochabamba, which ended with an agreement to continue negotiating at the National Congress. The Congress passed a law that authorized it to take up the new constitutional draft that had been approved in Oruro by the Constituent Assembly. This in effect, and perhaps unconstitutionally, turned Congress into a constituent body.

With OAS support, a Bicameral Commission of the National Congress, after tense negotiations, agreed to the new constitution, which included, at least two crucial political changes that would immediately affect the democratic process: one, it established a new electoral system by which a candidate could win the presidency with only 40% of the votes plus 10 points difference from the closest contender, and two, it reduced the autonomy of the Departments. However, a serious and significant controversy arose as Morales' party once again tried to approve the Constitution with a simple majority in the National Congress' joint session and not with a two-thirds majority as had been agreed. A crucial concession by Morales broke the impasse: his party agreed to a constitutional provision of no immediate presidential re-reelection. At this point, even though the United Nations and the European Union were observing the process, the OAS Mission's crucial role stood out as it directly facilitated the negotiations and the compromise—a role recognized by all the participants and observers. [13]

With that compromise, the plenary session of the National Congress approved the new Constitution (November 2008). An OAS/EOM observed the referendum on the new Constitution in January 2009, which passed with 61% of the vote. It also observed the December 2009 election, under the new Constitution, in which Morales was easily reelected with a substantial majority.

By 2013, however, Morales, still enjoying substantial public support and a legislative majority, decided to seek re-reelection. Violating the 2008 political agreement and constitutional provision against it, his loyal congressional majority interpreted that the two-term only re-election provision of the new Constitution did not apply to Morales, because his first term, they argued, began with the new Constitution approved in 2009. This notwithstanding the fact that a transitional provision in the new Constitution specifically stipulates that the previous presidential terms would count as his first term (Ortiz 2013). [14] The new and loyal Plurinational Constitutional Tribunal ratified the legislative action and Morales became eligible to run in the 2014 presidential elections, which he won handily with more than 60% of the vote.

This move by Morales was not accidental. It was part of an effort and pattern of increasing authoritarianism and erosion of the democratic order. As with the *chavista* regime, the pattern started with sound electoral victories provided by a historically excluded and destitute majority that closely identifies with the new charismatic leader and believes in his populist and nationalist promises and in his socially progressive programs and statist economic policies. Electoral triumphs are then used to change the Constitution (often illegally) to favor the centralization and accumulation of power in the executive branch, which leads to the control of state resources and of the legislative, judicial and electoral institutions—eliminating for all practical purposes the separation, independence and balance of power among the branches of government, so crucial for limiting power and safeguarding the vitality of the republican and democratic order (Wolf 2011) (Weyland 2013) (Mainwaring and Perez-Liñan 2013, 258–9, 261–262, 267–8).

Within such a framework, Morales' regime has used its increasing power to smother dissent or opposition. It has intimidated and/or persecuted political opponents, including "neo-liberal" former presidents and autonomist governors—accusing them of corruption and fabricated crimes, and forcing them into exile.[15] (Observatorio de Derechos Humanos 2013). The regime has even had violent and deadly confrontations with indigenous cooperatives that mine zinc, tin and silver from the highlands in Cochabamba and who resist the Morales administration's attempts to nationalize their business relations with private and foreign firms, and with indigenous peoples from the lowland departments (Beni), who oppose Morales' encroaching and violation of their rights and ancestral habitat (the Isidoro Sécure National Park and Indigenous Territory, known as TIPNIS), in order to build a highway and open up land for coca production[16] (Climate Connections 2014).

Morales has consolidated his power grab with the help of "progressive" social policies that in the short run benefited the previously marginalized majority. These policies include programs in education, health, sanitation, infrastructure, social security, employment and other sectors. He has been able to fund them thanks to a relatively well-run state and economy with moderate growth,[17] which has benefited in the last few years from high world demand for its minerals, gas and agricultural commodities such as soybean. The progressive social policies have increased his popularity and have generated a loyal state-dependent socio-political electoral base, which Morales and his Vice President, Álvaro García Linera (the ideologue behind Morales) utilize to mobilize and organize to win elections and referenda and remain in power.

But Morales' violation of the Constitution and of the fundamental democratic principles of separation of powers and limited elections, added to the regime's persecution of political and media opponents and violations of human rights, constitute clear signs of an alteration of the democratic order and disregard for the country's commitment to the Inter-American Democratic Charter. In addition, they detract from and taint his obvious success on the economic and social front. However, mainly because of Morales' electoral success, neither the Secretary General nor any member state has seen it politically and diplomatically fit to invoke the Charter or to bring these violations to the attention of the Permanent Council for, at least, a collective discussion of the matter. It is more politically convenient to look the other way and ignore the erosion of democracy in Bolivia and consider it an "internal affair", no matter how destructive or damaging it is to the collective commitment to promote and defend democracy.

Ecuador: From Unstable to Authoritarian Democracy

The political crisis that culminated in the congressional removal of Ecuadorian President Gutierrez on April 20, 2005 started in early December 2004, when Gutierrez contrived a congressional majority that removed the members of the Supreme Court, the Constitutional Court and the Electoral Court, and proceeded to appoint new provisional ones. What motivated this drastic move was the Supreme Court's ongoing investigation of government corruption and nepotism and the likely initiation of impeachment procedures against the President. This generated substantial political opposition, plus media and public discontent conveyed in large and violent street demonstrations in Quito and other cities, which called for the President's resignation.[18] The Army refused to obey the presidential orders to repress the demonstrations.

As a result of the growing political unrest, on April 20 a group of legislators called for a "special" meeting of Congress and, with 60 of 62 legislators present, adopted a resolution declaring that President Lucio Gutierrez had "abandoned his duties"—constitutional grounds for dismissal—and called for the succession mechanisms to begin. The special Congress reached its decision through an obscure internal parliamentary procedure that was enabled by admittedly unclear and confusing constitutional provisions for removing the President. But it definitely ignored the impeachment procedure (*enjuiciamiento político*) established in Article 130 of the constitution of the time, which required a two-thirds majority for removing the President from office. Nevertheless it did provide a constitutional façade. Most tellingly, the Army went along with the congressional resolution and put the President on a plane to Brazil. Subsequently, the National Congress named its own Vice President, Alfredo Palacio, as the new President of Ecuador, and received the support of the Armed Forces.[19] Strangely enough, the OAS Permanent Council accepted the new government without questioning the peculiar parliamentary procedures used to oust President Gutierrez, and passed a resolution entitled "OAS Support for the Republic of Ecuador" (CP/RES.880 (1478/05), which reaffirmed its commitment to the defense and promotion of the democratic values expressed in the IADC.[20]

The new Government invoked the Charter and asked the OAS for assistance in the process of selecting the members of the Supreme Court.[21] The Secretary General sent a mission of "good offices" to Quito, which facilitated negotiations and the acceptance of an ad hoc congressional procedure to select the new members of the Supreme Court. The new Court was installed in November 2005.

Nevertheless, despite the contribution of the OAS and its Democratic Charter to the eventual restoration of the democratic order in Ecuador, member states and the Secretary General failed to invoke or apply it in a preventive manner. Neither of them even raised the issue in the Permanent Council, for at least a collective discussion of the impending Ecuadorian political crisis, including the Ecuadorian Courts' views on the President's illegal and authoritarian dismissal of their members, which violated the Constitution and the IADC. Furthermore, President Gutierrez did not invoke the Charter nor did he ask for OAS assistance to resolve the conflict with the Courts—presumably because he knew he had acted illegally. Nor did he resort to the Charter when it was clear that the National Congress was about to oust him, also illegally or at least irregularly. Only once the transfer of power had been consummated did the member states notice with concern the "progressive deterioration of the democratic institutions and the rule of law in Ecuador." And only then did they proceed to encourage dialogue amongst all Ecuadorian sectors, to support the Ecuadorian government and to offer OAS assistance for its efforts to strengthen its democratic institutions, particularly the rule of law and the separation and independence of governmental powers.

Ten years later (2010), the Government of President Correa requested an urgent meeting of the Permanent Council, arguing that an uprising by police forces was threatening the life of the President and the constitutional order. In a special session, the Council hurriedly passed a resolution that repudiated the events and "any attempt to alter the democratic institutional system in Ecuador;" firmly supported the Ecuadorian government, and instructed the Secretary General to provide full support to its efforts to preserve the democratic institutional order.[22] The Secretary General traveled to Ecuador to express OAS support and solidarity with the government. This immediate OAS reaction to the political instability created by the police forces sent a strong signal to possible transgressors of the constitutional and democratic order, and possibly prevented its breakdown. In contrast to the situation of 2005, Correa's government enjoyed wide and strong support from public opinion and the armed forces.

However, Ecuadorian democracy, now more "stable," without an irregular transfer of power for the past few years, is now under threat from an increasingly authoritarian and personalized populist regime, with socialist inclinations, led by Rafael Correa (Weyland 2013) (Mainwaring and Pérez-Liñan 2013, 261–2, 267–8). He was elected first in December 2006 by a coalition of leftist parties including his own, *Alianza País.* His campaign promised a nationalist, progressive, anti-neoliberal/capitalist and anti-*partidocracia* revolutionary government. He won 56% of the vote in a run-off election. Following the Chávez model, he proceeded to manipulate the National Assembly, the Electoral Tribunal and the Constitutional Tribunal to call a referendum for a new Constitution, which was approved in September 2008 by 64% of the vote.

Under this new Constitution, which gave broad new powers to the executive branch, Correa easily won reelection in 2009, and with his broad "progressive" coalition came to control the legislative and judicial branches, as well as the electoral authorities. He thus obtained full control of the political institutions and state enterprises and resources, including its significant oil and mineral revenues from a global boom in commodities. This control enabled him to effect important distributive social policies in popular sectors such as health, education, housing, social security, public transportation, and the environment, which have reduced unemployment, poverty and inequality. He has proclaimed that his goal is a "citizens' revolution" for social justice. He has also expropriated foreign companies, distanced himself from the United States and joined the Bolivarian Alliance for the Americas (ALBA). These policies however, have not produced the same economic chaos as in Venezuela, because of Correa's sensible fiscal and monetary, financial and commercial policies, including maintaining a dollar economy.

As a result of these policies and his populist narrative, Correa was able to win reelection again in 2013 with 57% of the votes. But he has used his power and popularity to persecute and intimidate or denigrate as destabilizers and conspirators those who oppose him from the media (he has expropriated television channels), from traditional political parties and even from social movements like the Pachakutik, or those opposed to his mining or oil exploration policies, like indigenous miners (Confederation of Indigenous Nationalities of Ecuador), or indigenous peoples from the Amazon region.[23] As in Bolivia, this intolerant and authoritarian behavior detracts from his successful economic policies and progressive inclusionary social policies.

Correa's reactionary and authoritarian if not repressive policies have received broad international criticism from the Inter-American Press Association and the Inter-American Human Rights Commission (IACHR), particularly from its Rapporteur on Press Freedom[24] (Inter-American Commission on Human Rights 2014), but not from the Secretary General nor any member state in the OAS Permanent Council. Because of the Commission's persistent reports on violations of human rights in Ecuador and other members of the *chavista* alliance, Correa's government, along with his *chavista* allies, have attempted to silence the IACHR by accusing it of ideological bias and unfounded or distorted reports, attempting to limit the scope of its investigations and reporting, and even suggesting that its headquarters be moved from Washington, D.C. to Haiti or Panama (Aparicio and Perina, Amenazas a la Protección de los DDHH 2011) (Gaviria 2013).

Honduras' Interrupted Democracy

The Honduras crisis, pre and post the military coup of June 28, 2009, represents up to now the most dramatic application of the IADC, involving both
its preventive and restorative functions. On the one hand, the OAS (its member states and its Secretary General) failed to use the Charter in a preventive
manner to avert the coup; but on the other hand, it diligently used it to
suspend the coup makers from the Organization, the most extreme political
and diplomatic measure allowed by the Charter, until democracy was restored. The crisis also revealed the Charter's limitations and weaknesses, as
well as the inadequacy of the role that Secretary General and the Permanent
Council played in the crisis.

In early June, President Zelaya requested the Secretary General to send a
mission to observe a "public poll" (*consulta popular,* or referendum) to be
held on June 28, 2009, whereby the electorate would decide if the general
election of November 29 could include a referendum on whether or not to
convoke a Constituent Assembly to modify the Constitution, basically to
permit presidential reelection or expansion of the presidential term of office
(the *"chavista"* model). All political forces, including the President's own
Liberal Party, the Supreme Court, the Supreme Electoral Tribunal, the National Congress and the military strongly opposed this *consulta,* because it
was determined to be unconstitutional and was perceived as an attempt by
Zelaya to perpetuate his own power. Nevertheless, the Secretary General sent
an emissary to explain to President Zelaya that the OAS would not formally
observe the process but would "accompany" it, since it was only a "poll"
which had no legally binding force. All those who opposed the *consulta*
rejected the OAS mission, because it would legitimize the illegal referendum,
and the National Congress formally requested that the mission leave the
country (La Tribuna 2009).

On June 25, the Honduran representative asked the Permanent Council to
convene urgently to discuss the threats "to the political process and/or the
legitimate exercise of power," and requested its assistance in preserving the
democratic institutions of the country. The Council approved a resolution
that called on all political and social actors to respect the rule of law "in order
to avoid a disruption of the constitutional order" and instructed the Secretary
General to send a special mission to analyze the facts and promote a national
dialogue "aimed at finding a democratic solution" to the situation (Pemanent
Council 2009). The OAS mission sent by the Secretary General to support
President Zelaya essentially ignored the other branches' opposition to the
consulta, and did not have the capacity nor the time to promote dialogue,
negotiation and consensus-building amongst the protagonists. Those opposed
to the referendum interpreted the OAS presence as legitimizing a process that
the President would later use to call a referendum to change the Constitution

and engineer his re-election. Neither were the member states in the OAS Permanent Council disposed to invite the other branches of government to at least hear their grievances in its session of June 26, 2009. The Permanent Council meeting instructed the Secretary General to send a special mission, but it was indeed too little and too late.

The Secretary General and diplomats from the member states had all been well aware of the brewing political tension in Honduras caused by President Zelaya's intention to change the Constitution. The matter was a frequent subject of conversation during the OAS General Assembly that took place on June 2–3 in San Pedro Sula, Honduras. In fact, during those days, the Secretary General himself met with President Zelaya and the President of the Supreme Court to analyze the political situation. There was indeed an early warning and plenty of time for the Secretary General, through the political mission he sent, and/or for member states, through the Permanent Council, to engage all parties involved, not just the executive branch, in a process of dialogue, negotiations and consensus-building to avoid a breakdown of the democratic order, which was about to take place either in the form of an unconstitutional *consulta* or a coup d'état.

Despite the overwhelming opposition from all quarters, Zelaya, with the help of the Venezuelan government (for electoral logistics), decided to go ahead with his "non-binding poll" on Sunday, June 28. As the media had widely predicted, a coup did take place in the early morning of Sunday, when the military forcefully removed the President from his home, and dispatched him on a plane to Costa Rica. The National Congress appointed its own President, Roberto Micheletti, as President of Honduras (El Hage 2010).

Predictably, the reactive and restorative mechanisms of the Charter immediately kicked in. The day of the coup, the Permanent Council condemned it and demanded the safe return of President Zelaya to his constitutional functions. On June 30, a special session of the OAS General Assembly, convoked urgently for the occasion, declared that it would not recognize any government that emerged out of this constitutional rupture and instructed the Secretary General to begin diplomatic initiatives to restore democracy, but without any contact with representatives of the *de facto* government. On July 4, not having achieved the restitution of President Zelaya, it suspended the *de facto* government from the activities of the OAS, and instructed the Secretary General to reinforce its diplomatic initiatives to reinstate Zelaya (General Assembly of the OAS, special session 2009).

Even though a new Government was elected in fair and free elections on November 29—elections that had been planned and were on course before the coup—Honduras remained suspended from all OAS activities until June 1, 2011. Former President Zelaya returned as a citizen and managed his wife's failed electoral campaign for the presidency in 2013.

The Honduras case is emblematic. It shows the failure of the member states and the Secretary General to prevent the collapse of the democratic order—although as expected, they quickly reacted to the coup and suspended the transgressors from the Organization and isolated them diplomatically for about two years. However, despite their efforts toward the eventual restoration of democracy in Honduras, once again it must be emphasized that, as in Ecuador in 2005, neither the Secretary General nor any member state in the Permanent Council were willing to hear or invite to the Permanent Council the other branches of government or members of Zelaya's own party that vehemently opposed his illegal and authoritarian intentions to originally change the Constitution. Such a proactive initiative would have made the OAS a true forum for collectively "assessing the situation" and for facilitating a political dialogue that might have prevented the interruption of the democratic order.

Nicaragua's Eroding Democracy

A political/constitutional crisis that had been threatening Nicaraguan democracy as a result of a conflict between the *Sandinista*-led National Assembly and the President of Nicaragua, Enrique Bolaños, finally came to a breaking point in May 2005. The *Sandinistas* and other opposition parties (Arnoldo Alemán's Liberal faction), in control of the Assembly, passed a constitutional reform that limited the powers of the Presidency to name senior officials to State agencies. The Supreme Court followed with a decision siding with the legislature. President Bolaños rejected this attack on the executive branch as he considered it unconstitutional and a threat to his right to exercise his duties, and refused to publish the reform and make it official. Subsequently, the President invoked the IADC (Article 17) and requested assistance from the OAS to preserve Nicaragua's democracy.

The June OAS General Assembly took up the matter and adopted a Declaration (AG/DEC.43 (XXXV-O/05)) that instructed the Secretary General to send a special mission of "good offices" with the purpose of helping establish a national dialogue that would prevent the breakdown of democracy. The mission (June-October 2005), headed by Dante Caputo, OAS Secretary for Political Affairs, successfully helped avoid the rupture of the constitutional and democratic order and restore democratic governance.[25]

However, Ortega's return to the presidency, after winning the presidential election on November 2006 observed by the OAS, initiated a process to consolidate the *Sandinistas'* power, including control of the supposedly independent State agencies, the legislative and judicial branch and the electoral body. Thus, the *Sandinistas* have been able to manipulate the legislative, judicial and electoral institutions to alter the Constitution so that Ortega can be re-elected indefinitely. He can now be a "President for life."[26]

The *Sandinista* regime has thus become increasingly authoritarian at the expense of Nicaragua's democracy (Weyland 2013, 24) (Mainwaring and Perez-Liñan 2013, 261–2, 267–8). However, they have not mismanaged the economy like their allies in Venezuela and in fact have implemented sound economic policies that have produced a measure of economic growth (an average of 3.6% a year for the past decade or so) with declining unemployment and poverty, to the satisfaction of the business community (including many newly rich *Sandinista* "entrepreneurs" linked to Venezuelan oil and businesses), the International Monetary Fund, and the voting public, which keeps giving electoral victories to the *Sandinistas*. The "Liberal" opposition parties are disgruntled but hopelessly fragmented and unable to offer a political alternative or a serious electoral challenge to the *Sandinistas*, who are well organized, prosperous and in solid control of the State (Anderson and Dodd 2009).

Nevertheless, this significant and corrupt power grab and alteration of the constitutional and democratic order has tainted the *Sandinistas*' otherwise successful socioeconomic policies, much like in Ecuador and Bolivia. It has also been totally ignored by the inter-American community of democracies and no one has considered the possibility of calling attention to the *Sandinistas*' violations of the Inter-American Democratic Charter.

Venezuela's Altered and Fraudulent Democracy

The *chavista* regime, the hemisphere's emblematic pseudo-democracy, emerged from a substantive and undisputable electoral victory by Hugo Chávez in 1998. After that, he continued winning several national, legislative and local elections with a clear majority, but with increasingly questionable electoral practices. Today, Venezuela is run by an authoritarian, populist, statist, "socialist" and anti-imperialist regime, which is the result of the regime's slow but sure alteration of the democratic order—a perverse political phenomenon also known as a *coup in slow motion* (Kornblith 2013) (Mainwaring and Perez-Liñan 2013, 244–5 258–62, 267–8) (Weyland 2013).

The erosion of the democratic order perhaps began after the attempted coup of April 12, 2002. A faction of the armed forces ousted President Hugo Chávez, imprisoned him for 48 hours, and installed Pedro Carmona, a business leader, as provisional President.[27] Carmona proceeded to toss out the 1999 Constitution and dissolve Congress and the Supreme Court. As these events unfolded, Latin American Presidents and Foreign Ministers[28] immediately condemned the coup and asked for a meeting of the OAS Permanent Council to assess the situation in Venezuela and take the appropriate decisions, invoking Article 20 of the new Democratic Charter.

The following day, the Permanent Council unanimously condemned the "alteration of the constitutional order in Venezuela," and sent the Secretary

General to Caracas "to investigate the facts and begin the necessary diplomatic efforts, including good offices, to promote the immediate normalization of the democratic institutions." However, Carmona's drastic measures, along with his decision not to include in his cabinet opposition leaders from political parties, labor and civic organization, or moderate military leaders, led to his isolation and loss of critical support. Under these circumstances, and in view of condemnation of the coup by the Rio Group and the OAS, loyal "institutionalist" military groups rescued Chávez from his prison and returned him by helicopter to the government palace at 3 a.m. on April 14.

Secretary General Gaviria presented his report on April 18 to a special session of the General Assembly, whose resolution unanimously manifested, inter alia, the member states' determination to apply the Democratic Charter whenever necessary for the preservation and defense of representative democracy (AG/RES.1 (XXIX E/02). The resolution, negotiated with Chávez representatives, also expressed satisfaction at the reestablishment of the constitutional order in Venezuela and the return to power of the democratically elected Government of President Chávez; supported the government's initiative to convoke a national dialogue (a promise made many times since but never fully carried out); encouraged the government to observe and apply all the essential components of representative democracy; and offered any OAS assistance the Venezuelan Government might require to consolidate its democratic process. [29]

The situation was resolved quickly in favor of restoring the democratic order. But even though the crisis had been looming on the horizon and could have been easily detected by anyone paying attention, the Venezuelan Government did not ask for OAS assistance, nor did any member state or the then Secretary General, César Gaviria, invoke the Charter or convoke the Permanent Council to assess the situation collectively, thus missing the possibility of avoiding or preventing the coup and the temporary rupture of the constitutional democratic order. Following the coup, the regime became increasingly authoritarian and repressive, as resistance and opposition to it augmented from the political opposition, the independent media and the student movement. The country has subsequently become profoundly polarized in equally and bitterly divided contending parts: On one side, the monolithic government and its *chavista* followers (about 50% of the electorate), backed by the co-opted military and security forces; and on the other, the anti-*chavista* opposition.

The polarization cemented when the opposition (the *Coordinadora Democrática*) called for a Presidential Recall Referendum. The process leading up to it involved a long, complex and contentious process of negotiation and was marred by violent demonstrations, mutual accusations of attempting to rig or stop the process, and a controversial and disputed process of collecting the necessary number of valid voters' signatures. Secretary General Gaviria, along with the Carter Center and UNDP (United Nations Development Program) facilitated the process with the approval of both sides (Legler, Venezuela 2002–2004. The Chávez Challenge 2007).[30]

After months of mediated negotiations and intermediate agreements and declarations, in February 2004 they finally agreed to hold the referendum in August 2004, as an electoral and peaceful way to solve the lingering political crisis engulfing the country. Secretary General Gaviria sent Ambassador Valter Pecly Moreira, Brazil's Permanent Representative to the OAS, as Chief of the OAS electoral observation mission to monitor the referendum, which was held in August 2004.

The referendum confirmed Chavez' popularity and presidency, but at the same time it became a turning point, as opposition leaders challenged the results on the grounds of an alleged manipulation of the electronic results (Kornblith 2005) (McCoy 2005) (Legler, Venezuela 2002–2004. The Chávez Challenge 2007). From then on, the opposition began to deeply mistrust the electoral authorities and subsequent electoral processes.[31] This led to their refusal to participate in the legislative elections of December 2005. Both electoral events and the mistrust of the electoral authorities deepened and exacerbated the political polarization between the *chavistas* and the opposition—a polarization that has eroded the democratic political culture and the institutional framework to this day. The two camps have widely different and apparently irreconcilable visions of the country. The opposition's withdrawal from the elections left, for all intents and purpose, the state institutions in total control of the *chavistas* and led to Chávez' total domination of the political system. He used his electoral victories to claim a democratic legitimacy that he would manipulate to justify the introduction of profound socioeconomic and political changes, known as "the Bolivarian Socialist Revolution."

Using the huge, seemingly endless oil revenues, Chávez introduced progressive social programs known as "missions" in sectors such as housing, health, nutrition, education, social security for the vast and disenfranchised majority of Venezuelans. He nationalized and confiscated the hitherto efficient and prosperous oil industry, as well as most of the companies in the telecommunications, electricity, steel, and cement industries; and expanded the bureaucracy and government control over exports and imports, foreign investment and exchange. In the short run, these policies reduced poverty significantly from 50% to 20% (although four million Venezuelans, if not more given the worsening economic situation, remain below the poverty line). Unemployment has fallen to below 10% (although there is a huge underemployed population). Chávez has generated a persistent electoral majority of around 54% of the electorate (approximately 8 million voters). This state-dependent *chavista* "majority", well-organized and mobilized for political and electoral purposes by the regime, felt benefitted and empowered by its leader, whom they idolized and loyally voted for in every election until his death in 2014. Perversely, however, Chávez employed his electoral victories to extend his personal and centralized authority over the political system, to make it practically impossible for the political opposition to challenge him successfully. The regime controls and manipulates to its benefit all governmental institutions, beyond the executive branch and state enterprises, including the legislative, judicial and electoral branches, the politicized and partisan armed and security forces, the great majority of the media (television, radio and newspapers), as well as the majority of universities, governorships and local governments. There is no separation or independence of power among governmental institutions. *Chavistas* control all the state institutions and follow and execute *chavista* guidelines emanating from their supreme leader. There reigns but one political credo. The regime denigrates or vilifies and persecutes and/or harasses the independent media and opposition leaders, and accuses them of conspiring to overthrow its "legitimate" government and being subservient to the interests of the United States (the "empire"). [32]

However, the regime's ideological, misguided and corrupt management of the populist/nationalist, statized-and-centralized economy, including its deficit and public debt, have had disastrous socio-economic political repercussions for the *chavista* regime itself. In the last few years, popular support for the regime has wavered and its electoral majority diminished (the regime lost a referendum on reelection in 2008 and "rigged" the legislative elections in 2010), and polls show that more than 50% of the people are dissatisfied with the present conditions. This is basically the result of a growing discontent with rising lack of security (24,000 deaths in 2013) and impunity (92%) in the country, with rampant scarcity of food (28%) and medical and household supplies, with an inflation rate of over 50%, with an increasing international isolation and alliance and submission to the Castro regime, with the waste of oil resources in buying foreign allegiance (Petro-Caribe), and with the harassment of the independent media and persecution and imprisonment of opposition and student leaders (Inter-American Commission on Human Rights 2014). [33] The economic situation and accompanying discontent and unrest is likely to worsen as oil prices have plummeted from over US$100 a barrel to below US$40. Oil income is the State's main source of revenue and funds more than 90% of the national budget.

In view of the manifest popular dissatisfaction, the regime's authoritarian control of the state and its narrative were oriented to make sure that Chávez be elected indefinitely. Despite losing the 2007 referendum on changes to the constitution that would have allowed for his re-reelection, the regime nevertheless abolished the ban on allowing a sitting president to run for more than two terms by inserting the changes in the comprehensive constitutional reform referendum of 2009. Under the regime, elections are to be won at any cost and by any means[34] (Kornblith 2013).

Anticipating a probable defeat in the September 2010 parliamentary elections, the regime, with its hegemonic control of the National Assembly and the National Electoral Council, changed the representational rules and gerrymandered the electoral districts so that the less populated *chavista* districts would be overrepresented. In the election, the regime did not obtain the two-thirds majority it was seeking, while the opposition made significant gains and obtained 65 of the 165 seats in the Assembly, even though it won 52% of the votes. However, immediately after convening the new National Assembly and electing its authorities, the *chavista* majority changed the parliamentary rules so that they could pass major legislation with only a simple majority. This included a delegation of legislative power to the President, allowing him to legislate by decree without any participation of the opposition in parliamentary debate and negotiation, thus indicating once more the absence of separation of powers and the centralized, personalized, authoritarian and anti-democratic nature of the regime.

The latest expression of its desperate attempt to remain in power became evident during the obscure and unconstitutional procedures the regime employed to assure Maduro's election after Chávez' death on January 5, 2013, before he was supposed to assume his new term of office as President of Venezuela on January 10. Chávez' illness and departure catapulted the regime into a crisis. As Chávez had publicly handpicked his sitting Vice President, Nicolás Maduro, to succeed him, the question became how to transfer power to Maduro, since he was not elected (Vice Presidents in Venezuela are selected by the President and serve at his or her discretion). Article 233 of the Bolivarian Constitution stipulates that in case of the absolute absence of the elected President and his incapacity to assume power, the President of the National Assembly (in this case, Diosdado Cabello) assumes the presidency and calls new elections within the next thirty days.

However, the *chavista* Supreme Court (*Tribunal Supremo de Justicia*), in a twisted interpretation, decided that Maduro could remain in power beyond January 10 because Chávez had been reelected and that implied "administrative continuity," which not only extended the previous presidential term illegally but ratified Maduro as successor even though he had not been elected nor appointed as Vice President for the new term, and in fact was usurping the National Assembly President's mandate. This regime's "auto-coup" made Maduro a *de facto* President and assured the regime's control of the state and its continuity in power. He remained as "President in charge" and launched his candidacy for the April 2014 elections.

Maduro's government went on to manipulate the electoral process to his favor, undermining its validity. Vicente Díaz, the only non-*chavista* member of the National Electoral Council (CNE), described the electoral process as grotesque and shameless. The regime distorted the process from the beginning by utilizing state resources (petro dollars, state media, government officials, government facilities) for campaign expenses, mobilization of supporters, new subsidies and donations for its followers, and inauguration of new social services, schools and public works. In addition, Maduro's campaign perversely generated doubts about the integrity of the automated electoral technology implying that the government would know for whom voters would cast their votes, thus encouraging followers and intimidating opponents. This only increased the opposition's mistrust of the electoral authorities and of the electronic voting system. The regime also abused its huge media resources (it directly or indirectly controls about 80% of all media) to its advantage, to transmit its propaganda. It did not even agree to a debate between Maduro and the opposition candidate, Henrique Capriles.

These electoral abuses and distortions in favor of the official candidate violated the constitution and electoral regulations, as well as fundamental principles of fair and just elections agreed upon by all the democracies of hemisphere in the Inter-American Democratic Charter. Nevertheless, the *chavista* electoral authorities never denounced them or reprimanded Maduro's campaign. The regime also refused to invite the OAS or the European Union to observe the elections as had occurred in previous instances. Instead, it permitted its allies from UNASUR and ALBA countries to send observers to "accompany" the process. Those observers lacked independence, scope, rigor and experience.

The regime's transgressions were even the subject of an unprecedented declaration (April 2, 2014) by the Venezuelan Episcopal Conference, which condemned the Maduro Government's repression of street demonstrations led by student and opposition leaders since February 12, 2014. Straightforwardly, with remarkable candor, it also blamed the government for "press restrictions, lack of safeguards against judicial persecution, harassment of the private sector, and brutal repression of political dissidents, including threats, verbal attacks and physical violence to silence them," and for attempting to install a "totalitarian-style system of government, putting in doubt its democratic credentials." It also called on the government and the opposition to start serious dialogue to end the increasingly violent social and political unrest involving the country.[35]

The 14 April elections showed numerous and significant irregularities as reported by independent organizations and the Capriles opposition camp. But most revealing was the fact that the electoral authorities proclaimed Maduro's victory and swore him in with unusual haste, without a full audit of the polling places, as the opposition had requested,[36] even though the margin of victory was a mere 200,000 votes out of close to 15 million votes. Members of UNASUR and ALBA that "accompanied" the electoral process immediately recognized Maduro's victory. On account of the violations and irregularities observed, the elections became highly questionable and Capriles challenged them and did not recognize Maduro's victory (R. M. Perina, "Elecciones Inválidas en Venezuela" 2013) (R. M. Perina, "Elecciones Impugnadas en Venezuela" 2013).

Thus, the auto-coup, the absence of free and fair elections and rigorous electoral observations, the media harassment, the persecution of opposition and student leaders and the lack of real separation and independence of powers all constitute a flagrant violation of the Bolivarian Constitution and fundamental human rights. This is what makes Venezuela an altered and fraudulent democracy.

In addition, the erosion of the democratic order contravenes the democratic clauses of CELAC (Community of Latin American and Caribbean States), MERCOSUR (Southern Common Market) and UNASUR (Union of South American Nations), and of course the Inter-American Democratic Charter. In spite of this, however, the regime and its allies, the *chavista* alliance (Argentina, Bolivia, Brazil, Dominican Republic, Ecuador, El Salvador, Nicaragua and the fourteen oil-dependent Caribbean member states) have vehemently argued against any "intervention" from OAS member states that might question or call attention to these anti-democratic developments taking place in Venezuela. The alliance claims that the regime is democratic because it has won elections and must be left alone, willfully ignoring the fact that the regime has altered the democratic order by violating its own constitution and fundamental democratic principles, institutions, values and practices enshrined in the Democratic Charter.

The *chavista* regime even denounced the American Convention on Human Rights in 2012, reacting to the Inter-American Human Rights Commission's reports pointing to numerous violations of political and civil rights, including freedom of the press in Venezuela. However, these reports have been ignored by the political collective bodies of the Organization, allowing for the continuous deterioration of the democratic order in the country (Inter-American Commission on Human Rights 2014) (Kornblith 2013).

Remarkably and disappointingly, the fact is that until recently no member state nor Secretary General Insulza has been willing to invoke the Democratic Charter, as Art. 20 allows, or attempt to convene a Permanent Council meeting to collectively assess the Venezuelan situation, even though it is patently clear that an alteration of the democratic order has taken place, followed by increasing popular street demonstrations, violence and casualties, political repression and arrests and even with reports of torture. Against all odds, however, Panama (March 2014) endeavored to bring the Venezuela situation to discussion in the Permanent Council, only to be voted down by a majority of the member states (the *chavista* alliance), which even refused to have the meeting open to the public. Because of this "interventionist act," the *chavista* regime broke diplomatic and commercial relations with the Panamanian Government.

Secretary General Insulza, while supporting the Panamanian initiative, misleadingly and gratuitously commented afterwards that the "OAS will not intervene in Venezuela," as, according to him, conditions in that country did not warrant application of the Democratic Charter.[37] The majority of member states had already refused to even discuss the Venezuelan situation in a public session or to allow the National Assembly's deputy, María Corina Machado, to speak in the Permanent Council from the Panamanian chair, let alone take any collective action such as sending a fact-finding or dialogue promoting diplomatic mission.[38]

In addition, during his term of office (2005–2015), Secretary General Insulza, while occasionally receiving opposition figures and students leaders, has never attempted to bring the issue of Venezuela's eroding democracy for collective discussion by the Permanent Council, as the Democratic Charter or the Founding Charter would allow him to do. He is correct to say that the OAS would not "intervene", but only insofar as the present hemispheric correlation of forces in favor of the *chavista* alliance would not permit it. Nevertheless, he could, if he wished, use his mandate to call attention to the Venezuelan situation, even though his effort would be voted down by the *chavista* alliance. On the other hand, a collective action in defense of democracy, strictly speaking, would not be "interventionist" because it is a collective responsibility and commitment agreed to by all member states, including Venezuela. Thus, democracy, in a fragmented hemisphere that is lacking in leadership and consensus to promote and protect it as agreed to in the Democratic Charter, is allowed to erode slowly but surely in Venezuela behind the veil of a fraudulent democracy and non-interventionism (R. Perina, Hemisferio Fragmentado 2014) (R. Perina, "Ganadores y Perdedores en la OEA" 2014).

CONCLUSION WITH A CAVEAT

Despite the progress made in the development and application of new norms and instruments for the promotion and protection of democracy, most OAS member states have shown an alarming indifference and passivity, if not complicity with the pseudo-democracies' alteration of the democratic order and violations of the Democratic Charter.

The pseudo-democratic regimes have additionally formed a *chavista* alliance, encouraged and supported by Argentina and Brazil, which has successfully silenced any attempt by member states to criticize the "model" or their violations of the Democratic Charter, thus paralyzing and preventing the OAS from activating the Charter.[39] The alliance is the principal impediment to coherent collective responses to prevent the erosion and eventual collapse of the democratic order and the emergence of new tyrannies. It would pose an insurmountable obstacle to any member's attempt, under the IADC, to question or call attention to anti-democratic practices in pseudo-democratic regimes.

If, for example, the Secretary General or a member state were to invoke Article 20 to collectively "assess the situation" in a country that may be undergoing a political/institutional crisis that threatens its democratic order, and further assuming that a Permanent Council session is held for such a purpose, it would be a considerable challenge just to get a consensus, particularly if the affected state and its allies were opposed to it, on a resolution that would, minimally, call on the contenders in the crisis to start a process of dialogue to resolve their political differences, and/or permit a Secretary General's mission of good offices.

Decisions in the OAS Permanent Council are traditionally taken by consensus, and if consensus is not assured, a vote on the resolution would probably not even be called, as a vote is considered a polarizing practice that disturbs the harmony of the multilateral body. But if a vote were to take place, the resolution would still need a simple majority of eighteen members to pass, which may not be easy to obtain at this time in history. More substantially, the lack of consensus to analyze the situation when there is an "unconstitutional alteration of the democratic order" is based on a profound disagreement as to what exactly constitutes an "unconstitutional alteration." An "unconstitutional alteration" that violates the principles of the Charter and undermines democracy by using democratic means is a paradoxical process that does not elicit automatic consensus amongst member states to condemn it and propose collective action. Additionally, if a member state decides to convoke the Permanent Council to assess the situation in a fellow member state, without its consent, the affected government and its allies may consider such an action not only interventionism but an aggression, which could lead to the breaking of diplomatic and commercial relations, and polarize the region and the Organization. This possibility makes member states very nervous and reluctant to proceed in that direction.[40]

In short, given the likely rejection by the *chavista* alliance of any attempt to assess the political situation, it is highly improbable that in present conditions a collective decision could be reached to use the IADC to arrest the erosion of democracy in Venezuela or in any of its pseudo-democratic allies. Nevertheless, the erosion of democracy in these regimes and their violation of the IADC represent today the principal challenges, if not the failure, facing the OAS member states and the emerging Inter-American Democratic Regime.

NOTES

1. For a discussion of the process see Consejo Permanente de la OEA (2003, ix-xii, 37, 51–54; 101–108).

2. The concept is discussed in greater detail in Chapter 11.

3. Although other branches of government might consider it to be interventionist, as seen earlier, in February 1997, Ecuadorian congressional leaders and the mainstream media rejected OAS Secretary General Gaviria's visit to Quito in support of President Bucarám, and called it interference in the internal affairs of the country. Similarly, as we shall see later, the National Congress of Honduras called the Secretary Insulza's support for President Zelaya as interventionist also.

4. Theoretically, because even the assessment could be stopped if there is no consensus on the agenda of the meeting.

5. On the other hand, this may not be a weakness after all, since opening the Charter for a debate on its status and/or reform may be a Pandora's box, which may result in debilitating changes.

6. "Democratic paradigm" here refers to a mental structure or pattern of thoughts and values that generate and guide assumptions, ideas, questions, research and the quest for solutions, attitudes and behavior of individuals and states (Kuhn 1996).

7. This definition is one of the most accepted in the specialized literature. Also, according to Krasner, Hedley Bull, in *Anarchical Society: A Study of Order in World Politics* (Bull 1977), argues that "institutions contribute to the observance of rules, by formulating them, disseminating them, managing them, applying them, interpreting them, and giving them legitimacy." Krasner also states that international regimes are different from international agreements. The latter are ad hoc and specific, while regimes facilitate agreements and not only incorporate norms and expectations that facilitate cooperation but are a form of cooperation that goes beyond the pursuit of short-term self-interest. This coincides with the works of Robert Keohane and Joseph Nye (1977) and Robert Jervis (1983). Despite the stinging criticism from Susan Strange of the concept in "A Critique of Regime Analysis," (Strange 1983), it is fairly valid and useful to visualize and give meaning to a series of occurrences or patterns that are observed with increasing frequency in the conduct of the countries of the hemisphere in their inter-American relations, particularly with respect to the defense and promotion of democracy. Viron Vaky wonders whether member states would convert the OAS into an effective tool for regional governance and construction of an inter-American regime (Vaky and Muñoz 1993). This work argues that at a minimum, an inter-American democratic regime is in fact being created.

8. An idealist might even think that the regime provides grounds for renewing the notion of Pan Americanism or the "Western Hemisphere Idea" as the conceptual basis for integration of the hemisphere, an idea espoused by some continental leaders during the second half of the 19th century in various American or Continental Congresses (Panama 1826, Lima 1847, 1856, 1864). See Corrales and Feinberg (1999, 6–4) and Gil (1971, 144–183). In this vein, in a possible 21st century world of regions, the IADR could provide the foundation for a renewal of this idea. The OAS and other inter-American institutions could function as an integrating centripetal nucleus designed to institutionalize an inter-American democratic community with evolving democratic and political/security structure and incorporating norms and institutions that could actually include some features of an inter-American confederation of democratic countries (Whitaker 1954). On the conditions and processes for forming or integrating pluralistic political communities, see the classic works by Deutsch et al. (1968) and Nye (1971 and 1968).

9. The Inter-American Development Bank and the World Bank, at the insistence of their major democratic members (donors and contributors), have in fact warned of possible suspension of projects and financing in cases where democratic processes were interrupted.

10. The General Assembly, at its June 1999 meeting, decided to establish a Committee of the Permanent Council on the Participation of Civil Society in OAS activities. Although a U.S. delegation proposal for formal inclusion of NGOs in OAS activities was rejected at the 2005 General Assembly in Fort Lauderdale, they do now participate in informal forums organized around the holding of OAS General Assemblies.

11. See also a somewhat self-serving and uncritical report by the Secretariat for Political Affairs of the OAS (Secretariat for Political Affairs, General Secretariat of the OAS 2011).

12. The new constitution would allow Morales and his party, *Movimiento al Socialismo (MAS)*, to nationalize the gas and oil industries as well as all natural resources, reverse the much maligned neo-liberal and market-oriented economic policies, strengthen the state and the central government, grant more than one hundred new human and cultural rights based on the indigenous culture, introduce social policies to reduce poverty and inequality, increase the participation in governmental affairs of traditionally marginalized sectors like the indigenous communities, and reduce the autonomy of the rich and more "liberal" Eastern departments or states of the country such as the Beni, Pando, Santa Cruz, and Tarija, for example.

13. Much credit for this role corresponds to the head of the Mission, Raul Lago, an experienced and highly prudent and competent Uruguayan politician and diplomat.

14. This compelled some members of the opposition to question it and bring it to the attention of the Secretary General of the OAS as a possible overreach by the Morales government, since it was basically under its Mission's presence and facilitation that the no re-election provision was adopted in the 2008. See http://www.hoybolivia.com/Noticia.php?IdNoticia=83136&tit=oea_se_disculpa_de_bolivia.

15. See http://www.eldiario.net/noticias/2014/2014_04/nt140404/politica.php?n=70&-tres-politicos-exigen-garantias-tras-sufrir-ataques-y-amenazas.

16. See http://www.emol.com/noticias/internacional/2014/04/01/652942/un-muerto-y-40-heridos-en-choques-entre-policias-y-mineros-en-bolivia.html, and http://www.eluniversal.com/internacional/140404/aumentan-a-tres-los-muertos-por-protesta-minera-en-bolivia.

17. For the past ten years or so, Bolivia has had an approximate average growth of 3.5% a year. http://www.cepal.org/publicaciones/xml/5/51945/AnuarioEstadistico2013.pdf. Accessed November 17, 2014.

18. The Inter-American Commission on Human Rights (IACHR) pointed, for example, to "a series of acts of violence, harassment and threats against leaders of labor unions, social organizations, indigenous and political groups and students," which were expressing their public opposition to the government's actions. IACHR Press Release 8/5 of March 11, 2005.

19. It is worthwhile recalling that in 1997, President Bucarám was also overthrown by an irregular congressional procedure and not by a constitutional impeachment process.

20. With the Government's acquiescence, the Council sent a diplomatic mission to Ecuador, with the purpose of collaborating with the new Ecuadorian authorities and all sectors of society in their efforts to consolidate their democracy. The author, at the time a special advisor to the Department of Political and Democratic Affairs of the General Secretariat, presented a report on the political situation in Ecuador to the Permanent Council on April 22, 2005.

21. The follow-up resolution was also called "OAS Support for the Republic of Ecuador," May 20, 2005 (CP/RES. 883 (1484/05)).

22. CP/RES. 977 (1772/10), "Situation in the Republic of Ecuador."

23. For a comprehensive analysis of Correa's populism, see de la Torre's article (2013). In a bizarre development, not unusual in Ecuadorian politics, three political opponents of Correa that have been sentenced for defaming the President have sought refuge in an Amazon Indian community, and President Correa has angrily demanded the community leaders to turn them over or face the consequences. See: http://www.theguardian.com/world/2014/apr/30/ecuador-president-rafael-correa-demands-kichwa-sarayaku-defamors.

24. See: http://www.oas.org/en/iachr/docs/annual/2013/TOC.asp.

25. The mission facilitated the adoption of a mutually agreed upon legal framework that suspended implementation of the constitutional reform, arranged for the joint selection of State agency directors, set the conditions for the upcoming electoral process, and established a political roundtable to facilitate dialogue and negotiations amongst the contending political forces, with the presence of the Catholic Church and the OAS as guarantors.

26. See: http://www.csmonitor.com/World/Americas/Latin-America-Monitor/2014/0129/Nicaragua-s-Ortega-President-for-life.

27. The reasons for the coup were many, but suffice it here to say that by 2002, Chávez had become more authoritarian, and was accumulating and centralizing power through nationalization and expropriation of industries (oil and steel at first) and through increased personal and

chavista control of state agencies, the judicial and electoral system and the armed forces. He also had radicalized his populist, leftist socioeconomic polices in favor of the large, previously ignored underprivileged population, had begun to curtail the media who were criticizing him, scorned the political opposition and turned increasingly anti-American. As can be expected, this infuriated the traditional elite, the middle class and sectors of the armed forces—all of whom wanted his ouster and began to strike, protest, generate public unrest and plot to that effect (Smith 2005, 131–32) (Legler 2007, 204–9).

28. They were coincidentally meeting in San José, Costa Rica, at the annual gathering of the Rio Group.

29. Because of the uneasy relations existing between Venezuela and the U.S., some observers speculated that the U.S. Government had supported the coup, or argued that at least it recognized the coup makers too quickly, and only belatedly condemned it, when the coup was reversed. But the fact is that both the Permanent Council and the resolutions of the special session of the General Assembly, with the explicit U.S. vote, strongly condemned the unconstitutional rupture of the democratic process (De Young 2002) (Hakim 2002) (Shifter 2002) (Valenzuela 2002). Chavez reneged on these agreements and actually proceeded to radicalize his socioeconomic policies, became increasingly authoritarian, and polarized the political environment by accusing any and all opposition as conspirators and lackeys of U.S.imperialism.

30. The process actually began with an OAS General Assembly "Declaration on Democracy in Venezuela" (General Assembly of the OAS, special session 2002). Through a "Round Table for Negotiation and Agreements", the Government and the opposition agreed in November to appoint Secretary General Gaviria as the International Facilitator.

31. For an assessment of the OAS role in these elections, see Chapter 8.

32. The *chavista* regime is becoming to resemble more and more the dictatorial regimes of Alfredo Strossner in Paraguay (1954–1989), Anastasio Somoza (1967–1979) in Nicaragua and Rafael Trujillo in the Dominican Republic (1930–1961), but with the difference that the dictatorships would accuse the opposition as being "communist." Some of the most recent and prominent opposition politicians persecuted, exiled and/or imprisoned include Leopoldo López, imprisoned; Carlos Vecchio and Antonio Rivero, in hiding; Legislator María C. Machado, banned arbitrarily from her seat in the National Assembly; Daniel Ceballos, Mayor of San Cristóbal in the State of Táchira and Enzo Scarano, Mayor of San Diego, in the State of Carabobo, both ousted illegally and imprisoned; Ivan Simonivis, imprisoned; Carlos Ortega and Manuel Rosales, in exile, and María de Lourdes Afiuni, detained. Some 4,500 politicians, business people and students have asked for and received asylum in the U.S. since 2000.

33. The report has a special section on Venezuela.

34. The *chavistas* lost it by a slim margin, 51 to 49 per cent, but nevertheless it was a shocking wake-up call.

35. See: http://elpais.com/elpais/2014/04/03/inenglish/1396528231_890877.html.

36. In addition, Capriles' camp claimed that the audit performed on the 54% of the polling places was done irregularly without the presence of representatives of the opposition.

37. See: http://www.martinoticias.com/content/segun-insulza-en-venezuela-no-hay-condiciones-para-carta-de-oea/.

38. For her attempt to speak from the Panamanian chair, the President of the National Assembly stripped Machado of her congressional immunity and unconstitutionally expelled her from the chamber on charges (unproven) of treason—a decision quickly ratified by the *chavista* Supreme Court on March 31, 2014.

39. The alliance has even elected the Cuban dictator, Raúl Castro, as the President *pro tempore* of CELAC in 2012, violating it own "democracy clause."

40. Imagine what would happen to their commercial relations if Colombia were to propose a collective assessment of the situation in Venezuela. As we saw earlier, after Panama allowed Venezuelan opposition leader, María Corina Machado, to use its chair to speak about the deteriorating democratic order in Venezuela, President Maduro insulted the Panamanian President and broke off relations with Panama.

Chapter Seven

Technical Assistance
for Democracy Promotion

Theory and Practice

INTRODUCTION AND THEORETICAL ASSUMPTIONS

Up until now we have concentrated on the "high politics level" of promoting democracy; that is, on the legal/diplomatic norms and instruments member states have developed to promote and defend democracy, such as the amendments to the OAS constituent Charter, Resolution 1080 and the Inter-American Democratic Charter, as well as their applications, strengths and shortcomings.

Complementing this "high politics level," the OAS member states and the General Secretariat also developed a "low politics level" approach with tools to help promote and consolidate democracy. These include departments, units, commissions, programs and projects and a variety of technical instruments (toolbox) used to execute in the field the mandates and guidelines developed by the governing bodies of the Organization in their "high politics" instruments. These "executive" instruments of the Secretariat support member states in their efforts to promote democratic values and practices and preserve and strengthen their democratic institutions.

One such an instrument was the Unit for the Promotion of Democracy (UPD) created by the 1990 General Assembly and by a subsequent Permanent Council resolution in 1991. It was established "to respond promptly and effectively to member states that request assistance, providing advice or assistance related to the preservation and strengthening of their political institutions and democratic procedures."[1]

The UPD mandate presented a formidable intellectual and political/diplomatic challenge, but also offered opportunities for "low politics level" policymaking and technical cooperation for democracy promotion; that is, for practical experiences in the field. The mandate needed to be translated into program guidelines and these had to be implemented on the ground through technnical assistance instruments, which then had to be designed and applied in recipient countries.

The UPD's technical assistance included a set of instruments such as: seminars and workshops to exchange experiences, knowledge and best practices; technical advice on designing strategic projects or activities, strategizing on fund raising, and executing and/or supervising projects; horizontal cooperation to share specific knowledge and experiences (country-to-country, mutual visits), and research and publications to develop and disseminate new knowledge on democracy issues. The UPD tools also included training programs to promote democratic values and practices and share or transfer skills and techniques for political management in a democratic context; political/technical missions in country to observe, mediate and facilitate dialogue, negotiations (mediation/good offices) in political crises, and electoral observation missions. These instruments could be used separately or in combination. Sometimes technical assistance included financial support known as "seed money," to help a project at least begin design, planning and fund raising.

The UPD policy guidelines and technical assistance programs developed and executed through the years were guided implicitly by theoretical assumptions that can now be articulated in a systematic way and even postulated as a model approach to democracy promotion.[2] The underlying theoretical assumptions behind the guidelines and the programs may be described as follows:

a. The fundamental purpose of democracy promotion is to contribute to the strengthening and consolidation of democratic governance and liberal representative democracy. Their consolidation and viability depends on three interdependent variables: a democratic political culture; democratic, effective and legitimate political institutions, and democratic and effective leadership. This hypothesis is consistent with and incorporates theories about the role that each of those variables plays in the consolidation of democracy, as discussed below.

The predominance of these three variables in a society, whether together or separately, contributes to, if not determines, democratic governance and thereby the consolidation of liberal democracy. Or to put it another way: The consolidation and viability of democratic governance and liberal democracy depends on the prevalence of democratic values and practices (DVP) in the political culture, leadership and institutions of a society—three independent variables that are intimately and mutually inter-dependent. A liberal democracracy is consolidated when democratic values and practices predominate in a society, and when its institutions and leaders are highly credible and trusted and therefore legitimate. This, together with democratic elections and effective democratic governance are the foundation of democratic legitimacy: the principal capital of a consolidated democratic political regime.

b. The political culture of a society's citizenry is the cradle and the context from which political leaders and civil servants (bureaucrats) emerge and evolve. A political culture is transmitted through a process of socialization that imbues citizens and leaders with certain values, knowledge, skills and practices which condition if not determine their behavior in society but, most importantly, their attitudes and behavior in the political and bureaucratic institutions in which they may work and which they may eventually lead.

This theoretical construct about the interdependent relationship amongst the three crucial variables and their joint or independent impact on democratic governance provides solid grounds for articulating a theoretical approach to democracy promotion that focuses on all three variables (political culture, leaders and institutions) simultaneously or separately. It also offers a coherent and sensitive framework for the development of concrete technical assistance models designed to help strengthen and consolidate each of those independent variables (the "targets"). These models, based on the UPD/OAS technical assistance experience, are here postulated as effective, albeit complex and long term, instruments for the promotion, transmission and dissemination of democratic values and practices (DVP) among a society's citizens, leadership and institutions, with the intention of contributing directly or indirectly to the strengthening of democratic governance and the consolidation of liberal democracy.

This approach not only provides a clear understanding of the critical variables involved but also offers a strategic focus or target for intervention in the process of promoting democracy, through actual programs and activities designed to that effect. It shows policy makers and practitioners the strategic "targets" and a road map for an appropriate and effective policy of democracy promotion. While there are many targets in the field of democracy promotion, those identified here allow for the development of well-focused, strategic, concrete and practical technical assistance models designed to reinforce and/or consolidate them.

DEMOCRACY AND POLITICAL CULTURE

The promotion of democracy is a complex, multidimensional, slow and long-term task. It involves, in essence, the promotion and development of a democratic political culture. That is, the promotion, fostering, and teaching of values and practices that are essential for democratic governance and the sustainability of democracy—their inculcation, if you will, into the citizenry of a society.[3] In a democracy, citizens not only elect those who rule, but also consent to and legitimize (or not) their governance.

Ideally, to have a successful, effective policy and an effective strategy to promote and protect democracy, there must be a clear understanding of the target intended for promotion. Understanding the nature of the target facilitates the design and execution of effective policies, and helps identify the most realistic (in terms of political and cultural context, for example), concrete and effective instruments and approaches to achieve the desired end.

Democracy has been given many meanings or interpretations. In the broadest sense, one can view democracy as a particular political arrangement to organize and govern a society based predominantly on democratic values, practices and institutions—democratic governance, in short. More specifically, democracy is a system of government and institutions whose leadership is elected by periodic democratic elections, and represents the majority but respects the minority; that is, it governs within the framework of democratic institutions, values and practices, manages or resolves conflict and differences peacefully, and makes public policy choices to guide society and politics towards a desired ideal state of affairs–presumably a peaceful, prosperous and democratic society (Dahl, Shapiro and Cheibub 2003) (Sartori 1993) (Lipset 1993) (Peannock 1977) (O'Donnell and Schmitter, *Transitions from Authoritarian Rule. Tentative Conclusions about Uncertain Democracies,* 1986).

The search and struggle for democracy, however, is a never-ending, perpetually contested, dialectical political process in which political actors attempt to control the state in order to construct a more democratic society. It is a complex, interdependent process, which sometimes has to endure periods of crises and violence to protect and preserve it (O'Donnell, "The Perpetual Crisis of Democracies" 2007).

In today's Western world at least, the ideal end, that is, the desired and sought- after final democratic stage, is a liberal polity and society characterized by a political culture where democratic values and practices predominate. Both democratic values and practices are intimately related: values are what individuals in a democratic society treasure and aspire to most in their lives, which, to be meaningful or have any significance in a society and a polity, must be acted upon, practiced or pursued. Inter alia, DVP include fundamental freedoms, equality, justice, tolerance, moderation, cooperation, participation, competition, free and fair elections, pluralism, negotiations, compromise, mutual respect and trust, consensus building, probity, transparency and accountability; respect for human rights, the rule of law, majority rule with minority rights, and the sharing of power through checks and balances to safeguard against tyranny. Its citizens and leaders and its institutions are imbued with these DVP.[4]

Democratic rights (socioeconomic, cultural and political) and enjoyment and fulfillment of them are also considered to be significant components of a democratic political culture. In consolidated democracies, most of these rights are formalized or institutionalized in constitutions and practiced in daily political life. In fact, some scholars and international experts and officials have made a strong argument in favor of strengthening the state's institutions in order to expand and effectively guarantee the citizens' enjoyment of all those rights as a means of consolidating democracy. But I would argue that a citizens' democracy should be concerned not only with citizen rights and the state's obligation to guarantee them, but also with citizens' responsibilities and duties, as well as with political interaction amongst citizens themselves, an interaction that is conditioned by the nature (democratic or not) of the political culture. It is not just a question of state-citizen relationship, but also has to do with a citizen-to-citizen or citizen-to-leader relationship and vice-versa. If democratic values and practices predominate, the state will be more likely to guarantee the citizens' enjoyment of their rights.[5]

Contrariwise, a political culture may also contain anti-democratic values and practices, or authoritarian ones, if you will (incidentally, as individuals we are all imbued with a degree of both). Here the prevalent values and practices include intolerance, mutual distrust, violence, imposition rather than negotiation and consensus building, selfish individualism, disregard for sharing power or for the principle of separation and balance of power, suppression of or limited free markets and individual freedoms and rights, excessive patronage, cronyism, personalism and clientelism, electoral fraud, lack of transparency, corruption, disrespect for the rule of law, discrimination against minority or opposition rights, repression, and others.

But the crucial and vital question is which of these sets of values and practices predominate in a political culture, its citizenry, its leaders and institutions. As expected, a policy of promoting democracy would aim to contribute and eventually achieve the prevalence of democratic values and practices in a society and polity.

Because democracy is not just elections (as important as they are) but a way of life based on a democratic political culture, the consolidation of democracy depends largely on the extent to which that political culture is firmly rooted, solid and pervasive throughout a society, its leaders and institutions. A democratic political culture is the most significant and decisive variable in the development and consolidation of a democracy, but it is a variable that can only be changed in the long term. It depends on an effective process of socialization that transmits and consolidates democratic values and practices in its citizenry and leaders.[6] Furthermore, a democratic political culture conditions the international conduct of states and tends to encourage the development of relations marked by cooperation, security, and peace.[7]

But how do citizens and leaders acquire such values and practices? Citizens in general and leaders in particular acquire and internalize values and practices through a process of socialization. This is a complex, multidimensional, long-term, gradual process of teaching and learning. It involves promoting changes from preexisting authoritarian values and practices, for example, to new, more democratic ones, or reinforcing the latter values. Because these changes do not occur overnight, the process indeed may require generational changes in the citizenry and the leadership.[8]

The process includes several agents of cultural change, such as the school system, the universities, the mass media, civil society, the church, the family, interest group organizations, and, of course, political institutions (Dawson and Prewitt 1969). From the perspective of democracy promotion, this process provides a strategic focus or "target" that permits the development and implementation of a concentrated and effective, if long-term, strategic "low politics" approach to promoting democratic values amongst the citizenry and the leadership of a society. However, because of its nature, the impact of "low politics" strategic efforts to promote democratic values and practices would probably be noticed or appreciated only as they slowly become rooted or ingrained in a society's political culture, its leaders and political institutions. No one should expect an overnight success story.

This, of course, does not mean that a society would have to wait for the emergence of a new democratic citizenry and leadership before it holds elections to select its leaders, as the "pre-conditionists" would argue. On the contrary, democracies are born and/or periodically renovated with elections, whether or not democratic values and practices actually predominate in a society and its polity. If an electoral democracy is in place, no matter how precarious it is, national and international democratic forces must support, nourish and protect them; but they must also simultaneously be focused and persistent in their effort to expand and consolidate these values and practices. They must encourage civic and elected political leaders of newly established or re-established electoral democracies to implement public policies that support the process of socialization of democratic values and practices. And these leaders should also be responsible for practicing them in their daily political lives.[9]

Thus, in short, preventing the breakdown of democratic institutions and consolidating democracy essentially requires a long-term process of instilling and fostering a democratic political culture in its citizenry and leadership. In a democracy, a citizenry that is imbued with democratic values and practices is sovereign; it is the ultimate authority, watchdog and judge of the political system. It oversees and evaluates the performance of the state's institutions and its leaders. It is the guarantor of democracy. Its perceptions and actions legitimize or de-legitimize a government or a regime. Democratic governance requires its consent. Furthermore, the citizenry is the cradle out of which the socio-political leadership of a society emerges. It engenders and nourishes its leaders and determines their values and practices.

A Socialization Model

The UPD experience with its program on Education for Democracy can serve as a useful, practical and well-focused model that encourages and promotes the acquisition and/or transmission of democratic values and practices among a society's citizens and leadership, using technical assistance instruments. It involves a long-term approach and process to support socialization of them through the school system, in order to create or expand a citizenry imbued with a democratic political culture. [10]

In terms of the support for the socialization or transmission of DVPs through the school system, the model essentially attempts to show how to promote the effective teaching and learning of democratic values and practices through the school system (one of the principal agents of socialization). The model goes beyond or in addition to the traditional civics education, which emphasizes the teaching of national history, the epics of independence, the constitution, political institutions, the national anthem, the flag, and other national symbols. It focuses rather on encouraging the teaching of and learning about democratic institutions, values and practices in order to promote and facilitate their acquisition and internalization beginning at the earliest stages of life, through agents of socialization such as the school system, the family and the community. Its goal is to ensure the continuous transmission and predominance of democratic values and practice among the citizenry and the leadership of a society (Mejía and Restrepo 1997) (Pizarro and Palma 1997) (Patrick and Leming 2001).

The model is comprehensive, with interdependent components and multifaceted processes that require long-term commitment on the part of the international "promoters" and the national counterpart. It begins with a multinational or regional (Central America, for example) conference, organized jointly with the Education Ministry of one of the countries of the region. Its purpose is to share information and experiences about how democracy, its values and practices are taught and learned in each of the national school systems of the region. More specifically, however, the purpose of the conference is to obtain information about whether or not the subject is taught and if so, how it is taught and learned; the place, role and significance the subject has in the school curriculum, the teaching methodology and philosophy employed, as well as the materials (books, technology) used, and the teachers' preparation and qualifications to teach the subject. Regional conferences are frequently also an efficient and effective way to assess the needs of a region or a country on a specific subject. [11]

Based on the knowledge and information obtained, the "promoter," an international organization such as the OAS/UPD, an international non-governmental organization or a government agency involved in democracy promotion (USAID, for example), can attempt to provide a series of technical assistance services that would encourage and support the Education Ministries of the region in their efforts to develop and/or strengthen their capacity to transmit and teach DVPs.

The technical assistance may include most if not all of the instruments in the democracy promotion toolbox identified above. Thus, for example, it would involve, first and most commonly, providing the counterpart national agency with technical advice on designing a national or regional (multinational) program or project, and its rationale, objectives, activities, budget, and so forth.

Assuming that funding is obtained, the program or project (the model) would require, at a minimum, conducting research to develop specific knowledge and information on the different modern methodologies, content, resources for teaching and learning democratic values and practices in elementary and secondary schools, followed by technical advice on designing students' books and teachers' manuals. It would also require technical advice for developing training programs for current teachers and organizing workshops and seminars for that purpose. Significantly also, it would necessitate providing technical advice to Education Ministries and teacher training colleges on developing new curricula to train new teachers. Teacher training is the first link in this long chain of the formal education component of socialization (Patrick and Leming 2001) (Pizarro and Palma 1997).

If similar technical assistance programs are implemented simultaneously, or have been carried out in different countries, it would be beneficial for all involved if the program or project were to organize horizontal cooperation activities (mutual visits, regional workshops) to share knowledge and best practices. The model would also require a final phase of observing and evaluating the implementation of the program/project. The success of the program or project would not only depend on the timely achievement of its objectives but also, most importantly, on the capacity of the national counterparts to assume complete responsibility for it.

As modest and limited as the "target" appears to be, the training of teachers is nevertheless the first link in the long chain of the process of promoting democracy that begins with the "high politics" rhetorical pronouncements, negotiations and decision making in the political and diplomatic spheres, and ends with the "low politics" level of implementation of programs and projects on the ground. The instruments employed, on the other hand, represent the whole gamut of technical assistance instruments provided by international donors such as USAID, CIDA, the World Bank, the IDB, the OAS and others. They are also the tools used in the following focus areas of democracy promotion.

LEADERSHIP IN A DEMOCRATIC SOCIETY

If the consolidation and viability of a democracy depends on the predominance of a democratic political culture among its citizens, its values and practices must also predominate in its leadership.

As O'Donnell points out, "democracy is ultimately based...on citizens," (O'Donnell, The Perpetual Crisis of Democracies 2007), while in his work with Schmitter, they stress the "vital significance of political leadership and judgment, and the role of single individuals in complex historical processes" like the transition and consolidation of democracy (O'Donnell and Schmitter 1986, ix). [12] Thus, I would argue that a high quality democratic leadership is central to democratic governance and the consolidation of democratic institutions, and that democracy's strength, effectiveness and consolidation depend on this type of leadership. [13]

Leaders emerge out of the citizenry, and in many ways reflect and represent the prevailing values and practices, although not always faithfully. This is why it is crucial for the sustainability of democracy that both its citizenry and leaders be imbued with democratic values and practices to a similar degree. A citizenry and a leadership with different political values and practices (or both) permeated with predominately anti-democratic or un-democratic political culture are dysfunctional to democracy and a formidable challenge to democracy promotion efforts.

If it is citizens who are the focus of "low politics" democracy promotion efforts through the school system's formal socialization process, then the political leadership stratum of a society must also be the focus of complementary and/or additional but specific and concentrated efforts to imbue it with democratic values and practices, as well as with political management and professional skills that would contribute to the development and consolidation of a democratic and effective leadership—that is, a high quality leadership.

High quality democratic leadership essentially refers to democratically elected leaders that perform crucial leadership functions, such as: a) leading and governing a country within the framework of democratic institutions, values and practices; b) integrating society's various strategic actors that have diverse and competing interests, and building consensus amongst them around a compelling vision of a nation, state or locality; c) solving or managing domestic and international challenges peacefully; d) satisfying the citizenry's demands and expectations for a prosperous, safe, just and free society; and e) protecting and strengthening the nation's democratic institutions.

In short, democratic leaders not only have to be elected in free and fair elections, but also have to govern democratically, skillfully and effectively.

Democratic governance depends on the existence of this type of leadership in charge of political institutions. This kind of leadership generates and sustains the legitimacy of a democracy, and vindicates the role of politics and politicians, at least in Latin American democracies where their performance and legitimacy are severely questioned. Conversely, the lack of this type of leadership generates instability and mistrust in politicians and governmental institutions.[14] High quality democratic leaders are strategic resources that democratic institutions need, and must be stimulated, nourished, and developed. Leaders are in effect an important component of the social capital of a nation.

Thus, because of the centrality of leaders and civil servants in institutions, emerging and or consolidating democracies required a consistent and focused effort to assist and encourage the development of young, upcoming social and political leaders, particularly those already involved in democratic politics as members of political institutions and organizations, whether governmental or nongovernmental. Young people must be the focus of attention in democracy promotion. They must be trained and imbued first with democratic values and practices so they can govern democratically and assure their predominance in political institutions, and second, with knowledge and skills to manage those institutions and govern their society effectively.

A Model Approach for Promoting High Quality Leadership

These theoretical assumptions about leadership provide the conceptual framework to articulate and propose a technical assistance model for the development of high quality leadership (strategic resource). The model, also based on the UPD/OAS experience, supports long-term national and regional programs to continuously train and update society's young leaders in the nature of democratic institutions, values and practices as well as in political management skills to improve their political competence.[15]

The aim of these programs is to increase and refine the leaders' understanding of and commitment to democratic values and practices learned in their socialization process; and to enhance their capabilities or skills to lead and run political institutions and organizations more effectively, so that they can be more responsive to the needs and aspirations of citizens. The expectation is that these programs would ultimately generate more trusted institutions and leaders and in doing so, increase democracy's legitimacy.[16]

The training programs include lectures, workshops and simulations with practical exercises in democratic values and practices and democratic institutions, as well as political management skills such as negotiation and consensus-building techniques, the design and use of polls, the significance and use of new technologies in politics, organizational skills, communications and media skills, campaign strategies, electoral organization and observation, and others.[17] They emphasize an interactive and participatory methodology, instead of using traditional teaching and learning methodologies and subjects (such as the study of socioeconomic and political reality, public policy analysis and political philosophy/party orientation). The immediate outcome (impact and change) of these training programs can be measured by testing the change in knowledge and/or skills that participants exhibit before the activity and afterwards. On the other hand, measuring long-term changes in political culture is much more complex and almost impossible to carry out within the lifespan of a project.

The UPD/OAS experience with these training programs showed that there is considerable interest in and demand for these types of programs, because participants perceive them as relevant, practical and useful for their political development. As such, they should therefore be a permanent feature of democracy promotion efforts. But, as in the previous examples of model approaches to promoting democracy, executing these training programs for young political leaders from an international organization such as the OAS is a complex and challenging endeavor.

In short, leaders and civil servants permeated with democratic values and practices are the central, vital and most significant resource or capital that democratic political institutions possess. Their prevalence in such institutions is essential for democratic governance and the consolidation of democracy. Or, in other words, the consolidation of democratic institutions depends on their having democratic leaders and civil servants that are permeated with democratic values and practices.

DEMOCRATIC INSTITUTIONS

Democratic institutions are the third critical variable that offers policy makers and practitioners a strategic focus or concrete "target" for "intervention" in the process of promoting democracy through technical assistance programs designed for that purpose.

In Latin America, academic studies and national and international surveys (such as *Latinobarómetro*) have pointed frequently to the weaknesses and the scant credibility and legitimacy of the region's political institutions. They are perceived as unrepresentative, corrupt and ineffective, disrespected, flawed in design, and vulnerable to corrupt internal and external forces and attempts to misuse, ignore or dismantle them. Analysts and observers see their political culture and leadership as characterized by a lack of transparency, accountability, integrity and independence; and by the incapacity or incompetence of the leadership to resolve conflicts peacefully, build consensus and manage successfully the problems of their society, and satisfy citizens' demands for better social services and a more just, free and prosperous society. These institutional weaknesses are thus one of the major challenges of democracy promotion in the region (Smith 2005, 303–310; Navia and Walker 2010, 261; Mainwaring and Scully, "Democratic Governance in Latin America: Eleven Lessons from Recent Experience" 2010, 375; Levitsky and Murillo 2013, 93–105; Drake 2009, 37–46). This fragile institutional reality has led many academics, political leaders and democracy promotion practitioners to point to the need for and importance of domestic and international efforts in institution building or institutional strengthening. But scant attention has been given to what exactly is institution building and how exactly it is carried out in practical, operational terms.

THE NATURE OF POLITICAL INSTITUTIONS

An adequate focus on institutions can provide clarity of purpose for high politics policy pronouncements and for low politics technical assistance efforts on the ground to promote democracy. It would also allow international and national promoters and practitioners to concentrate on practical assistance programs that stimulate and have an impact on institution building.

Truly democratic political institutions are supposed to embody, reflect, promote and protect democratic values and practices in the performance of their functions. They are the means and ends of democratic politics. Society needs them to structure, organize and process political interactions among its individuals and groups. They are vital strategic instruments for the promotion, consolidation and exercise of democracy. Democratic governance and democracy's sustainability depend on the robustness and effectiveness of well run democratic institutions. Here is why:

Institutions, analytically speaking, and in the broadest abstract sense, may refer to a pattern of well-established informal or formal structures with rules, norms, and values that condition or govern behavior. In a more limited and concrete sense, political institutions may also be thought of as political organizations, with formal and informal norms, rules, roles and purposes around specific issues or areas, which reflect and are the actual, observable expression of the values and purposes of those who created them. To facilitate and simplify the analysis, and because the concepts are closely related, political institutions here are also intended to mean political organizations. [18]

Political institutions are crucial to the political process because they provide a legal and organizational framework for the policy-making process that translates society's demands into public policy. They help structure or give meaning to political behavior and relations; they provide the channels for moderating, negotiating and constructing consensus amongst competing or conflicting demands and interests, and between society and the state. They facilitate the business of politics. Furthermore, in practice, they manage society and are ultimately responsible for its wellbeing, its safety and security, its prosperity, its stability, its democracy. Political institutions are the permanent features of a society, while the officials, practitioners, politicians and leaders who manage them come and go.

Good democratic governance (the practice of governing democratically and effectively) and "governability" (capacity to govern) depend on the existence of solid political institutions in all areas of government. Political institutions become solid when they are valued and respected because they perform their functions adequately and effectively and meet citizens' expectations. Ideally, they should be independent of special interests; responsive to the needs, demands and expectations of the general public; mutually respectful of each other's role and limits in the institutional framework, and accountable to the electorate and public opinion. Solid, consolidated institutions provide legal certainty and political stability (Huntington 1968, 6–39).

Long-term economic development also depends on the strength of political institutions and the rule of law, as Douglass North has shown. They reduce risks and uncertainties, inefficiencies and the transactional costs of investing and doing business, which in turn encourages economic development, employment and reduction of poverty (North 1990, 6 *et passim*). More specifically, in well-established democracies, governmental institutions (national and local) share responsibility for performing different political functions. They "manage" a society in the context of certain democratic principles, values and practices. For example, in a democracy where political power is divided, shared and balanced to avoid its excessive concentration and possible abuse, the legislative, the executive (the presidency, its ministries and agencies), the judicial and electoral institutions, normally and duly observe this basic democratic and most cherished principle and practice in their interactions.

Moreover, political institutions are not just intellectual or analytical constructs; they have concrete human dimensions because they are, in fact, human entities or groupings (Etzioni 1964, 3) (North 1990, 5 *et passim*). They exist as result of human behavior. Human beings conceptualize, create, conduct, manage, reform, use, abuse, weaken or strengthen them. These are citizens, in general; but in particular, they are political leaders such as presidents, ministers, judges, legislators, administrators, consultants, and politicians who perform daily their respective institutional functions and duties. Their performance and success or failure have profound consequences for society's wellbeing, aspirations, needs, interests, demands and expectations. Moreover, the legitimacy, consolidation and sustainability of democratic institutions depend on the confidence and trust that their performance is able to elicit from the citizenry.

Democratic political institutions prevail and consolidate as those individuals who work in and/or lead them are imbued with democratic values and practices and as they become reliable and legitimate. The legitimacy of democratic institutions is acquired as citizens become more identified with them because they are perceived as performing their role properly, and as citizens trust and value them. They are consolidated when no one questions them or proposes an alternative institution to govern society. Legitimate political institutions are the foundation of a consolidated democracy.[19] But in the final analysis, one must not lose sight of the fact that, in the broadest sense, the business of promoting democracy is indeed a human development enterprise. It is a citizenry and leadership issue all around, along with their democratic values, practices and institutions.

Strengthening Democratic Institutions

The task, then, for democracy promotion is to focus on supporting efforts to strengthen the capacity of democratic political institutions to fulfill their roles, functions and responsibilities in a democratic society. No doubt, as has been said before, there are many ideas and efforts, at both the academic ("high politics") and "low politics" levels, about how to strengthen political institutions (institution building, capacity building) as a way to promote and consolidate democratic political systems.

Prominent political scientists explicitly or implicitly have suggested ways to go about institutional strengthening. In his seminal work, *Political Order and Changing Societies*, Huntington presents a very useful set of criteria to measure the levels of institutionalization of political organizations: adaptability, complexity, autonomy and coherence (Huntington 1968, 8–32), but without going into how, precisely, to achieve them. Di Palma also has very useful suggestions for political leaders on the kinds of rules of the game they have to create to achieve successful transitions to democracy, and on how, in general, international actors promote democracy (di Palma 1990, 8–10 183–199). In his postcript to *Polyarchy*, Dahl also proposes a foreign policy strategy of technical assistance to strengthen democratic conditions in countries with already established polyarchies (R. A. Dahl 1973, 208–227). Larry Diamond calls for revolutionary changes in institutions (Diamond, "Comments on A Quarter of Century of Promoting Democracy" 2007) (Diamond, "The Democracy Rollback" 2008).

Other works on the subject of promoting and protecting democracy propose mostly "high politics" level measures. These include generic suggestions for policy makers to, for example, change the constitutional and institutional design to strengthen democratic governance and prevent its breakdown; to adopt democratic norms for membership in international organizations, and provide incentives and punitive measures for those who comply with or violate them; to link development assistance to compliance with democratic standards like transparency and probity; to ensure domestic ownership of democracy assistance and fine tune it to national needs and circumstances; and, perhaps the most concrete of all, to carry out electoral monitoring. Some also recommend structural changes such as democratizing the economy, assuring majority rule with minority rights and encouraging political decentralization (Consalvi and Fernández 1996) (Piccone 2004) (Peeler 2004) (Pevehouse 2005) (McMahon 2006).

Although these are valuable contributions to our understanding of democracy promotion, neither of these works, however, nor many others reviewed, tell us how exactly to strengthen those institutions, in concrete practical terms; or how exactly to produce, on the "ground", the institutional reforms or changes suggested. There is no clear indication as to what the instruments to be used are and how to use them and for what specific purpose, and none indicate the complexities involved in such an effort. Furthermore, none addresses the human dimension of institutions, that is, the leadership's values, skills and practices that are so crucial for the performance and orientation of institutions.[20]

Cheema's work, on the other hand, based on his UNDP experience, is one of the more detailed and comprehensive attempts to show how democracy promotion is or should be carried out. He identifies electoral systems, parliaments, decentralization processes, human rights protection, administration of justice as "target areas" for democracy promotion, and even points to modalities used in democracy assistance (workshops, seminars, experts consultancies on institutional design and restructuring, skills training courses, equipment donations), all of which, according to him, contribute to strengthening the capacity of government. But, he asserts, they "do not reshape the internal contextual factors that make democracy work or collapse--culture, ethnicity, the balance of political power, including civil and military relations, the incidence of the media, poverty and the vested interests of the ruling classes." (Cheema 2005, 246). He ignores, however, the role political actors (leaders) and institutions may have in shaping the contextual factors he mentions, and does not go far enough in showing how exactly the technical assistance modalities should be used to produce the reform or the changes that he implicitly suggests are needed to strengthen and build democratic institutions and processes he accurately identifies. There is little theoretical or practical guidance as to what exactly institution building or strengthening is, and how it is carried out and accomplished, in practical terms on the ground, in the recipient country.

A Different Approach

The focus proposed here, however, is supported by the theoretical construct described above and by a gradual, long-term and sober technical assistance model (based on the UPD experience) aimed at producing changes in the values and practices of the citizenry in general, and of civil servants and political leaders in particular as they manage and lead institutions. This approach explicitly connects the three variables of the construct: political culture, leadership and institutions. It is not a dramatic, glamorous, or pretentious approach that would produce drastic institutional changes overnight, as sometimes demanded by transitory senior officials of donor agencies or international organizations. Resulting changes would only be perceived in the long run, and may be measured by the degree to which institutions and political leaders become respected, trusted and valued, and not regularly challenged, criticized or disdained.

The leadership of a society can and will occasionally attempt to make significant changes to the political institutions or the institutional architecture of a country in a short period of time, in a dramatic and drastic manner. It can formally introduce fundamental institutional changes in a constitution and have them quickly approved in a referendum and proclaim the birth of a new democratic order containing new democratic institutions (recent cases: Bolivia, Ecuador, Venezuela). But if the values and practices that prevail in a political culture are predominantly anti-democratic, it is highly improbable that the leadership or the civil servants of the new institutions would be imbued with democratic values and practices, and the institutions therefore would not perform as the new modern, democratic and effective institutions that democrats and democracy promoters would expect. The consolidation of democracy requires congruence between the predominant political culture and the existing political institutions, its leadership and staff. Otherwise a country may transition through a long period of instability or "ungovernability."

The point here is that the strengthening and consolidation of democratic political institutions does not happen overnight, through drastic and dramatic change. Rather, it is the result of a process of incremental change, which essentially involves a process of modernization, understood here as the introduction, adoption and internalization of changes in values, norms, structures, procedures, and practices of an institution, which are envisioned, designed, prompted and produced by a modern leadership and a cadre of civil servants imbued with democratic values and practices (DVP) and with modern political management skills (PMS). For democracy promoters, it implies working with and concentrating efforts on the leaders and the staff of these institutions, since they are the ones who will produce the changes that will modernize, strengthen, and protect the democratic political institutions that will consolidate and sustain democracy. After all, institutions, as indicated before, are human endeavors and human enterprises.

The theoretical construct used here allows us to postulate a model technical assistance approach that focuses on the human dimension of political institutions. This approach is a concrete, practical and useful instrument to contribute to the strengthening and consolidation of democratic political institutions. It is applicable to political institutions such as the legislative, judicial and electoral institutions, political parties, national and local governmental institutions, and nongovernmental organizations.[21] Here the model is applied to the legislative institution, drawing on the experience of the UPD/OAS work with the legislature.

THE LEGISLATIVE INSTITUTION

The legislative institution is a crucial component of representative democracy. It is a key institution in the democratic system of separation, independence and balance of powers that guarantees individual liberties, limits the power of the executive branch and prevents its inclination to accumulate and abuse power, particularly in presidential democracies.[22] It is not possible to have a solid and strong democracy if the legislative branch is weak. A weak legislature only leaves the door open for arbitrary action, usurpation and abuse of power and impunity by the executive branch.[23]

To perform properly this crucial constitutional role, legislatures must be capable of adequately performing their functions and discharging their responsibilities; that is to say: genuinely representing the citizenry, legislating rigorously, and appropriately controlling or overseeing the performance of the other branches of government, especially the executive branch.

But to do so, they need credibility and legitimacy. These attributes in turn depend on the representativeness of their members, and on the strength of their institutional capacity (technical, organizational, administrative and drafting of legislation) to propose and discuss public policy, to draft laws and evaluate their impact, to represent the interests of the constituents, to watch over the actions of the other branches of government, and to maintain their own political weight vis-à-vis that of other state authorities.

Legislatures in Latin America

The return of democracy at the end of the 1970s and the early 1980s in Latin America did not necessarily mean that the legislative bodies immediately became strong or that citizens had the most favorable perception of legislative institutions.

Research, surveys, technical assistance, and workshops carried out by academics and the UPD/OAS on these subjects from 1994 to 2004 showed a widespread consensus regarding the weaknesses, deficiencies and needs of most legislative bodies Latin American states. It was generally agreed that legislatures and their members (and politicians in general) lacked representativeness and were marred by corruption, lack of transparency and accountability, subservience to the executive branch, and incompetence and ineffectiveness in the performance of their role and functions, all of which were thought to undermine their credibility and legitimacy.[24]

In Latin America, this lack of representativeness, perceived both by citizens in general and experts and politicians alike, is essentially linked to the nature of the electoral representation systems and to the decisive but not very democratic role played by political party bosses in choosing candidates for the legislative bodies. The criticism typically points to the proportional representation regimes based on lists of candidates for national, regional, provincial or state legislatures who are unknown to the great majority of voters. When these candidates are elected, they are not politically independent: invariably they act in accordance with party discipline, rather than the demands or interests of their constituents.

In some countries of the region (Bolivia, Colombia, Venezuela, Mexico), changes have already been made to combine proportional electoral representation systems based on closed lists with uninominal, simple majority ("first pass the post") candidacies. The uninominal (single district/single-person) system, or a mixture of this with the proportional system, helps make the legislature more representative and strengthens its role. Uninominal districts reduce the geographical and political area the legislator is to represent and bring him or her closer to constituents and their interests. The candidate must be from the district and, theoretically, has to be known in order to win, has to represent and adequately reflect the values and interests of the district, has to act with probity and effectiveness in his functions and must periodically be accountable to the constituents that elected him or her (Katz 1980) (R. M. Perina 1984).

Additionally, the lack of representativeness has also been associated with the lack of or inadequate use of institutional mechanisms for interaction with voters, such as public hearings, televised or public debates, legislative offices in their constituencies, and easy and open relationships with the press. These mechanisms facilitate legislators' interaction with society and contribute to better understanding of their role and activities. They allow citizens to better evaluate the performance of their representatives and to make sure that their interests are properly represented. They tend to enhance the image constituents have of legislative bodies.

Latin American national legislatures have been noted for their insufficient institutional capacity to perform their fundamental functions to the fullest. These insufficiencies are linked basically to organizational and technical shortcomings related to, for example, the administrative services of the institution, the legislative rules and procedures, the legislative archives, the information and data available for drafting bills, the legislative drafting techniques, the parliamentary rules on procedures for debates, the advisory staff systems and others. Thus, legislators do not have the necessary or sufficient administrative, technical, informational and staff resources to perform their functions adequately. Frequently, they also lack appropriate professional technical advisory services, which are often provided by political advisors with limited technical understanding of legislative procedures or substantive issues that require legislation. These institutional deficiencies frequently result in legislation lacking proper comparative study or precedents, with serious conceptual voids or missing information that often duplicate, contradict or invalidate existing laws, rendering their application difficult. [25]

To address these deficiencies and weaknesses in performing the legislative role and functions in most Latin American countries, the UPD/OAS developed and executed between 1994 and 2005 a program of support for legislative institutions, focused on technical assistance and advice for legislative modernization and inter-parliamentary cooperation, as a means of strengthening their role and function. [26] Other multilateral institutions such as the Inter-American Development Bank and the World Bank, among others, also carried out programs to promote stronger legislative bodies, within the broader framework of the modernization of the state and governance (The Inter-American Development Bank 1996) (The World Bank 1996). [27]

A Model for Legislative Technical Assistance

The UPD experience in support of modernization and strengthening of legislatures in Latin America can be articulated and postulated as model of technical assistance that can be useful for institution building efforts in general and for legislative institutions in particular. The model's main objective is to strengthen and modernize the capacity of legislative institutions to perform their functions adequately and effectively, and thus reinforce their significant role in the democratic system governance. Ultimately, this means strengthening the institutions' credibility and trust and thus their legitimacy.

Capacity-building in a legislature, however, requires a clear understanding of the internal and organizational nature and dynamics of the institution. The following internal structures and functions are useful target areas for technical assistance: a) the administrative and technical structures and functions (internal norms and procedures, personnel units, internal program-budget units, security units, communication and information systems units, with their corresponding staff; and b) the technical or substantive departments or offices related to, for example, political/legislative advisory systems, public relations, communications, budget analysis and legislative oversight, legislative and drafting methods, Webpage and Internet services, and others. Both of these areas provide administrative, technical and political support to the political/legislative structures and functions, such as the different legislative leaderships, the multiple caucuses, the committees and the individual legislators themselves, who study, draft, propose, negotiate, debate, approve or reject declarations, resolutions, bills and legislation.

Those internal structures provide the focus or the target for the technical assistance model to work on modernizing and strengthening the institution's capacity to perform its functions. To that effect, the model involves a strategy that uses technical assistance instruments (the "toolbox") to generate and develop the strategic resources (institutional capital) that are required for capacity building in each of the areas/structures identified. There are at least three types of interconnected strategic resources: 1) cognitive resources, including knowledge, information, values and skills; 2) technology, and 3) human resources, the staffers and legislators who administer, run and lead the institution and who must learn, adopt, internalize and use those resources. In short, legislative modernization and strengthening is a complex, sensitive and long term capacity building process that focuses on the development of strategic resources.

The technical assistance tools may involve, among other things, advisory and consulting services, workshops and training programs to: a) design strategic projects to support the legislative leadership's desires and efforts to modernize the institution; b) develop a fundraising strategy for the project; c) develop resources such as guidelines, manuals, strategies, information systems, communications techniques, web pages, codes of ethics, legislative techniques and internal regulations, and d) train or update administrators, technicians, advisors and legislators to help them acquire and internalize the knowledge, information, values and new skills needed to strengthen and modernize the institution and to improve their performance—particularly in terms of how to represent their constituencies, communicate with citizens, negotiate, debate and legislate, control and supervise the executive, and promote horizontal cooperation amongst national legislatures to share knowledge and best experiences in legislative modernization. Technical assistance may also involve support and academic advice on research, workshops and publications to create and disseminate a critical body of knowledge and information on issues related to the role and functioning of legislative institutions as well as to modernization and strengthening—which can in turn be used to train new experts (academics and practitioners) in legislative modernization.

The proposed technical assistance model concentrates on crucial substantive subjects or areas of legislative affairs, with the purpose of providing concrete, practical products or outputs that can be used to produce modest changes (outcomes) and contribute to capacity building. These products or outputs of technical assistance would include, for example, model legislation for new or revised national legislation on urgent and relevant issues; methodologies for parliamentary control and oversight; design of a strategic plan for implementing a legislative modernization project, guidelines for incorporation and application of new communications and information technologies ("e-Congress"); models of parliamentary advisory services; guidelines for legislative techniques and parliamentary negotiation; blueprints and strategies for training programs for capacity building (virtual and/or real); guidelines for legislative-executive relations; institutional strategies for relations with constituents; guidelines for strategic communications and press relations; institutional design on electoral regimes for parliamentary elections; strategies for adopting international treaties, conventions and agreements; a model parliamentary code of ethics; a model legislative interactive Web page for national and regional networks; software design for databases on comparative legislation and issues of legislative interest; software design and guidelines for the development and standardization of parliamentary procedures and on-line legislative drafting, and others. [28]

But producing those outputs is not sufficient to produce change, an impact or effect (outcomes) in the political culture of an institution. The ultimate objective of a democracy promotion project then, in theory, should be to contribute to changes in the political culture, that is, in the behavior of its citizens, leaders and institutions. The problem is that those changes are not measurable in any meaningful way in the short or even medium term, let alone over the lifetime of a project. So, objectives should be modest, concentrated on a few concrete, realistic, relevant and strategic objectives that would contribute over the short- to medium-term to promoting, but not directly causing, behavioral changes in those who work, manage and direct legislatures. Thus, technical assistance activities must be planned to produce the type of outputs described above, and must ensure that those outputs are then adopted or enacted to have an impact or effect. For example, for an output to produce an impact or change, a model legislation to reform the electoral system must first be enacted or a code of parliamentary ethics must first be adopted and then implemented by the legislature.

Another way to help strengthen and modernize the role of the legislative institution is to encourage inter-parliamentary cooperation to share knowledge and experiences. This can be accomplished through horizontal cooperation or mutual technical assistance and exchanges of expertise in legislative modernization and in collaborative strategies for the collective promotion and defense of democracy and human rights observance. [29]

In the broader field of teaching and research, there is also a need to expand empirical and comparative studies on the role, functions and organization of legislative bodies in Latin America. This would include issues such as: a) the performance of legislatures in terms of their principal constitutional and institutional role and functions; b) the relationship between the legislative branch and the executive branch (conflict, cooperation, submission, and so forth), plus the debate about presidential vs. parliamentary systems;[30] c) the degree of representativeness of legislators and electoral representation systems for legislatures; d) the relationship of the legislature with the citizenry in general and specific constituents in particular, including the constancy, closeness and form of that relationship; e) the degree of legislative responsiveness to the problems of society; f) the legislators' relationship with their political parties; g) the credibility and legitimacy of the legislative branch; h) the relative and comparative influence of internal factors in the performance of legislatures, such as technical deficiencies, poor information and knowledge among legislators and advisors, limited understanding of legislative procedures, meager technology infrastructure, lack of competent technical/political advisors, political fragmentation, corruption, the reigning political culture, political parties and so forth); and i) alternative strategies for strengthening the legislative branch.

Research and studies into these crucial legislative topics would significantly contribute to the development of a better understanding of the systemic role, functions and operation of legislative institutions in Latin America. This body of knowledge and information would in turn be useful for training advisors and legislators, academic experts, democracy promoters and institutional designers. It would also help develop a legislative discipline, which could serve as the intellectual foundation for institution building and stronger and more effective legislatures.

In short, the model of technical assistance suggested, supported by a sound theoretical construct, is an example of a "low politics" technical assistance approach intended for recently established or re-established electoral democracies whose leaders request assistance for their own efforts to strengthen democratic institutions such as the legislature. In the case of legislative institutions, the model aims at the development of strategic resources necessary to build the institution's capacity to perform adequately and effectively its systemic role and institutional functions, and contribute to democratic governance.

Finally, the model postulates that all these technical/political services, plus the generation, transfer and sharing of knowledge and skills, are transformational learning experiences, which, once adopted, internalized and utilized, do produce changes (albeit incremental) in the political culture (DVP) of those who lead and work in legislatures. It also proposes that these changes would tend to fortify the institutional capacity of legislatures to perform their role and functions, which would in turn significantly contribute to increasing their credibility and legitimacy, and thereby strengthen and consolidate their central role in representative democracy. Ultimately, the viability and vitality of democracy depend on the strength of institutions such as legislatures and the capacity of their leaders to lead and provide "good" democratic governance and democratic governability. Because of their significance in representative democracies, legislative institutions, particularly in emerging or recently reestablished democracies, should be the focus of greater continued attention by the academic world, political leaders and the international community of democracy promoters.

As mentioned earlier, the technical assistance model proposed here is based on the UPD/OAS experience. That experience indicates that providing technical assistance, particularly from a multilateral intergovernmental organization such as the OAS, is complex, multilayered, and politically and diplomatically very sensitive, given the political significance and political nature of the legislative institution and its leaders.

A CAVEAT: THE COMPLEXITY
OF DEMOCRACY TECHNICAL ASSISTANCE

Strictly speaking, the assistance is "technical," but it also involves diplomatic, political and bureaucratic complexities, particularly if it is provided by a multilateral, intergovernmental organization like the OAS, and more so if it involves significant political institutions such as legislatures, political parties or governmental institutions. Democracy "technical" assistance encompasses a complex transnational process with several international and domestic actors that demand frequent diplomatic, political and technical consultation and negotiations.

The process cannot be imposed from above. Rather, it should respond to a request for assistance from a domestic or national actor. In the case of the OAS, it requires an official communication from an institution of a member state asking for assistance. The request must be transmitted from the country's Foreign Ministry and its diplomatic mission (which must approve it or at least not obstruct it) to the appropriate office of the OAS General Secretariat. This in itself can be a complicated and politically sensitive process, as there are different actors and institutions involved with likely different political interest and ambitions in the requesting member state.

Before the request ("project") is approved for implementation, it normally needs technical consultation with the domestic counterparts to fine-tune it according to internal OAS guidelines and requirements. The project then goes through a bureaucratic maze within the General Secretariat, including evaluation and budget analysis phases. Implementation of the project requires the signing of an agreement with the counterpart institution, which in turn necessitates negotiations on the components of the technical assistance to be provided, including, for example, its content, budget, modalities, activities, objectives, sequence, timing, and the responsibilities of all involved, in addition to the complex and politically sensitive issue of identification of technical experts to be contracted for the delivery of the technical assistance.

Experts not only have to meet the obvious expertise requirements, but also have to be culturally and politically sensitive, with knowledge of the country or the region and fluent in the language of the country.[31] An international "promoter" like the OAS, not strictly speaking a funding agency, would likely also have to provide technical assistance on fundraising with institutions such as the Inter-American Development Bank or pertinent U.S. agencies—although the OAS can occasionally provide "seed money" to start a program or project.[32] The search for funding for democracy promotion of the sort proposed here is a challenge, as donors are not usually willing to provide funding for long-term projects, although that is precisely what is needed for effective implementation of technical assistance programs. Donors and their bureaucracies, like politicians or senior policy makers and managers in international organizations, want to see "results" in the short term, during their watch.

Like other international organizations, the OAS and its area of democracy promotion is always constrained by the scarcity or inadequacy of human and financial resources, and is also conditioned by the limits imposed by member states on its autonomy, as it may only take action at their behest, approval or instructions.

CONCLUSION

The purpose of the present Chapter has been to suggest an approach to promoting democracy based on theoretical assumptions that link, in an interdependent fashion, democratic values and practices (democratic political culture), democratic and effective leadership, and democratic institutions. The assumption is that the virtuous interaction among the three variables is a necessary precondition for democratic governance and the sustainability of liberal democracy.

The approach also includes "low politics" technical assistance models of democracy promotion that are concrete, realistic instruments that can be used to promote the consolidation of a democratic political culture, the strengthening of democratic institutions and the development of democratic, skillful and effective leadership. These models are based on the OAS experience.

Essentially, the "technical" approach emphasizes the domestic human political dimension of democracy promotion, and gives democracy promoters and practitioners a focus and three strategic targets for "low politics" technical assistance efforts. It proposes that policy and strategy concentrate on identifiable and concrete variables such as political culture (DVP), leaders, and institutions. It permits the development and application of practical action plans and programs for democracy promotion, however gradual and long-term, and avoids what critics have identified as lack of theoretical coherence and dispersion of efforts, and sidesteps the obsession with short-term results. The consolidation and viability of democracy ultimately depend on the strength and performance of those three fundamental variables and their virtuous interaction. This approach attempts to correct the methodological deficiencies pointed out by Carothers, and coincides with Diamond's suggestion that democracy promotion requires working with political culture and institutions (T. Carothers 2004, 2–35) (Diamond, 2006, 114–115 and 119–120).

This approach also recognizes that external forces involved in the "high politics" efforts of the international community of democracies (resolutions, declarations, policy guidelines and actions, academic and observers' rhetoric and recommendations, funding and technical assistance) do provide an essential supportive context: they put pressure on and offer incentives for the internal forces to maintain and strengthen the democratic path. But external forces can also discourage or obstruct democratic developments if the domestic actors perceive their efforts as interference, irrelevant, too abstract or insensitive to national values and practices. Thus, democracy assistance turns out to be not only "technical" but eminently political/diplomatic, and a complex international bureaucratic process as well—a caveat that democracy promoters frequently ignore or do not recognize.

NOTES

1. As one of the special advisors to Secretary General Baena Soares at the time, the author was responsible, along with Baena's Chief of Staff, Ambassador Hugo de Zela, for designing and proposing the structure and programmatic areas of the UPD. From 1991 until 2005, the author directed the UPD's program of support for the promotion of democratic values and practices (education for democracy and leadership training), and institutional strengthening (legislative institutions and decentralization and local governance). The UDP was updated to the Secretariat for Political Affairs in 2005, and became more of a political/diplomatic office for conflict resolution and crisis management, discarding most of the democracy promotion programs that had been the flagship and hallmark of the Organization up until then, except for its focus on electoral observation missions.

2. For a detailed description of the activities and products of the UPD, see the quarterly *Reports of the General Secretariat on the Activities of the UPD to the Permanent Council*, the annual reports of the Secretary General (General Secretariat 1991–2010) and Secretary General César Gaviria's memoires (Gaviria 2004, 19–36).

3. A political culture is normally understood to consist of a set of values, norms, beliefs, attitudes, customs that motivate, condition if not determine political behavior of individuals and institutions. But in the interests of brevity, I have reduced this concept to values and practices. On the significance of a political culture and its definition, see Almond and Powell, *Comparative Politics* (1978), Inglehart and Welzel (2005), Almond and Verba, *The Civic Culture Revisited* (1989).

4. For additional various views on a democratic political culture, see Chapter 3 in Dahl, Shapiro and Cheibub (2003), Dahl (1973), and Russell, Shin and Jou (2007). Institutions are included as component of a political culture because they embody and express political values

held in a society and polity. In consonance with James McGregor Burns (1978), some of these values could be categorized as instrumental "modal values", or behavioral values (e.g., tolerance, compromise, consensus building, probity, transparency and accountability); and others as "end values", that is higher or ideal values that are constantly sought after (e.g., liberty, equality, justice).

5. For a full discussion on significance of these rights, see UNDP's report *Democracy in Latin America* (2004). The report, however, does not fully discuss citizens' duties and responsibilities in a democracy.

6. With regard to the role of political culture in the strengthening of democracy, see O'Donnell (1998), Fukuyama (1996), Putnam (1996), Lagos (1997), and the classic Dawson and Prewitt (1969).

7. On the relationship between political culture and the conduct of States, see Katzenstein (1999, 674), Duffield (1999), and also the democratic peace theory literature referenced in Chapter 5.

8. On how political activist acquire political beliefs, see Dawson and Prewitt (1969); Almond and Powell, *Comparative Politics* (1978, 102–103) and Dahl (1973, 167–188).

9. Electoral democracies are those polities whose leaders have been elected by legitimate elections but have not developed as yet into full liberal democracies, characterized by the predominance of democratic values, practices and institutions. Some current Latin American democracies would fall under this category (Diamond 2003). This is consistent with the view of liberal democracy stated by Zakaria (1997). It is worth noticing, however, that this "preconditionist" argument is rebutted by Plattner (1999).

10. Concerning the role of education in constructing a civic culture, see Almond and Verba (1989, 24).

11. At the UPD, the author coordinated the conceptualization, design and implementation of various activities intended to generate knowledge and information about the teaching and learning of democratic values and practices in Latin America. This included, for example, a series of national workshops in Asunción, Paraguay in 1994–1996, at the request of the Ministry of Education, with the objective of developing a program of education for democracy, which contemplated a training program for teachers and the development of teaching materials. Also, a regional MERCOSUR workshop, organized by UPD in Asunción, Paraguay in October 1995, identified the need in the region to implement an education reform that would incorporate the teaching and learning of democratic values into the formal school curriculum (General Secretariat, annual report 1996–1997). A similar workshop was held in San José, Costa Rica in August 1997 for the Central American region, and yet another in Montevideo, Uruguay in July 2003, in cooperation with the Uruguayan Ministry of Education (Department of Democratic and Political Affairs 2004). In 2005, the program was transferred to the Office of Education and Culture in the OAS Secretariat for Integral Development, changing its name to Inter-American Program on Education for Democratic Values and Practices. See: http://portal.oas.org/Portal/Topic/SEDI/EducaciónyCultura/EducaciónenValoresyPrácticasDemocráticas/tabid/1227/Default. For continuous efforts in this direction in Latin America, see Levinson and Berumen (2008), Amadeo and Cepeda (2008) and the online publication on Education in Iberian-America: http://www.rinace.net/reice/numeros/vol7num2.htm. See also publications of the Center for Civic Education, www.civiced.org. and Cox, Jaramillo and Reimers (2005).

12. See also Huntington (1991, 107).

13. Mainwaring and Pérez-Liñan's theory shows the centrality, significance and impact of political actors' normative preferences on regime outcome, *Democracies and Dictatorships in Latin America. Emergence, Survival* (2013, 289–292), and *Lessons from Latin America. Democratic Breakdown and Survival* (2013).

14. This high quality leadership requirement is consistent with the notion that formal authority, even if achieved by a democratic election, is not the same as leadership. For a discussion of this and other leadership functions, see Peannock, *Democratic Political Theory* (1977, 472, 484–493); Dahl (1973, 124–188); Huntington (1991, 36–39); Schumperter (1975, 289–296) and Almond and Powell (1978, 102–3). For indicators of low levels of satisfaction with and mistrust of political parties and politicians, see the 2006 *Latinobarómetro* (www.Latinobarometro.org).

15. For several years (1997–2005), at the then Unit for the Promotion of Democracy of the OAS, the author coordinated the conceptualization, design and organization in Latin America of around fifty subregional and national programs and workshops to train some two thousand young leaders from political parties, nongovernmental organizations and the media, irrespective of political orientation or affiliation. For their content and methodology, see Riquelme (2000), Galán (2000), Pressacco (2002) and Caetano and Perina (*Democracia y Gerencia Política. Innovación en Valores, Instrumentos y Prácticas* 2006).

16. There are, of course, international foundations related to political parties that promote democracy through training programs for political leaders around the world. German foundations such as the Friedrich Ebert, the Friedrich Naumann and the Konrad Adenauer Foundations were pioneers in that effort since the 1960s in Latin America. These "party" programs are tailored to develop leadership based on a particular democratic political orientation, such as social democracy or liberal democracy. Since the 1990s, United States' political parties have also supported political leadership programs through the National Democratic Institute for International Affairs (NDI) and the International Republic Institute (IRI).

17. The concept, but not necessarily the content and methodology, is similar to what is offered at the Graduate School of Political Management (GSPM) of George Washington University.

18. For a fuller discussion of political institutions, structures and organizations, see O'Donnell, Delegative Democracy (1994), Almond and Powell, Comparative Politics (1978, 12), Etzioni (1964) and North (1990, 3–10, 273).

19. Huntington argues that political institutionalization occurs when "political organizations become valued and stable" (Huntington 1968, 12).

20. This is consonant with Carothers' contention that, for example, the U.S. government has focused far too much on formal institutions (constitutions, parliaments, political parties, elections) as the essential elements of democratization, at the expense of values and processes and has ignored "complex and more important underlying realities of political life" (Carothers 2004, 35). Piccone also recognizes that the "shortcomings of existing on the ground support can undermine the efficacy of overall international democracy promotion efforts." (2006, 19). The argument here is that what is needed is a more concerted effort focused on the human dimensions of institutions, their leaders and their political culture's context, and on the practical instruments to effect, on the ground, the institutional changes suggested in most of the literature on the subject.

21. Aspuru et al. suggest "empowering civil society and domestic actors" as an approach to promoting, consolidating and defending democratic governance, but offer no details on how exactly this can be done; that is, how exactly does one empower cititzens to do that? This indeed is a question that democracy promoters have had a hard time answering, and which this book attempts to address (Azpuru 2008).

22. Concerning the institutional strengthening of legislatures in Germany, Canada, the United States, England and France, see Ornstein (1986).

23. A weak legislative institution can lead to what Guillermo O'Donnell has called "delegative democracy," in which the executive branch *de facto* takes on almost authoritarian powers and basically directly or indirectly writes the laws. See O'Donnell, Delegative Democracy 1994.

24. Close (1995), Leiva (1997), Tickner and Mejía Quintana (1997), Caballero and Vial (1994), Valencia (1995), CADEL (1999), Caetano and Perina, *Mercosur y Parlamentos* (2000), Rodriguez, *Experiencias de Modernización Legislativa* (1999). Drake calls them "legislative Lilliputians" (2009, 37). Even the U.S. has been criticized for not performing its functions properly. See *The Best-Do-Nothing Congress Money Can Buy* (1997); Mann and Ornstein (2006) and http://www.commentarymagazine.com/2013/12/05/two-cheers-for-a-do-nothing-congress-bills-passed.

25. On the weakness and deficiencies of legislatures in Latin America, see Alvarez and Rodriguez, *El Poder Legislativo en la Democracia y la Integración* (2001); CADEL (1999); Caballero and Vial (1994); Cevasco Piedra (2000) (R. M. Perina, *El Fortalecimiento del Poder Legislativo* (1997); R.M. Perina (2005); Rodriguez, *Experiencias de Modernización Legislativa* (1999); Muñoz (2003); Rodriguez, *Los Parlamentos de Centroamérica* (2001); Senate of the

Republic of Mexico (2005). While it is true that most legislatures today can exhibit certain degree of modernization in terms of the incorporation of modern technology such as computers, information and communications systems, electronic voting systems, web pages (first generation reforms), it is unclear whether this has indeed meant that legislatures have corrected their weaknesses and deficiencies in the performance of their more political role and functions. A more current survey would more than likely show that most legislatures in Latin America still fail to perform adequately their role and functions, and are still perceived as unrepresentative, corrupt, incompetent and ineffective. I would argue that they still require technical assistance to strengthen and consolidate them, even though it would probably be more focused on the "political" aspects of modernization, that is, promoting the adoption of democratic values and practices as well as political management skills in those who lead and staff the institution. For the so-called second generation of reforms, see Caetano and Perina, *La Segunda Generación de Reformas Parlamentarias* (2004).

26. Fulfilling official mandates, the OAS-UPD and later the Department of Democracy and Political Affairs' (DDPA) Program of Support for Legislative Institutions (PAFIL) had the mission of supporting member states' efforts to strengthen and modernize their legislative institutions, as well as to collaborate with national legislatures and regional parliaments in the promotion of inter-parliamentary dialogue and cooperation. From 1991 to 2005, the UPD provided technical assistance to the national legislatures of Argentina (including the legislature of the autonomous city of Buenos Aires), Bolivia, the Dominican Republic, Ecuador, Guatemala, Honduras, Paraguay, Peru and others, as well as to regional parliamentary institutions such as the Joint Parliamentary Commission of MERCOSUR (CPCM) and the Forum of Presidents of the Legislative Branches of the region (FOPREL MERCOSUR); the Andean Parliament and its Andean Center for Legislative Development (CADEL) as well as the FOPREL Andino; the Central American Parliament (PARLACEN), the Forum of Presidents of the Legislative Branches of Central America (FOPREL Centro-Americano) and its Central American Institute of Legislative Studies (ICEL). In addition, several academic institutions received assistance to collaborate in this effort, including the Department of Political Sciences of the Pontifical Universidad Javeriana of Colombia; the Legislative Studies Program of the Latin American Center of Human Economics (CLAEH) in Uruguay; the Political Science Institute of the University of Uruguay; the Department of Political Science of Torcuato Di Tella University in Argentina; the Political Science and International Relations Department of the University of Brasilia; the Law School of the American University of Paraguay; the Parliamentary Training Institute (ICAP) of the Chamber of Deputies of Argentina; the Pontifical Catholic University Madre y Maestra (PUCMM) of the Dominican Republic, and the INTERLEGIS program of the Brazilian Congress, among others. For a complete description of technical assistance activities in the legislative area, see Unit for the Promotion of Democracy (2004).

27. The IDB carried out legislative modernization projects in several countries: Nicaragua ($1,700,000), Panama ($2,800,000), Dominican Republic ($490,000), Paraguay ($730,000), Ecuador ($750,000) and Colombia ($6,000,000). Legislative modernization was considered to be a necessary component of the State's reform process, which included the judicial branch and governmental structures of the executive branch. The purpose was to guarantee legal stability and the rule of law, transparency and the quality of the legislation that was required for reforms (downsizing) of the public sector, as well as promoting savings, domestic and international, investments and socioeconomic development. The IDB support focused on providing non-reimbursable technical assistance and soft substantive loans for modernizing the organization and administration of legislative institutions, including technical assistance and equipment for data systems, communications and computers, electronic voting machines, and administrative management systems, legislative advisory systems, legislative training for staff, procedures, techniques and control of legislative quality, among other matters.

28. For example, the technical assistance provided by the UPD Program for Support of Legislative Institutions contributed to the development of useful products such as manuals and guides for application in different areas of legislative work. These included: *Guía para el Control Político y la Fiscalización Presupuestaria; Guía para el Análisis Presupuestario; Manual sobre Técnica Legislativa y Negociación Política; Guía sobre Negociación Política Parlamentaria; Manual de Estrategias de Comunicación Política para Parlamentarios; Manu-*

al de Relaciones Legislativas con la Prensa; Guía para la Relaciones entre Diputados y la Sociedad Civil; Analisis del Proceso de Tratamiento Presupuestario en Centroamérica; Analisis sobre el Uso de Nuevas Tecnologías en las Instituciones Legislativas (Congreso Electrónico); and *Manual de Técnica Legislativa, Codigo de Etica Legislativa* (Unit for the Promotion of Democracy 2004).

29. Inter-parliamentary cooperation could also involve technical assistance to support and develop a sustainable institutional capacity to deal jointly with challenges of mutual interest such as natural disasters, drug trafficking, corruption, terrorism, education, public safety, migration, among others. These "*inter-mestic*" challenges (partly international and partly domestic) invariably require legislative answers; that is, legislation minimally harmonized, at least at the regional or subregional level, and compatible with regional and international legal instruments such as treaties or conventions.

30. (Liphart 1992) (Linz, *The Perils of Presidentialism* 1990) (Linz, *The Virtues of Parliamentarism* 1990) (Linz and Valenzuela, *The Failure of Presidential Democracy* 1994). I would argue that because of the tradition, history and political culture of Latin America, a presidential system is best for democratic governance and stability but it needs a strong legislative institution that fulfills adequately its role and functions (R. M. Perina 2005).

31. See Fukuyama on the importance of understanding local norms, habits, constraints and opportunities (Fukuyama, *State Building, Governance and World Order in the Twenty-First Century* 2004, 82–91).

32. The World Bank and the Inter-American Development Bank have provided substantial financial support for reform of the state. Similarly agencies of developed countries, including the United States, Canada, Spain, Sweden, Norway and others, have made important contributions to democracy promotion efforts in different areas.

Chapter Eight

Electoral Observation

Between Relevance and Interference

INTRODUCTION

Election observation a combination of both high politics and low politics approaches to democracy promotion. It involves negotiations, decisions, guidelines and actions at the highest political/diplomatic levels, followed by politically sensitive agency in actually organizing and carrying out the electoral observation missions (EOMs) on the ground. It has become one of the main tools of democracy promotion since the beginning of the "third wave" of democracy. Advanced democracies, international organizations and non-governmental organizations employ electoral observation constantly to foster the transition from authoritarian/totalitarian regimes to democracy and/or to further support consolidation of it. [1]

EOMs are important for the simple reason that elections are important. Democracy was an important feature of the early history of the independent republics in Latin America, even if restricted to males and the literate and propertied class, as their leaders attempted to introduce it, citing the United States as a model of the new form of free government in the continent. For Paul Drake, "from the throes of independence onward, Latin Americans held amazingly widespread and frequent elections." Most countries "excelled at elections, often unfair, un-free, and narrow, but sometimes astonishingly open from the beginning—and increasingly so in the twentieth century." Even dictators like Batista, Somoza, Stroessner and Trujillo used "elections," if fraudulent to the extreme, to pretend they had the consent of the people and thus justify their arbitrary and repressive rule. However, since the late 1970s

141

and early 1980s "elections gradually became more regular, secret, direct, obligatory, participatory, equal and free and fair." (Drake 2009, 40–44).

The purpose of this Chapter is to assess the evolution of the OAS/EOMs, identify the challenges they face and propose ways to strengthen them as a significant inter-American collective instrument to promote democracy.

THE ORIGINS OF OAS ELECTORAL OBSERVATION MISSIONS

Prior to 1989–1990 and since 1962, the OAS conducted electoral observation activities in an ad hoc manner, at the request of a member state and following specific Permanent Council resolutions. In general, for these missions, the Secretary General, in consultation with the Government concerned, which paid the mission's expenses, appointed three or four high-level officials and distinguished political figures like former presidents of member states. The "observers" would then travel to the country of observation one day before election day, when they visited several polling places and then reported to the authorities that requested the observation (Baena 1994, 137, 141).

An exception to this type of mission—in terms of its number and "private" nature—occurred following the political/military crisis that engulfed the Dominican Republic in 1963–66 after the overthrow of left-leaning President Juan Bosch by a right wing military junta, and the defeat of a pro-Castro military uprising by the Inter-American Peace Force. At the request of the Dominican transitional president Héctor R. García Godoy, the OAS Meeting of Consultation of Foreign Ministers authorized the Secretary General to send a forty-one member mission to "observe" the elections of June 1966. Even though the Organization paid for the mission, its members could only "observe" the process as private invitees and not in any official capacity. They sent their "private" report to the President of the Republic and it was published by his office (Baena 1994, 138–9).

In essence, at least up to the 1980s, most member states, many of which were under semi-democratic civilian rule, one-party authoritarian regimes, or under direct military rule, refused to give the OAS any substantive responsibility for monitoring elections. The Mexican delegation exemplified this position as it argued that such an activity represented a violation of state sovereignty and of the sacrosanct principle of non-intervention. In this restrictive context, the General Secretary would only be able to recommend names of observers as they would be invitees of the government that requested the observation, which was responsible for their expenses and safety. Moreover, the observers could not be considered to belong to or represent the OAS; their report or conclusions were personal and to be delivered to the national authorities that invited them, not to the governing bodies of the Organization. The Ecuadorian delegation, on the other hand, represented the minority's views when it stated that the request for observers constitutes a free, sovereign act of a member state and could not be considered interference in its internal affairs (Baena, 1994, 144–45). A few years later, the *chavista* Venezuelan Government and the Nicaraguan Government of Ortega would express similar views against EOMs.

The nature and scope of EOMs, however, changed drastically with the approval of the "Human Rights, Democracy, and Electoral Observations" resolution by the 1989 OAS General Assembly. A formal request by the *Sandinista* Nicaraguan Government to the Secretary General to send an EOM for the upcoming general election in February 1990 triggered arduous diplomatic negotiations between those member states that had serious reservations about these Missions, and those that viewed electoral observation as an instrument to promote the consolidation of democracy and peace, particularly in Central America, where the OAS and the United Nations had facilitated the peace agreements that had ended decades of war in the region.[2] Those in favor of this new role for the Organization were supported by the 1985 reforms to the founding Charter itself, which established that one of the main purposes of the Organization was now to "promote and consolidate representative democracy." This great achievement for democracy in the hemisphere had been made possible by the fact that most member states had already returned to democracy by that year. Additionally, the entry of Canada as a full member of the OAS in 1989 strengthened those who favored a more active role of the Organization in promoting democracy.

This watershed resolution in 1989 marked a significant step in favor of electoral monitoring, expanding the power of the Secretary General. For the first time now, member states recommended that the Secretary General, at the request of a member state's government, organize (selecting his own observers) and send an official OAS Mission to observe all the phases of an electoral process, not just the day of the election. It also instructed the Secretary General to report the findings and conclusions to the Permanent Council. Today, EOMs are a fully recognized instrument for the collective promotion and consolidation of democracy in the Inter-American Democratic Charter where the general standards for them are established.

THE SIGNIFICANCE OF ELECTIONS

Free and fair elections are undoubtedly one of the fundamental components of representative democracy. Every attempt by prominent scholars and their disciples to define democracy invariably includes them as necessary conditions for its existence (Schumpeter 1975) (Dahl 1975) (Sartori 1993) (Tilly 2007) (Mainwaring and Scully 2010). Elections are the central pillar and the foundation of democracy. While democracy is not just elections, without elections there is no democracy. As Dieter Nohlen puts it, "democracy is inconceivable with elections." (Nohlen 1993, 9). Democracy begins with elections, and they renovate and strengthen democracy.

In Latin America, they became the principal instrument to consolidate the democratizing transition process from authoritarian rule. The call for elections triggered euphoric liberalizing changes in the polity. It mobilized political parties and organized labor, freed public opinion and political prisoners, diluted the power of the military, and generated excitement and uncertainty about the future government and society in general (O'Donnell and Schmitter 1986, 57–64).

In general terms, however, an election performs several functions for a democracy: a) It is the principal civic instrument a society has to select and legitimize a government periodically, and to resolve political differences collectively and peacefully; b) it compels political forces to define, compromise, agree and commit to certain rules of the game for selecting governmental leaders—electoral codes that must be impartial, equitable, transparent and legitimate for fair political competition; c) it provides the context for and the opportunity to participate and decide collectively about the direction of society; d) it offers the occasion to exercise fundamental rights such as freedom of expression and association and universal secret voting; e) it is an opportunity for open debate and fair competition among different ideas, visions for a country and policy proposals; f) it requires (compels) tolerance for political pluralism and for divergent proposals of public policy; and g) it requires participants to know how to win with certain modesty and lose with dignity—today's winners may be tomorrow's losers.

In short, elections provide a unique opportunity for the exercise of democratic values and practices. But internalizing it as the only game in town necessitates much practice and time, and that is why there are never too many elections. Holding periodic elections contributes significantly to the consolidation of democracy. But elections alone do not make a democracy. Elected leaders must also follow with democratic governance; that is, they must also respect democratic institutions, values and practices.

THE NATURE OF THE NEW OAS EOMS

Electoral Observation Missions merit special mention because they are one of the primary and most visible activities of the OAS in its new role of promoting democracy. They have become a permanent feature of the electoral process of many member states. Since 1989, the Secretary General has dispatched more than 200 EOMs to about 50% of OAS members. Indeed, today the Organization is best known and recognized for its EOMs: they are the Organization's flagship in its mission to promote representative democracy.

EOMs are a powerful instrument with the potential of having immediate impact on the democratic process, particularly in electoral processes that are questioned, doubted or mistrusted by some of the contenders. Their reports could have calming and reassuring effects about the results and thus legitimize the newly elected authorities, or could have de-legitimizing consequences if the elections are reported to have been marked by widespread and significant irregularities that make the process invalid, as in the Dominican Republic in 1994 or in Peru in 2000. On the other hand, an EOM could have a damaging impact on the credibility of the OAS itself if its performance in observing an election is perceived as validating or legitimizing an irregular, unclear or fraudulent process, as in Venezuela in 2004 and 2006, Honduras in 2009 or Nicaragua in 2012.

The nature and scope of these electoral observation activities has varied depending on the situation in the country. The most important EOMs are those that are known as "comprehensive" and deploy a large number of specialized observers to as many voting locations as possible. They remain in the country throughout the different phases of the electoral process, including voter registration, campaigning, electoral preparation, voting, and the post-electoral phase, which includes the proclamation of the winners. [3]

In terms of the organization of the Mission itself, observers are normally placed strategically throughout the country. They are sent to major population centers, from which they try to cover as many urban and rural electoral districts as possible. They are distributed according to criteria of population, contentiousness, accessibility, etc. But in the final analysis, particularly in presidential elections, it is the location of each of the 50–70 statistical samples that determines where an observer is stationed. Observing the performance of the polling places where the samples are located and obtaining their results (and a copy of the official tally or *acta de escrutinio*) of each and every one of the samples is essential and crucial for the success of the statistical projection (misnamed "quick count"), especially in highly contested or contentious elections. Projections were quite useful, for example, to the Missions in Nicaragua in 1990 and Venezuela in 2000. They helped calm and normalize the process of declaring the winner.

The Mission's authorities and coordinators provide observers with appropriate information about the country, including its constitutional and political system, its electoral regime and its media landscape, as well as with a communications system and adequate transportation in order to facilitate coordination and execution of its activities. The Mission also trains observers in OAS observation methodology, questionnaires and survey forms and code of conduct (Misión de Observación Electoral, Venezuela 2005). Missions are usually composed of an international multidisciplinary team of experts in

informatics, statistics, communications, logistics, political science, law, electoral systems, education and other disciplines.

Observing elections requires belief in and commitment to the Mission,
discipline, and cultural and political sensitivity. It involves long hours of
often arduous, tiring and demanding work. On Election Day, observers must
be present at the opening of a specific polling place, as they are compelled to
observe and obtain the official results from it. Sometimes they have to go to
difficult places in the countryside, traveling by either all-terrain vehicles,
river boat, mule or helicopter, or by long walks through inhospitable places,
to get to their polling places samples. There have been cases when observers
were shot at, caught in demonstrations, stoned, insulted, ridiculed by the
press, accused of electoral tourism, or worse yet, kidnapped by guerrilla
forces, as occurred in Colombia. Sometimes they had to be evacuated for
health or security reasons, or even expelled from the Mission for misconduct.

Objectives of the EOMs

Although the SG/OAS would occasionally send a small number of observers
for Election Day, since 1989, EOMs have developed into sophisticated missions with standardized methodology and technology (Unidad para la
Promoción de la Democracia-UPD 1998).[4]

The largest and longest comprehensive EOM took place in Nicaragua, to
monitor the electoral process that culminated in the surprising defeat of the
Sandinistas in February 1990. The EOM consisted of more than four hundred
observers who stayed in the country for more than nine months, covering
most of the country's electoral districts (Baena 1994, 147–171). This election
was not only paradigmatic in terms of electoral observation but also in that it
marked a transition from a communist regime, led by the *Sandinista guerril-*
leros who had taken over the government by force from the Somoza dictatorship in 1979, to a democratically elected civilian government. In the last few
years, however, most Missions range from twenty to a hundred observers and
last an average of about twenty days, depending on the type of election.

Their formal, stated objective is to observe and inform the Secretary
General (SG/OAS) and the Permanent Council (PC/OAS) about the electoral
process. This is supposed to guarantee non-interference in the internal affairs
of the "observed" country. But, in reality, its underlying if implicit purpose—
the raison d'être of an EOM—is to contribute, by its presence and tasks, to
the integrity of the electoral process; that is, to a process that is universal,
free, fair, impartial, competitive and transparent.[5] Simultaneously, it is also
to contribute to the strengthening of the country's electoral institution and
thus to the consolidation of democracy. Missions thus seek to generate in the
citizenry a sense of confidence and credibility in the electoral process, which
in turn would bestow final legitimacy on it. If they are effective in achieving

these purposes, EOMs are considered effective and therefore successful and relevant. If not, they are irrelevant.

In pursuit of the objectives, the EOMs' fundamental task is to verify whether the protagonists in the electoral process (political parties, candidates, electoral and governmental authorities, the media and others) behave according to the established laws and regulations. In this sense, an electoral observation is inevitably an evaluation exercise, no matter how much member states and OAS authorities insist or pretend that EOMs do not pass judgment on electoral processes—since that would violate the principle of non-intervention and would mean interference in the electoral process of the country. The fact is, however, that they do assess the integrity of the electoral process, except that they do not it with external models or international standards, but with domestic electoral standards established in domestic electoral laws, and that is why it is hard to argue that electoral observation is an act of interventionism.

While a special ad hoc group within the office of the Secretary General designed, organized and deployed the Nicaraguan EOM, by 1990 these functions had become the responsibility of the newly created UPD. In 2005, the recently established Secretariat for Political Affairs assumed that responsibility.[6]

Functions of the EOMs

In pursuing their objectives, EOMs perform technical as well as political functions, as seen below.

a) *Technical functions.* Observers perform a variety of daily "technical" functions. They examine in great detail the Constitution of the country and its electoral law and regulations; interview all the protagonists; attend political meetings and campaign rallies; examine campaign financing; analyze press coverage and the observance of press and other freedoms; receive complaints about irregularities, bring them to the attention of electoral authorities and follow up on their responses. They monitor the electoral authorities' organization of the process, including the designation and training of polling places officials; the preparation and distribution of the voters' registry and electoral material; the adoption of security measures; the public information campaign; analyze the technology used for voting, transmitting and tabulating results; and observe their audits after if needed.

On Election Day, they observe the voting process from beginning to end, in as many polling places as possible, with a questionnaire to check every aspect of the process. Observers fill out a questionnaire with questions that include: a) Was the polling place opened on time? b) Did the polling place authorities arrive on time? c) Were party representatives or delegates present? d) Were the polling materials (ballots; voting registry, voting machines) in place at the time of opening? e) Were the voting machines functioning and connected properly? f) Was there any violence or conflict in the precinct? g) Did the polling place close on time? h) Were the tallying procedures executed properly? i) Were records kept and sent properly to central authorities? j) Was there access to the national information and computing center (where national tallying takes place)? Missions that observe a presidential election would likely organize a complex operation in the field to gather this information and the official tallies of polling places that form part of the statistical sample for the so-called "quick count", or a projection of results, which is used as a parallel counting device to check official results. These functions are described in detail in OAS documents and EOMs reports.[7]

The information collected on Election Day, as well as that collected during the pre- and post-election phases of the electoral and observation processes, forms part of the reports that observers have to prepare periodically if not daily, which is subsequently analyzed and integrated by a core group to produce press releases and the final report of the Mission.

It is worth pointing out that most EOMs report irregularities or deficiencies in the electoral process that do not necessarily affect the validity of the election. The most frequent irregularities encountered are organizational and logistical, including inconsistencies in the voter registry, lack of clarity or contradictions in rules, misdistribution of voting materials, inaccessible voting places, delays in opening polling places, lack of training of electoral authorities, mistakes in calculating results, inconsistencies or voids in the electoral code, lack of compliance with the electoral schedule, delaying informing about the results, the use of state resources, among others. But if these irregularities are few and random or isolated, they do not threaten the integrity of the process; that is, they would not constitute a pattern that would affect the results or indicate the possibility of fraud. Fraud is defined as a premeditated manipulation of the electoral process or its results to favor a particular candidacy.

b) *Political functions.* Although OAS officials constantly repeat that the Missions' role is only to observe, anyone who has participated in an EOM knows they do more than that. Particularly in contentious elections, their role is political in many respects.

Some specific political functions of EOMs include facilitating negotiations and consensus building amongst stakeholders, acting as a go-between or conciliator amongst them; and helping authorities solve organizational or logistical problems—but only at the request of the interested parties. These functions sometimes help clarify confusing and conflictive situations, and discreetly help correct irregularities or prevent attempts to unduly alter the process. These tasks can be effective in highly competitive or contested elections in that they can add to a general sense of greater transparency, impartiality, tolerance and confidence in the electoral process. If so, they can also enhance the relevance and image of the EOM. The EOM experiences in Paraguay (1991–1993), Dominican Republic (1994), Peru (2000) and Venezuela (2000 and 2005) illustrate this point. [8]

Lest the nature and scope of an EOM be misunderstood, it is important to underscore that an EOM is not an electoral judge or police, nor an electoral administrator. It can investigate allegations of irregularities and present its findings to the stakeholders, but it cannot enforce them. Only national authorities can implement changes or solutions to the issues that arise during the contest. Nonetheless, EOMs cannot escape the fact that they are players too, although not the deciding one, as some would have it. Nevertheless, in performing these functions, it is not unusual for observers in remote polling places to be asked by officials to mediate and/or find solutions to disputes about issues that must be resolved *in situ*. There have been occasions on which observers have "had to" even help with the counting and tallying of the results.

Ultimately, however, EOMs present their reports to the Secretary General and the Permanent Council or the General Assembly. If the report concludes that significant irregularities, including fraud, have compromised the integrity of an election, it behooves those collective bodies to decide whether the election is fraudulent and invalid, and if it violates the Inter-American Democratic Charter. They may collectively assess the situation and take appropriate action.

c) *Tension and Balance.* In performing their functions, EOMs struggle with the tension between irrelevance and interference. Their challenge is to strike a balance between being relevant without being interventionist, or between being not interventionist and irrelevant.

In that balancing act, Missions must seek to be objective, neutral, independent and respectful of national laws and customs, as now formally established in the IADC. They must be proactive but not the center of attention or be excessively protagonist. Their behavior must be measured, marked by a spirit of cooperation with all the participants, and always cognizant that ultimately the national actors are the only ones that can guarantee the integrity of the electoral process. EOMs must not unduly legitimize the electoral authorities, nor overly question them, so as to avoid erosion of public confidence in the process. Neither must they disqualify or validate the electoral process or the electoral authorities a priori–that is, before analyzing the process thoroughly. Moreover, Missions must always be skeptical of conspiracy theories and must play the devil's advocate. And, of course, observers must not show preference for particular candidates—a frequent temptation.

RELEVANCE AND CONTRIBUTIONS OF THE EOMS

Since their inception in electoral processes, EOMs have demonstrated their relevance by making significant contributions to the integrity of elections and the strengthening of electoral institutions in several countries of the Americas, as detailed below.

a) The first few years of comprehensive EOMs provided the experience for developing observation methodologies and a code of conduct for observers, which became the standards for monitoring elections; they were published and distributed through their election reports and observers' manuals. They were shared with the United Nations, the African Union, the European Union, the Organization for Security and Cooperation in Europe, as well as with nongovernmental organizations like the Carter Center, the National Democratic Institute (NDI), the Swedish International Institute for Democracy and Electoral Assistance (IDEA), and others—all of which have also developed similar standards and codes (The Carter Center 2007) (IDEA 1998) (NDI 2007) (Organization for Security and Cooperation in Europe 1999). Some of these institutions, however, employ international standards for organizing and administering democratic elections that may or may not be entirely compatible with local electoral laws, regulations or electoral codes. The OAS, on the other hand, strictly adheres to local norms and traditions to evaluate elections, and has the advantage, at least in theory, of having the Inter-American Democratic Charter as reference for definitions and standards of representative democracy, democratic elections, and electoral observation. And this is not a minor or insignificant detail or difference, since the Charter has been signed and committed to by all of its member states.

b) The mere presence of observers is frequently a factor dissuasive of possible irregular or fraudulent activities. An EOM is a window to the world; people being observed do not want to be identified as fraudulent or incompetent in organizing an election. Its presence provides the public and stakeholders reassurance and confidence in the electoral process. It may even encourage moderation, transparency, and genuine efforts to organize elections competently and to assure their integrity.

c) Frequently, EOM technical assistance and advice prior to the electoral process, as well as their post-electoral recommendations, also have contributed to the strengthening of electoral institutions. These are intended to improve the organization and administration of elections, including the updating of the electoral code and the electoral registry, the modernization of electoral technology, the revision of campaign financing laws, the professionalization and training of human resources, and more. In this vein, the OAS provided assistance to Bolivia, Costa Rica, El Salvador, Nicaragua, Paraguay, Peru, Dominican Republic and others. Until recently, improvisation, disorganization and political corruption in electoral organization and administration created confusion and mistrust, particularly amongst the opposition, and seriously threatened the integrity of elections in many of those countries.

d) More significantly, there are some notable cases in which EOMs' good offices showed their relevance and impact on the ground by taking a stand against fraud, facilitating the resolutions of political/electoral crisis or making recommendations for changes to improve the electoral system. As such, they contributed to the strengthening of democratic electoral processes, which in turn provided the foundation for sustained democratic development and consolidation in several member states. The following section examines some of these cases.

SOME RELEVANT EOMS

The first significant and comprehensive electoral observation took place in 1990 in Nicaragua. More than four hundred observers observed the process for about nine months, amidst a polarized political environment with the *Sandinista* Ortega's Government confronting the liberal coalition supported by the *Contras.* The EOM not only observed the process thoroughly from its very beginning, but at the end was instrumental, along with the United Nations and the Carter Center, in assuring the acceptance of the results. Secretary General Baena Soares' diplomatic skills and his Mission's "quick count" convinced Ortega to accept, reluctantly, his defeat. Many of the EOMs suggestions for improving the integrity of the process were later implemented by the Nicaraguan authorities (Baena 1994, 147–71).

The EOM in Paraguay in 1993 (with one hundred and ten observers and four months in country) facilitated the signing of a Democratic Coexistence Agreement amongst the principal candidates, which committed them to respect the prevailing rules, to reject any notion of interrupting the electoral process, and accept the results. The agreement took on particular significance as rumors spread of a military coup and there were calls to postpone the elections. The Mission also facilitated arduous negotiations amongst legislators of the multiparty Congressional Bicameral Commission responsible for verifying the results and proclaiming the new authorities. Congress ratified the Commission's final unanimous decision, which resulted in a legislative body controlled by the opposition. All of this legitimized the electoral process. The EOM also made numerous recommendations that were later implemented by the new Supreme Electoral Tribunal (Misión de Observación Electoral en Paraguay 1996).

In the Dominican Republic in 1994, the EOM observed significant irregularities, which compromised the final results of the general elections and generated a political crisis. The Mission, in cooperation with the Catholic Church, adroitly facilitated negotiations between the opposition parties and the ruling party, which culminated in a "Democracy Pact." This momentous agreement called for new elections in eighteen months, the appointment of new independent electoral authorities, and significant changes in the electoral system. These were later implemented and helped consolidate Dominican democracy (Misión de Observación Electoral en República Dominicana 1997) (Graham 2011).

Similarly, in Peru in 2000, the EOM detected serious, widespread organizational, logistical and computing deficiencies and irregularities in the first round of the presidential and congressional elections held on April 9. The electoral authorities and Fujimori's Government, however, ignored the OAS's good offices and corrective recommendations for the second round (May 28). The Peruvian Government also refused to postpone briefly the second round, as requested by observers and the opposition candidate, to allow for enough time to rectify some of the flaws in the system. This intransigence and the opposition candidate's decision to boycott the election led the EOM to reduce its presence drastically and basically desist from observing the second round. The Mission presented an unfavorable report to the OAS General Assembly meeting in Canada (June 4–5), which in an unusual resolution stated its concern over the credibility of the process. This collective pronouncement delegitimized Fujimori's victory. A diplomatic/ political mission sent to Peru facilitated negotiations for new elections in November 2001. However, amid revelations of pervasive corruption and bribery schemes within his inner circle, Fujimori abruptly resigned and went into exile in Japan (Misión de Observación Electoral en el Perú, 13 de diciembre de 2000). The November democratic election, observed by the OAS, paved the way for the development and consolidation of Peruvian democracy.

In Venezuela, five days before the May 2000 elections, the EOM observed significant delays in the organization and preparations for the so-called "mega-elections" for President, national, departmental and local legislators, governors and mayors, and parliamentarians for the Andean and the Latin American Parliaments. The electronic/automated system designed for the occasion was not ready to process the voting and tallying adequately, and was judged by the Mission as likely to produce unreliable, questionable results that could cause a political crisis. As the Mission recommended, the government and the electoral authorities postponed and divided the elections into separate manageable events. Elections for national offices and for the regional parliaments were held on July 30 and for local offices on October 1 (Misión de Observación Electoral en Venezuela 2001).

For the legislative elections of 2005, the EOM made a significant effort at facilitating the negotiations between the opposition parties and the electoral authorities around electronic voting notebooks and digital fingerprint scanners, which the opposition rejected, alleging that both had the potential of violating the secrecy of the vote. But despite the National Electoral Council's agreement to suspend use of the digital scanners, the opposition withdrew from the elections. The Mission's report identified significant deficiencies and irregularities in the electoral system as well as weaknesses in the political system, which needed to be corrected for the consolidation of Venezuelan democracy, and which implied that the election and the newly elected legislature lacked full legitimacy. The Venezuelan political and diplomatic authorities strongly scorned and rejected the preliminary and final report, as they considered it an act of interference in the internal affairs of the nation (Misión de Observación Electoral, Elecciones Legislativas de diciembre 2005 en Venezuela, 26 Abril 2006).

As head of the OAS/EOM, the author's preliminary oral report to the Permanent Council on the 2005 legislative elections pointed out the opposition's mistrust of the electoral authorities as one of the major causes of the opposition's withdrawal and of the growing political/electoral polarization in the country. The government and its Representative in the Permanent Council, Ambassador Valero, considered it a biased and unfounded report, accusing the author of representing the views of the opposition and of the U.S. Government. However, no other member state followed the Venezuelan delegation in its questioning of the integrity of the Mission, and the Secretary General actually supported its performance and report (R. M. Perina February 1, 2006). Strangely enough, Venezuelan electoral authorities kept the final report for several months on the CNE web page and eventually adopted many of its technical recommendations. The political opposition, on the other hand, failed to use the report to question the validity of the elections and the legitimacy of the elected representatives. Nor did any of the member states or the Secretary General delve into the serious flaws of the election and their detrimental effects on the Venezuelan democracy.

In Haiti, for the November 2010 presidential and congressional elections, the Joint OAS-CARICOM Electoral Observation Mission (JEOM) identified considerable irregularities in the process, including mismanagement and disorganization, ballot stuffing, intimidation and vandalism in polling stations and a mistrust of electoral authorities. These irregularities generated violence from followers of the opposition candidates, who alleged massive fraud, challenged the results and called for cancellation of the elections. On December, President Préval requested the OAS to send an expert commission to verify the results, whose January 2011 report concluded that candidates Manigat and Martelly were the two top finishers in the November vote, ahead of governing party candidate Jude Celestin who had been placed second in the preliminary count. For the run-off, the electoral authorities implemented the technical changes suggested and accepted the recommendation concerning the final placing of the candidates (Expert Verification Mission January 13, 2011).

THE CHALLENGE OF IRRELEVANCE

However, serious questions have emerged in the last few years about the effectiveness and relevance of OAS electoral observation missions. Critics have pointed to Missions that have been sent unnecessarily to observe elections that are not vital to the member states' democracy—their presence being pointless. In some cases they have been perceived as unduly partial to the ruling party or the Government (i.e., the President); while in others, they have been accused of arriving too late, of inconsequential performance and of doubtful reports that do not reflect reality, and of being too cautious and deferential to the incumbent government—legitimizing questionable elections, with detrimental consequences for their own credibility and the democratic order of the country involved.

Any or all of these elements can generate the perception that an EOM is weak or ineffective and that it does not contribute to the integrity or validity of the electoral process. This in turn debilitates the prestige and relevance of the EOMs, and devalues their usefulness as an instrument to guarantee democratic elections and strengthen the democratic order. A few recent EOMs illustrate these challenges, as described below.

a) As a result of negotiations between the Venezuelan Bolivarian Government and the political opposition that followed the attempted coup of 2002, both protagonists jointly decided in November to appoint Secretary General Gaviria as International Facilitator. After months of OAS-mediated negotiations and intermediate agreements and declarations, in February 2004 they agreed to a Presidential Recall Referendum, as an electoral and peaceful way to solve the lingering political crisis engulfing the country (Gaviria 2004).[9]

OAS Secretary Gaviria named Ambassador Valter Pecly Moreira, Brazil's Permanent Representative to the OAS, as Chief of the OAS/EOM for the referendum, held in August 2004. Chávez defeated the recall with 58% of the vote and remained in power. Pecly's and the Carter Center's reports on their observation of the electoral process became very controversial. Both claimed the elections had been free and fair, with some technical irregularities that did not affect the validity of the results, while the opposition claimed that the election was fraudulent and marred by irregularities, including the electronic manipulation and distortion of the results by the electoral authorities, who were under the control and direction of Chávez (McCoy 2005) (Kornblith 2005) (Legler 2007) (Misión de Observación Electoral de la OEA al Referendo Revocatorio Presidencial en Venezuela 2004).

The referendum nevertheless confirmed Chávez' popularity and presidency, and also became a turning point in the Venezuelan political process. Henceforth, the opposition started to deeply mistrust and reject the electronic electoral system introduced and operated by the *chavista* regime, but more significantly it distrusted the *chavista* electoral authorities, who managed the system with little transparency and even less impartiality, making it more difficult for the opposition to trust the electoral process, to the point of, mistakenly, refusing to participate in the legislative elections of 2005,[10] leaving, for all intents and purpose, the State institutions under the total control of the *chavistas*. Both electoral events and the mistrust of the electoral authorities deepened and exacerbated the political polarization between the *chavistas* and the opposition—a polarization that has contributed to the erosion of Venezuelan democratic political culture and the institutional framework to this day, and has made democratic governance almost impossible.

For the presidential elections of 2006, Secretary General Insulza dispatched sitting Uruguayan Permanent Representative to the OAS, Ambassador Juan E. Fisher. Both his and the Pecly-Moreira Mission in 2004 reported that the process was basically "normal and tranquil," with some technical irregularities and flaws in the electoral norms (dispersion, lack of clarity and precision, omissions, outdated), but considered not serious or widespread enough to merit questioning the validity of the election. Both Missions even remained in the country after the election to observe an (incomplete and non-transparent) audit of the results. (Misión de Observación Electoral de la Organización de los Estados Americanos al Referendo Revocatorio Presidencial en Venezuela 21 September 2004) (Misión de Observación Electoral de la OEA en Venezuela 10 September 2008).

However, the political opposition and the independent media viewed both Missions as being partial to the Government and rather timid in reporting or denouncing the Government's abuse of state resources and media, and the political and technical irregularities that marred the electoral process. The Missions were perceived, at best, as irrelevant and, and at worst, as obsequious and legitimizing the incumbent's controversial and even doubtful victories.

The appointment by both Secretaries General of the two sitting diplomats as Chiefs of Mission was unusual, ill-advised and controversial. Both ambassadors came from member states with ideological affinity to President Chávez, and with a traditionally strong commitment to non-intervention. Neither had any experience in electoral politics or electoral observation. Rumors had it that Gaviria wanted to placate Chávez' ire for his role in bringing about the recall referendum. And Insulza did not want to antagonize Chávez any further, since the Venezuelan President had repudiated the 2005 EOM's report, and had strongly supported his bid for the OAS Secretariat.[11]

But the fact is that their appointment and performance compromised their Missions' independence, effectiveness, integrity and credibility. [12]

Nevertheless, all these EOMs from 2004 to 2006 had one thing in common: They all pointed to a polarized Venezuelan polity marked by antagonism, confrontation and mistrust, all clearly expressed in the electoral process; which indicated the imperative need for a serious dialogue between the Government and the opposition, while failing, however, to observe the Government's abuse of power and state resources and to assign a greater responsibility to the *chavista* Government for not bringing about the promised dialogue with the opposition.

Lamentably, however, all these Venezuelan EOMs failed to even moderate Chávez and his followers' arbitrariness, abuses and manipulation of the electoral process and the political process more generally. The *chavista* regime continues to control the electoral and judicial institutions, denigrate, persecute and jail the political opposition, harass and intimidate the independent press and ignore civil liberties and the rule of law, not to mention the Inter-American Democratic Charter (R. M. Perina, "Elecciones Impugnadas en Venezuela" 2013) (R. M. Perina, "Elecciones Inválidas en Venezuela" 2013).

Neither electoral reforms nor the political moderation and dialogue the EOMs proposed have had any impact on the increasingly polarized political process in Venezuela. The regime's aggressive rhetoric and actions have indeed widened and hardened the division and polarization in the country. The dialogue with the opposition that Chávez had promised the inter-American community in 2002 in order to reduce the growing violence and the polarization in the country has not really materialized and has only been a periodic façade used to calm international criticism.

b) In Honduras, in June 2009, at the request of President Zelaya, the Secretary General, José Miguel Insulza, sent an emissary to inform the President about the plans to "observe" a referendum on a constituent assembly that would change the Constitution to allow for presidential reelection. The National Congress, the Supreme Court and the President's own political party had rejected the referendum as unconstitutional. In view of the opposition to it, the emissary publicly suggested that the referendum was indeed a non-binding poll with no significant consequences. As those opposed to the referendum/poll interpreted the OAS presence as legitimizing a process that the President would later use to engineer an unconstitutional change that would allow his reelection, the National Congress asked the OAS observer to leave the country. The President nevertheless insisted on holding the referendum (or so-called poll), now with support from the Venezuelan Government, which provided the logistics for the event. As a result of this, he was ousted by military force and sent to Costa Rica in exile. [13] The obsession to observe and the temptation to always and automatically accept an invitation by a

President led the Secretary General to miscalculate the situation and send a misguided mission, which arguably augmented the tension between the President and those opposed to the referendum/poll and precipitated the coup.

c) In 2008, President Ortega of Nicaragua refused to invite or request an OAS/EOM for the municipal elections, arguing that EOMs were interventionist and controlled by the United States. However, for the presidential election of November 2011, Ortega's Government did invite the OAS to send an EOM, amidst strong and persistent questioning from the opposition about the constitutionality of his candidacy. Through an irregular procedure and questionable criteria of human rights violations, the Supreme Court had allowed Ortega to seek reelection—even though it was expressly prohibited by the Constitution.

The Mission arrived in Managua at the beginning of October. Although it faced certain obstructions to its work on Election Day, the Mission detected serious irregularities in the accreditation of opposition parties' poll watchers, in the issuance of voting identity cards to voters, and in the uneven political composition of electoral authorities in polling places. It also reported that despite rumors of impending violence, the voting was peaceful and relatively normal. But the Mission did not challenge the validity of the process, which had been tainted from the beginning by Ortega's unconstitutional candidacy (Electoral Accompaniment Mission in Nicaragua January 25, 2011). In addition, national observers and the European Union Mission had corroborated the opposition parties' claim that the electoral authorities were not impartial, transparent or very collaborative with the observer teams.

By accepting the invitation to observe, the Secretary General also accepted the distorted and questioned political/electoral context, as though one could separate in real life the pre-arrival context from the electoral process in progress after arrival. From the beginning, this conditioned and compromised the credibility and relevance of the EOM in the eyes of the opposition and in much of public opinion. The Mission arrived too late in the game and faced an irrelevance/interference dilemma: If it questioned Ortega's candidacy, it would be interfering in internal affairs, but if it did not, it would validate a flawed electoral process, condemn the Mission to irrelevance, and abort the possibility of contributing to containing the erosion of the democratic order in Nicaragua. It chose not to comment about the constitutional transgression or about the perils of indefinite reelection. Worse yet, its presence gratuitously validated not only the questionable political context but also Ortega's anticipated victory—which had all the advantages of incumbency.

d) In the Dominican Republic's presidential election of May 2012, the EOM arrived late, only a few days before Election Day. Its seventy-one observers monitored the voting and the organization of the event in a statistically representative sample of polling places, obtaining their tallying sheets for the "quick count," which allowed it to make an accurate projection of the results. In its post-election press release, the EOM correctly concluded that, in general, the election was well organized and that people voted in a relatively peaceful atmosphere. But it also detected some irregularities such as the buying of voters' IDs and lack of regulation on the "use of state resources, campaign financing and equal access to the media." Based on these findings, it recommended to the electoral authorities that they "establish clear limits on the duration of the campaigns as well as effective mechanisms to control their financing and their expenditures; create the conditions to guarantee equal access to media outlets and approve the proposal for a new organic electoral law" (R. M. Perina 2011) (Misión de Observación Electoral de la OEA 26 septiembre 2013).

This is all well and good but not sufficient to contribute to the strengthening of electoral and democratic institutions. In the Dominican Republic (and Nicaragua), the focus of the EOM was mistaken. In today's Latin America the significant irregularities do not necessarily occur during the balloting. The alteration or violation of fundamental principles of a democratic election now frequently takes place before Election Day and significantly conditions the electoral process in favor of a candidate (usually the incumbent's). To ignore these "structural" irregularities is to validate or legitimize pernicious practices that tend to erode democracy. To argue that an EOM, as in Nicaragua in 2011, can comment only on what it observes during its presence in the country is disingenuous, and in that case it is better not to arrive in the country at all.

To be relevant, an EOM cannot concentrate its monitoring only on the week before the election and on voting day. In the Dominican Republic, the Mission arrived too late and did not comment on the "structural" distortions that were evident before Election Day. For example, it did not point out the use and abuse of state resources by the campaign of the candidate favored by the Government—a practice which had been identified in previous EOMs reports in 2004, 2008 and 2010 and had been notorious even during the EOM's preparatory visit. This significant irregularity, which violated standards stipulated in the IADC, was public and well documented by the impartial nongovernmental organization, Participación Ciudadana (Participación Ciudadana 2012).

It is no secret that greater campaign financing and expenditures increases the probability of victory. The use of state resources and the Government's increased expenditures on social programs and on inauguration of public works for electoral purposes distorted the process in favor of its candidate. On the other hand, opposition candidates questioned the composition and partiality of the electoral authorities (*Junta Central Electoral*), including their prohibition of electoral monitoring by national organizations and their ban on electoral alliances by the opposition parties.

Also, identifying irregularities and making recommendations to correct them after the elections have taken place cannot contribute to the perfecting of the current electoral process, and thus makes the EOM irrelevant and even counterproductive. It actually validates a flawed process. The recommendations advanced in the final reports to the Secretary General and the Permanent Council can also be irrelevant or useless if they are not taken into account by future EOMs to the country or by its electoral authorities. This practice or approach devalues the EOMs as useful instruments to contribute to the strengthening of electoral processes and the consolidation of democracy. Democracy is not only well organized and peaceful balloting on Election Day.

e) Other EOMs have also faced a variety of challenges that threatens their effectiveness and relevance: One is the obsession to observe, referring to the Secretary General's temptation to accept (or informally request) invitations to all kinds of elections, including some that are not crucial for the sustainability of a democracy, even when EOMs are clearly not necessary or when it is too late or too close to the election day. The most common and significant Missions are the ones sent for general presidential elections. Yet observers have been present in several primaries (e.g., Honduras and Paraguay), legislative elections (e.g., Venezuela, Dominican Republic, Mexico), provincial and local elections (e.g., Bolivia, Peru, Colombia, Nicaragua), constituent assemblies elections (e.g., Paraguay, Bolivia, Ecuador), referenda on revoking a presidential mandate (Venezuela), on energy policy (Bolivia), on the construction or enlargement of the Panama Canal, and others. An EOM was even sent in 2011 to Bolivia for a national election of judges, without serious consideration of the flawed electoral method employed, let alone of the implications such an election has for the country's democracy.

Another challenge EOMs face is late, irregular and insufficient funding, which frequently determines that Missions are improvised, poorly organized and staffed, and arrive too late in the electoral process—all of which condition their performance in the field. It also makes Missions dependent on a few donors, which may affect their political independence or impartiality. In addition, the European Union, UNASUR and other international or domestic nongovernmental organizations have begun to compete for the limited funds available for electoral observation. Scarce funding also prevents EOMs from proper analysis and follow up of their own previous reports and recommendations, which limits their effectiveness in improving the integrity of the electoral processes and tarnishes their own reputation.

Yet another challenge is a recent reluctance by some countries to invite OAS/EOMs. Nicaragua and Venezuela have argued lately that these Missions are controlled by the United States and are "interventionist." The real objective is to avoid critical, independent observations. Venezuela has opted to invite electoral authorities from friendly countries, or from regional organizations such as UNASUR. These "observers" are lavishly hosted, arrive two or three days before the election, have guided tours of polling places and their reports—if they make one—must be pre-approved by the Venezuelan authorities. They have no credibility and their presence has been branded as "electoral tourism." Of course, there are member states (Brazil, Argentina, Chile, Uruguay, the U.S. and Canada) that have never invited EOMs, as they consider them unnecessary.

These recent examples of misguided practice point to an increasing and generalized notion that EOMs are losing their usefulness and relevance as one of main instruments available to the OAS and its Democratic Charter to promote the consolidation of democracy in its member states. In the last couple of years, however, as a new leadership has been appointed in the Secretariat for Political Affairs and the Department of Electoral Cooperation and Observation (DECO), the tendency has been reverted with new more relevant guidelines, methodologies and practices.

CONCLUSION

EOMs are important because of the centrality of elections in a democracy; they are indeed useful instruments to promote and contribute to the integrity of elections and the consolidation of democracy. Therein lies their relevance. Yet, it is essential to keep in mind that, even if an electoral process is valid and legitimate, an election does not make a democracy whole. Democracy also requires democratic governance. That is, those who are elected democratically must also govern democratically, respecting the fundamental democratic values and practices agreed by all member states and established in the Inter-American Democratic Charter.

EOMs are complementary, if fundamental, instruments to the high politics and low politics OAS instruments that are available to the Organization and the member states themselves to protect, restore and promote representative democracy as the preferred system of government in the Americas. So, in many ways, when the effectiveness and relevance of EOMs are questioned, the OAS effectiveness and relevance are also in doubt. And that is why they must be fully supported and funded, properly employed and continuously strengthened. A few suggestions for strengthening EOMs will be made in the final chapter of this book.

NOTES

1. See various "democracy promoters" identified in Chapter 4.
2. Mexico continued to oppose EOMs for its own traditional reasons, but strangely enough so did the United States delegation. The U.S. Government mistrusted Baena Soares' relationship with Daniel Ortega, as it believed that the Secretary General was too lenient or accommo-

dating to the *Sandinista* leader. Ortega asked for observers because he was convinced that he would win the election handily and needed the OAS to legitimize his victory. He also thought his victory would be questioned by the *Contras* and the United States. Argentina, Canada and Venezuela strongly supported the resolution.

3. Examples of comprehensive Missions are the ones headed by the author in Paraguay and Venezuela (Misión de Observación Electoral en Paraguay 1996) (Misión de Observación Electoral en Venezuela 2001) (Misión de Observación Electoral. Elecciones Legislativas en Venezuela de diciembre 2005 26 Abril 2006). See others in http://www.oas.org/es/sap/deco/moe_informes.asp.

4. Recent versions of this Manual do not change the essential standards established then as a result of wide and significant experience in the field.

5. This kind of process essentially constitutes what Munck and others call "democratic elections" (Munck 2005).

6. As a Special Advisor to the Secretary General and Coordinator of the section on institutional strengthening at the UPD, the author was appointed by the Secretary General to head OAS/EOMs in Paraguay (1991–93), Colombia (1994), Guatemala (1995), Venezuela (2000 and 2005) and Dominican Republic (2006).

7. See for example the Manual for observers used for the legislative elections in Venezuela in 2005 (Misión de Observación Electoral, Venezuela 2005).

8. The author directed the OAS/EOMs in Paraguay and Venezuela.

9. It is interesting to note that Secretary Gaviria spent almost a year and a half in Venezuela facilitating the dialogue and observing the process of recollection, verification and validation of the signatures for the referendum. It was highly unusual for a Secretary General to spend so much time away from headquarters.

10. See also oral report on the 2005 parliamentary elections (R. M. Perina February 1, 2006), and the full report (Misión de Observación Electoral. Elecciones Legislativas en Venezuela. Diciembre 2005, 26, Abril 2006).

11. Diplomatic and media comments also had it that Insulza did not want to upset and alienate his Socialist Party associates in Chile.

12. It is also noteworthy that Gaviria's report on his Mission to facilitate and observe the entire process of the Presidential referendum was never officially published. His views on the actual referendum in the unpublished report are more critical of the political situation than Pecly Moreira's report, although both signal the existing political polarization and the need for moderation and dialogue. Notably, Fisher's report was not published until September 2008, almost two years after the election. His role on the process up to the referendum is described in detail in his memoires (C. Gaviria 2004).

13. Chapter 6 provides a more detailed account of these events in Honduras.

Chapter Nine

The Survival of Democracy and OAS Relevance

INTRODUCTION

We can now draw some positive lessons from the preceding chapters about the evolution and survival of democracy in the Americas since the birth of the new republics in the early 1800s, and about the revival and new role of the OAS in defending and promoting democracy in the mid 1980s.

THE SURVIVAL OF DEMOCRACY

In general terms, one can conclude with relative certainty that democracy is gradually taking root and consolidating in the Americas, and is probably here to stay, but with likely difficult tests and challenges along the road. The ideal of and aspiration for democracy has been around in the hemispheric republics since their independence and inception in world affairs, having survived many external and internal challenges since their early days in the 1800s.

As shown in Chapter 2, the young republics at first had to face external challenges in the form of European military interventions, attempting to regain their lost colonies in the early-mid 1800s or impose new imperial rule in the early twentieth century, and later they had to confront ideological political and military penetration and subversion by Fascism, Nazism and Communism. This was compounded by U.S. interventionism (Gun Boat and Dollar Diplomacy), ostensibly to stop or prevent European penetration and guarantee the U.S.'s own growing security and economic interests in the region, particularly around the Caribbean basin and the Panama Canal (Newfarmer 1984). The democratic sectors of the new republics also had to contend with domestic challenges, such as civil, borders and territorial wars, *caudillos'* nationalism and dictatorships, oligarchical rule, populist dictators, revolutionary leftist waves, communist rural and urban guerrillas (Castroism) and military dictatorships.

But democracy survived, and by the 1980s it had become "the only game in town" throughout the hemisphere, except in Cuba. Thus, it is not unreasonable or unduly optimistic to postulate that democracy is here to stay as the prevailing governing systems in the member countries. Today no one questions its validity or proposes an alternative system of governance that does not result from the will of the people expressed in democratic elections. This preference for democracy was manifested dramatically in the Inter-American Democratic Charter when all the countries of the hemisphere established that "the peoples of the Americas have a right to democracy and their Governments have an obligation to promote it and defend it."

In addition, there are significant promising signs of this trend towards democratic continuity, if not consolidation. Communist guerrilla forces (urban and rural) that once threatened to take over the continent are no longer operative and in many cases (such as El Salvador and Guatemala in Central America, and Argentina, Chile and Uruguay in South America) have abandoned their revolutionary armed struggle to establish a communist or socialist state, have signed peace and reconciliation agreements and have become political actors vying in democratic electoral contests for their ideals. Even the long-standing guerrilla forces in Colombia (the FARC) are now engaged in final peace talks with the Colombian Government. Coup attempts or the illegal *de facto* governments that emerge from military, auto-coups or parliamentary coups are condemned and not recognized domestically and regionally (Haiti in 1991, Peru in 1992, Guatemala in 1993, Paraguay in 1996, Ecuador in 2000, Venezuela in 1992 and 2002 and Honduras in 2009). Today, the great majority of Latin American countries have well-organized elections and, with few exceptions related to abusive intervention to assure re-reelection, fraudulent elections are things of the past, just as are full-fledged, repressive dictatorships. After a period of instability and uncertainty when presidents would not finish their terms because of discontent and unrest, stemming from unpopular economic policies, corruption and ineffective governance, most governments in the last few years have finished their terms and transfer power even to the opposition (Valenzuela 2005).

Most of these governments (except for Venezuela, and Argentina to a certain extent) have managed their economies' growth sensibly with prudent fiscal and monetary policies, along with progressive policies of social inclusion that have reduced poverty. Economic development, unemployment reduction, and increasing social inclusion and services have provided a sense of prosperity and hope for the future to a growing middle class. This has helped avoid the economic instability and stagnation that once used to fuel social/labor discontent and unrest that perturbed oligarchs and generals, which in turn caused political instability and threatened the permanence of governments and the durability of democracy itself. According to *Latinobarómetro,* the majority of people in most Latin American countries today support democracy and prefer it (56%) to any other form of government, with greater support, on average, in South America and Mexico (60%) than in Central America (49%).[1] Moreover, recent research indicates that most Latin American countries have shown unprecedented democratic stability since the 1990s, which suggest "a probability of continuity into the short-to medium-term future," although some countries (Argentina, Bolivia, Ecuador, Nicaragua and Venezuela) show disturbing signs of democratic stagnation and erosion, which makes it "premature to proclaim the definitive triumph of democracy." (Mainwaring and Perez-Liñan 2013, 261–7).[2]

THE NEW OAS STRENGTHS AND RELEVANCE

The OAS, albeit presently debilitated and questioned by critics from both "the left and the right," is still unquestionably the principal forum for dialogue and cooperation in inter-American affairs.

During the 1980s and 1980s, it showed significant strengths that emanated from the fact that all of its active members were democracies (regime congruence), which were determined to apply the OAS norms and instruments they themselves created for the promotion, defense and consolidation of democracy in the hemisphere. Its strengths also resulted from the increasing obsolescence of the coup d'état, the gradual but not linear waning of the non-intervention principle, the emergence of the Inter-Amerian Democratic Regime (IADR) and the presence of the U.S. and Canada in the Organization.

New Norms and Instruments

Because of the new norms and instruments member states have developed and used to promote and defend democracy, one can expect them not only to condemn an attempted coup or an illegal interruption of the democratic order, but also to repudiate, impose economic and diplomatic sanctions and even suspend from the Organization a *de facto* government if democracy is not quickly restored (Haiti, Peru, Guatemala, Paraguay, Honduras). This will likely isolate the trangressor government and can have a significant disruptive impact on its country's internal affairs and external relations. Moreover, as we saw in Chapters 5 and 6, members have developed and institutionalized a clear and specific pattern of "high politics" collective response that involves a set of complex and gradual steps and escalating pressures designed to persuade if not force transgressors to restore the democratic order.

This well-established pattern should be a warning to potential transgressors. That is, there are inter-American norms and procedures in place to protect democracy that, if violated, will be applied and will have serious consequences for them and their country. If government leaders and military officers perceive these new inter-American norms, instruments, and procedures as having real consequences if not respected or complied with, then they effectively will serve their preventive purpose. However, if they choose to ignore them, then the hemisphere will continue, sporadically, to see coups or attempted coups, but they will be condemned and not recognized and will eventually collapse as in Venezuela in 2002 or Honduras in 2009. Finally, the collective norms and instruments created for the promotion and protection of democracy must be understood not only as a warning (red light) against violations of the democratic order, with likely serious consequences for transgressions, but also as norms and instruments to prevent or restrain the U.S. Government's temptation to invervene unilaterally, as in Panama in 1989. If collective action to protect or restore democracy works, there is no need for unilateral intervention.

Likewise, the OAS experience with promoting democracy at the technical assistance level (the "low politics" approach) enriches our understanding of the endeavor. As seen in Chapter 7, experience shows us that democracy promotion is a very complex process, which is difficult to plan, organize and implement, as it involves many actors and processes, both national and international. The OAS efforts in this field also teach us that, because of its complexity and sesitivity, democracy assistance requires a clear theoretical focus with a well-identified dependent variable (i.e., the democracy component that the assistance seeks to promote or strengthen), as well as a practical, relevant and effective strategic approach to successfully complete the assistance. The experience also provides the foundation for building a theoretical model which can be useful in analyzing and assessing democracy promotion policies and practices, and can also be used to develop and execute programs designed to promote the consolidation and strengthening of democratic values, practices and institutions. The model offers possibilities for a more clear and focused strategy based on sound theoretical foundations related to political culture and institution-building.

Thus, using and applying "high politics" juridical and diplomatic instruments, as well as "low politics" instruments of technical assistance, member states, through the OAS, have contributed significantly to the development of a useful and effective methodology for the promotion and consolidation of democracy in the hemisphere. As result, the institution gained considerable usefulness and prestige in the mid 1980s and through the 1990s. This renewed relevance had been lost as several dictatorships, military or otherwise, plagued and fragmented the hemisphere during the 1960s and 1970s, essentially paralyzing the Organization and compelling it to concentrate on technical issues of socioeconomic development and cooperation, along, of course, with its traditional role of guaranteeing security and the peaceful resolution of conflict.[3]

The OAS Has Extended Its Reach

The new role of the OAS in the defense and promotion of democracy represents a significant expansion of its traditional competency to "strengthen peace and security in the hemisphere" in the face of external aggression—originally assigned to it in the Rio Treaty of 1948, and in the OAS Charter as modified in 1967.[4] Today, the OAS role has expanded to include the promotion and protection of democracy against *internal or domestic* aggression or threats to its existence. In contrast to collective defense against external aggression, however, there is no institutionalized provision for the OAS to use force to protect democracy from its internal enemies, except in a hypothetical case in which an internal aggression (e.g., communist guerrilla insurgency or military coup) overthrows the democratic order in one member state and turns into an external threat to another member state. In this case, conceivably, democratic member states would collectively or individually come to the rescue of the deposed democratic authorities, would imposed sanctions on the transgressor, and would even use force or the threat of force to restore democracy. Nevertheless, these fundamental and unprecedented changes represent profound challenges to the traditional concepts of sovereignty and non-intervention.[5]

Moreover, because of its new role and experience with promoting and defending democracy, the OAS has become a leader and model regional organization in developing and applying norms and practical instruments for democracy promotion, and as such, it has contributed to, and is an integral part of the global network and effort to promote and protect democracy around the world. In 2002 and 2007, for example, the OAS and the National Democratic Institute (NDI) organized an international meeting on electoral observation with representatives from several likeminded institutions to share experiences and develop common standards and methodology for electoral monitoring, and to implement efforts to continue to ensure the integrity of EOMs.[6]

The Obsolescence of Coups d'état

One lesson and corollary that surfaces from the member states' application of the new OAS norms and instruments to promote and protect democracy is that coups d'état will no longer be accepted, domestically or regionally, as a means of changing governments. Member states will not recognize governments that overthrow legitimate constitutional governments through violence (coups) or irregular, illegal and unconstitutional procedures (auto-coups or legislative coups). As we have seen, given an irregular interruption of the democratic process anywhere in the hemisphere, members will take immediate and decisive collective action through the OAS, or individually (if capable of doing so), to attempt to reverse it. Or, if there is an attempted coup in progress, members will seek to stop it and prevent the breakdown of the democratic order. Transgressors will be sanctioned and suspended from participating in OAS activities. Whatever action is taken, it will almost always entail the invocation and application of the Democratic Charter. The lesson is that there is no longer any room in the Americas for military governments or for governments that result from an unconstitutional takeover as in the past. [7]

The Waning Principle of Non-intervention

The collective commitment to promote and protect democracy is also a welcome challenge to the traditional absolute and all-inclusive principle of non-intervention. This is a positive development in inter-American affairs and reflects the strength of the new OAS norms and instruments. Although the non-intervention principle remains a bedrock at the core of the inter-American system, in recent times it has been challenged and eroded by the democracy principle that, arguably, has gained supremacy in inter-American affairs. In this view, collective "intervention" to protect democracy and human rights has superseded the traditional notion of non-intervention. Violations of human rights and interruption of the democratic order are no longer exclusively internal affairs. Their promotion and protection have become regional, hemispheric and international concerns as well as the obligation of member states. Democracy, like human rights, is indivisible; if violated in one place is violated everywhere. Illegal or unconstitutional governments that violate either or both can no longer hide behind the principle of non-intervention or absolute state sovereignty. [8] To paraphrase Thomas Franck, states that agreed voluntarily to join a democratic community that promotes and protects democracy and human rights do not have the right to invoke the principle of non-intervention when they themselves violate these principles; that is the price they must pay for belonging to a democratic community (Franck, "The Democratic Entitlement" 1994, 2) (Franck, "The Emerging Right to Democratic Governance" 1992). The invocation (mainly for domestic consumption) of the non- intervention principle by governments intent on preventing collective monitoring of their violations of democratic principles and norms that every member states has voluntarily agreed to promote and defend becomes unjustified and disingenuous.

The principle of non-intervention is no longer supreme or operative when human rights and the principles of democracy are violated. In today's interdependent world, collective or unilateral political/diplomatic "intervention" to protect democracy and human rights is justified and seems unavoidable. Even humanitarian military interventions are likely to be legitimate if gross violations of human rights occur. Although less probable today, military interventions, collective or unilateral, can be expected in extreme cases of violation of the democratic order. This is particularly likely after collective threats of or actual sanctions fail to prevent the collapse of democracy or to restore it, and if the violations are gross and the new *de facto* regime appears to threaten regional peace and security. Nevertheless, there will be governments that will abuse it for internal purposes, to try to cover up violations of democratic practices and human rights.

Moreover, in recent years, the principle of non-intervention has lost some of its absolute force and has gradually receded in the face of the inexorable reality of globalization, interdependence, transnationalism and the process of integration itself. In fact, some observers are already claiming that the international system has by now accepted a degree of "interventionism" as legitimate and even "legal" or permitted by international norms.[9] In its extreme expression, this manifests itself in humanitarian military intervention, on a collective basis, authorized by regional organizations such as the OAS, the North Atlantic Treaty Organization (NATO) or the United Nations. From this perspective, this new interventionism is motivated and justified by serious violations of human rights, and by the collapse of the rule of law and constitutional democracy—conditions which in turn are perceived as a threat to the peace and security of neighboring countries or to the region as a whole. Interestingly enough, the existence of this kind of threat in the Americas was recognized as early as 1959 at the Fifth Meeting of Consultation of Ministers of Foreign Affairs in the Declaration of Santiago.

Notwithstanding the limitations posed by the use and misuse of the non-intervention principle, it is perhaps a promising and significant sign that, in the context of the new democratic paradigm that has emerged since the mid-eighties and reflected in the Democratic Charter, the collective "interventionist" decisions and actions taken in application of the existing instruments to promote and defend democracy, in the final analysis, have proven to be useful and effective in several cases. As shown in Chapters 5 and 6, those collective "interventions" in favor of democracy have contributed significantly to reversing institutional breakdowns, as in Peru, Guatemala, Venezuela and Honduras or to avoiding them, as in Paraguay and Bolivia. In Haiti, although these actions did not have the desired effect immediately, pressure was maintained and served as a basis for decisions by the United Nations Security Council authorizing the use of force to oust General Cédras' *de facto* government.[10]

In short, arguably, the non-intervention principle has been losing ground as absolute and all-encompassing, as it has been undermined and even superseded by the democracy principle.

The Doctrine of Collective Security for Democracy

From a realist perspective, the joint principles of absolute sovereignty and non-intervention wil be challenged and not respected if the security of the democratic order in a member state is in imminent danger. This is illustrated by recalling the Colombia's armed forces' violation of Ecuadorian territorial sovereignty on the occasion of their hot pursuit of FARC guerrillas forces, on March 1, 2008, when its leader, Raul Reyes (Mono Jojoy), was killed.

Most OAS member states viewed this incursion as a military intervention in a neighboring country and as "a violation of the sovereignty and territorial integrity of Ecuador" and thus proceeded to condemn and reject it.[11] On the other hand, from a realist angle, this event can be interpreted in terms of the supreme obligation any government has to safeguard the existence of its own state, guarantee the security of its citizens and defend its vital interests and values, such as freedom and democracy. As such, the military attack and killing of the guerilla leader could be considered an act of self-defense consistent with its supreme obligation—an incursion that was just and appropriate for the defense of the Colombian democratic state, threatened by the FARC. Furthermore, it is consistent with Art. 23 of the OAS Charter which asserts that "measures taken for the maintenance of peace and security...do not constitute a violation of the principles set forth in Arts. 19 and 21," which refer to the non-intervention principle and the territorial inviolability of a member state.

Moreover, arguably, the military attack was not against the Ecuadorian government, its armed forces or people; it was not intended to invade, occupy, acquire, or annex territory or to appropriate resources. Neither was it an attempt against the sovereignty or political independence of the Ecuadorian government. The true enemy and target was not Ecuador but the FARC, the principal threat against the Colombian democracy, given their use of torture, assassinations, kidnapping, bombings, their manifested anti-democratic ideology, and their connection to narco-trafficking. The FARC, with camps in Ecuador, are the real violators of its territorial integrity and sovereignty (unless their presence had the consent of the Ecuadorian government), the true aggressors and threat to security, peace and democracy not only in Colombia but in the region.

The Colombian action can also be explained by what can be called the doctrine of "democratic realism" and its corollary, "collective security for democracy." This doctrine is based on the premise that (1) democracy is a principal political value or public good, and the preferred form of government in the Americas; that (2) the people of the Americas have the right to democracy and their government "the obligation to promote it and defend it" as established in 2001 in the Democratic Charter; and (3) that a threat to any democracy in the inter-American system, by an irregular force such as the

FARC, intent on overthrowing the government, is indeed a threat to all democracies in the hemisphere, as well as to its security and peace; and 4) that countries will act unilaterally if they perceive their security and democratic regime threatened and no collective cooperation is forthcoming (in this case from Venezuela or Ecuador).

However, for many members in the OAS, the Colombian military incursion into Ecuador violated the non-intervention principle and generated significant tension in the hemisphere, particularly with its "leftist" neighbors and those member states which still hang on anachronistically to an inflexible conception of the non-intervention principle, and who frequently misuse it to cover up or disguise their own violations of the democracy principle. Nevertheless, no coalition or majority of member states could be gathered to activate sanctions against the Colombian government, except for an innocuous Permanent Council declaration condemning the incursion. Security (democratic, in this case) trumped non-intervention, again.

In short, from a "realist" perspective, in today's hemisphere, "interventions" are inevitable when democracy, security and peace are at stake, whether or not analysts, international officials or some governments consider them illegal, unfair and contrary to elemental principles of a peaceful and "democratic" international coexistence. The doctrine of collective security for democracy will trump the principle of non-intervention, particularly when there exist extreme situations that exhibit a clear and present danger to the security and peaceful existence of a democratic state or the region. In these cases, extreme violations of the democratic order and of the non-intervention principle by a non-democratic regime will trigger the application of coercive economic/financial and commercial sanctions and/or military intervention from a group of concerned states or unilaterally from a powerful individual state, to eliminate what is perceived as a threat to their collective vital national interests, and to preserve or restore democracy.

Thus, violations of the dual non-intervention and absolute sovereignty principles by those states concerned with the security of the democratic order in a member state will inevitably generate tensions and friction with those states that anachronistically cling to these principles, but also with those states that blatantly misuse them to cover their own violations of fundamental principles of their own democracies and of their commitment to the IADC.

The Presence of the U.S. and Canada

One of the main strengths of the OAS today has to do with U.S and Canadian membership, which makes the Organization truly inter-American and the only forum where all the countries of the hemisphere can gather to dialogue, negotiate and cooperate in relevant inter-mestic issues that periodically challenge the hemisphere, but particularly in those related to democracy, human rights, peace and security. This inevitably enhances the Organization's relevance, due to the significant presence of two of the most powerful developed democracies in the world. Canada entered the OAS in 1990 and ever since has provided leadership and strategic financial support for the OAS role in promoting and defending democracy and human rights in the hemisphere (Major 2007) (Cooper 2003). The U.S., on the other hand, as we have seen, has been a prominent player in inter-American relations (both conflictive and cooperative) and in the foundation of the OAS in 1948. And, as expected, the U.S. has been one of the major promoters of democracy in the region as an active participant and strong supporter (diplomatically and financially) of the development and application of the OAS norms and instruments to promote democracy and the observance of human rights.[12]

As of late, however, superpower status in the hemisphere has not translated into diplomatic victories at the OAS. U.S. diplomats are not always able to achieve Latin American consensus for their objectives. For example, an American proposal to strengthen mechanisms for preventing constitutional breakdowns was widely and publicly rejected during the 1999 General Assembly in Guatemala. Nor could the Bush Administration obtain consensus, at the June 2005 General Assembly in Fort Lauderdale, Florida, on a proposal to allow the Permanent Council to monitor and assess the evolution of democracy in the Americas and to have nongovernmental organizations more involved (by advising and testifying) in the proceedings of the Organization when dealing with democracy crises (Hawking and Shaw 2007, 28–29). In November of that year, the U.S. push for a Free Trade Area of the Americas (FTAA) was soundly rejected in the Summit of the Americas in Mar del Plata, Argentina.[13]

Neither is the presence of the superpower in the Organization always necessarily negative or counterproductive. The U.S. (and Canada) has played a significant and decisive role, multilaterally and unilaterally, in protecting and restoring democracy in the cases examined in previous Chapters—even if some critics are not totally convinced of U.S. commitment to democracy in the Americas and elsewhere,[14] and even if it is impossible to prevent intervention by the U.S. when its security is threatened. The presence in the OAS of the most powerful democracy in the world, whose foreign policy usually promotes democracy for moral/ideological and strategic reasons can not only be a force for the survival and consolidation of democracy in the Americas, but can also be a guarantee for the security of its members.[15]

CONCLUSION

As it is, then, the OAS today remains the central and most important institution of the inter-American system. It draws its strengths from its norms and instruments, and also from the context they helped create, as reflected in the emergence of IADR and the Doctrine of Collective Security for Democracy. It is still the only multilateral institution where all the democratic countries of the hemisphere can assemble to dialogue, negotiate and cooperate. It is the main source of legal and historical reference for the most important hemispheric norms, mechanisms and instruments institutionalized in conventions, treaties, declarations, and resolutions that regulate and condition the interaction of the hemisphere's nation-states.[16] In this increasingly globalized and interdependent world, where crucial *inter-mestic* issues and challenges (such as democracy, human rights protection, peace, and security guarantees) cannot be managed unilaterally but require cooperation and multilateral action, the relevance of international organizations like the OAS cannot be ignored or dismissed (Keohane 1998). International organizations and multilateral cooperation do indeed provide the fora and the mechanisms that help generate order in this virulent and turbulent transnational world, where the state is no longer the exclusive actor. Furthermore, despite its present limitations and weaknesses (addressed next), the OAS is the hemispheric focal point for collective efforts to dissuade attempts to disrupt the institutional and democratic integrity of member states, or to restore democratic institutions if interrupted. It legitimizes and immediately triggers inter-American and international cooperation and "intervention" in reaction to imminent or actual institutional breakdown.

NOTES

1. http://www.latinobarometro.org/documentos/LATBD_INFORME_LB_2013.pdf. It is interesting to note, however, that this preference does not translate into equal satisfaction with democracy, which has been standing at around 40% in the last few years, and, which, incidentally, is similar to the satisfaction with democracy in Europe. Likewise, satisfaction with or approval of governments is moderate (49%).

2. Ten years ago, in his chapter "The taming of democracy," Smith argued that electoral democracies no longer pose a threat to the traditional oligarchies, the socioeconomic elites from the upper and middle classes or to the military sector, and were likely to survive but not necessarily thrive in the short run. According to his somewhat pessimistic assessment, at that time, Latin American democracies still faced daunting socioeconomic challenges as reflected in popular disenchantment with continuing poverty and inequality, as well as formidable political challenges from the undemocratic orientation of the majority of citizens, from their mistrust of politicians and democratic political institutions and from the very weakness of these institutions (Smith 2005, 313–46). On the hand, Professor Drake, with a somewhat more sanguine architectural analogy, concluded that while the foundation of democracy has been built (as symbolized by the pervasiveness of elections), it remained to be seen whether the edifice constructed upon it will "stand the test of time" or whether it will be tumbled "once more by anarchy or tyranny" (Drake 2009, 249).

3. It must be noted here that the hemisphere has been a relatively peaceful region for much of the twentieth century. While the hemisphere experienced various geopolitical and traditional territorial/border wars and disputes (such as the 1932–35 Chaco war between Bolivia and Paraguay; the five-day "soccer war" between Honduras and El Salvador in 1969, and the Ecuador-Peru border conflict in 1995), as well as low-intensity, ideologically-driven guerrilla warfare that spilled over national boundaries in Central America up to the late 1980s, they did not erupt into fully-fledged regional wars. Moreover, the long-standing inter-American instruments for peaceful resolution of conflict, including the Rio Treaty (1947), the Pact of Bogotá (1948) and the OAS (1948), have played a significant moderating role to that effect (Nye 1968) (Infante 1977) (Orrego-Vicuña 1977). But with the end of the ideological Cold War and its belligerent repercussions throughout the hemisphere, and the collapse of military regimes and the subsequent emergence of democratic regimes, the likelihood of traditional armed conflict in the hemisphere has declined considerably, although there remain long-standing territorial disputes that are, however, in the process of peaceful resolution under international law. For a description of these lingering conflicts/disputes from a relatively pessimistic (realistic?) perspective characteristic of the early 1980s, see (Child 1985) (Morris and Millan 1983).

4. It should be borne in mind that the Rio Treaty was not intended only to defend the hemisphere and its members from an armed attack emanating from outside the hemisphere, as some critics claim, but rather as a system of collective defense against an attack by any state, hemispheric or otherwise, on a member state. In fact, the Rio Treaty has been invoked and applied *only* in the case of intra-hemispheric conflicts, and particularly among states that comprise the wider Caribbean region. See "Aplicaciones del TIAR" and it relation to democracy in García Amador (1981, 811, 852).

5. The beginnings of this analysis can be found in (Farer 1996), and particularly in Tesón's work (1996).

6. Participants included the European Union, the Organization for Security and Cooperation in Europe (OSCE), the United Nations, the Organization of African Unity (OAU), the Asian Network for Free Elections (ANFREL), Elections Canada, the Carter Center, the International Foundation for Electoral Systems, (IFES), the Commonwealth Secretariat, the Institute for Democracy and Electoral Assistance from Sweden (IDEA) and others.

7. The reference is to the resolution "Support for Democratic Government in Venezuela," CP/RES.576 (887/92) of February 4, 1992, and is in keeping with the statement of Strobe Talbott, the U.S. Under Secretary of State, at the meeting of the Permanent Council on the attempted coup in Venezuela, in which he made it clear that "the days of dictatorship are over."

8. The concern over violation of them is not part of an imperialist and interventionist plot as Presidents Morales, Ortega and Chávez/Maduro have frequently claimed or would like us to believe; it is a genuine concern of the democrats of this hemisphere.

9. See the excellent analysis of this issue by Fernando R. Tesón, who proposes that collective and humanitarian military intervention, authorized by the United Nations for the purpose of remedying serious violations of human rights, is legitimate in current circumstances (1996, 29–51). For Slater, collective action in defense of democracy should not be regarded as Interventionism; see his chapter "The OAS as Anti-dictatorial Alliance" (Slater 1967, 183–216). On the other hand, consider Nye's warning on the perils of this kind of interventionism (The New National Interest 1999.

10. See Vio-Grossi (1998, 113). According to T. Franck, the decision of the U.N. Security Council established a precedent by permitting the use of force, on the grounds that violations of human rights and the right to democracy constituted a threat to the peace of the region (Franck, "The Democratic Entitlement" 1994, 9).

11. See Consejo Permanente de la OEA 5 de Marzo, 2008; Meeting of Consultation of Ministers of Foreign Affairs 4 April 2008. The U.S. delegation added the following statement to the Foreign Ministers' resolution: "The United States of America supports this resolution's effort to build confidence between Colombia and Ecuador to address the underlying crisis. The United States of America is not prepared to agree with the conclusion in operative paragraph 4 in that it is highly fact-specific and fails to take account of other provisions of the OAS and United Nations Charters; in any event, neither this resolution nor CP/RES. 930 (1632/08)

affects the right of self-defense under Article 22 of the OAS Charter and Article 51 of the U.N. Charter."

12. See also Corrales and Feinberg (1999), A. Valenzuela (1997), Vaky and Muñoz (1993), Major (2007), Shaw (2007), Villagran (1993), Smith (2005), Diamond (2008), and a speech by the U.S. Secretary of State, Madeleine Albright, at the School of Advanced International Studies, SAIS, January 17, 2000.

13. See also Slater (1967, 242–51 and 274–5).

14. See Carothers, *Revitalizing Democracy Assistance. The Challenge of USAID* (2009), Diamond (2008), Piccone, "The Democracy Agenda in the Americas: The Case for Multilateral Action" (2011) and A. Valenzuela (2002). On the U.S. role promoting democracy see also Chapter 4.

15. In this context and in that of the IADR, the U.S. could play a significant political/ security and economic role, along with other hemispheric "powers," in promoting prosperity and guaranteeing security in the hemisphere. In a likely twenty-first century world of regions and transnational turbulence and insecurity, this is not a possibility to be dismissed lightly, particularly in the face of increasing transnational terrorism and cyber-war, climate change and natural disasters, not to mention a possible future of inter-regional and global conflict, made possible by the new technology in weapons (including space weapons) and transportation, which has made any region of the world reachable from anywhere and susceptible to aggression. However, in order for the IADR and the Western Hemispheric Idea to become a reality and viable entity, the U.S. has to be more engaged in promoting and defending democracy and in cooperating and developing partnerships to generate prosperity and stability, and would have to abandon its anachronistic Cuban embargo, which has been a source of criticism and unnecessary tension with many Latin American Governments. Two recent U.S. regional initiatives, one for prosperity in Central America and the other for energy security in the Caribbean, may indicate movement in this direction. This is, of course, in addition to free trade agreements with several countries in the hemisphere, which can be the foundation for revisiting the 1990s idea of a free trade zone for the Americas.

16. Although for many critics of the Organization, the resolutions of the General Assembly are meaningless, superficial, or irrelevant, the process of final approval is complex. These resolutions are usually the result or conclusion of a long process of debate, analysis, and negotiation, which begins with informal and committee level talks among Foreign Ministers and representatives of the countries in the Permanent Council and General Assembly meetings. Only after considerable drafting and efforts to achieve consensus are they finally forwarded to the plenary session of the General Assembly. At any rate, the point is that the resulting regulations (Resolution 1080, for example) do end up influencing the external and internal conduct of member states.

Chapter Ten

Institutional Tensions and Weaknesses

INTRODUCTION: BASIC TENSIONS

Despite its newly regained relevance and strengths, as a result of the adoption of norms and instruments to promote and defend democracy, and the considerable progress made in their application, the Organization and the IADR still face some institutional challenges, derived mainly from basic tensions and limitations inherent in it, and more broadly, from the current ideologically-fragmented state of affairs in inter-American geo-politics. These represent weaknesses or shortcomings and contextual constraints that limit the OAS effectiveness and potential for preventing the erosion of democracy in certain member states.

The tensions the Organization faces are overlapping and intimately related to the ubiquitous all-embracing principle of non-intervention: One is between institutional autonomy and dependency, embodying tensions resulting from the frequently uneasy relationship between the collective bodies (member states) and the General Secretariat, mostly around issues of management and leadership, and from the exclusive domination of the executive branch over other branches of government of "equal" power in the affairs of the Organization. Another tension results from the interaction between institutional obligations and non-compliance with norms, which includes violation of the bedrock principle of non-intervention and non-compliance with the new collective commitment to promote and defend democracy (the "democracy principle"). And finally, there are the tensions and limitations resulting from hemispheric ideological/political differences and fragmentation, which impede multilateral consensus, and paralyze and marginalize the Organization from effectively performing its role of promoting and preserving democracy.

TENSIONS BETWEEN INSTITUTIONAL DEPENDENCY AND AUTONOMY

The OAS (including its collective bodies and the Secretary General) is not an autonomous multilateral entity that can act unilaterally without the consent of its member states. It is not a supranational body, independent of its members, nor is it monolithic institution. This nature of the Organization tends to limit or constrain what it can do in performing its new role of promoting and defending democracy. OAS critics frequently ignore this fact and demand from it actions that have a very low probability of being carried out.

The Collective Governing Bodies

Like most intergovernmental institutions, the OAS is a political/diplomatic Organization of thirty-five member states, with various collective decision-making organs such as the General Assembly, the Meeting of Consultation of Ministers of Foreign Affairs, the Permanent Council, and others, which are the governing bodies of the Organization. But ultimately, the collective pronouncements and actions of these bodies depend on the decisions of each member state's Permanent Representative (Ambassador), who follows his or her Foreign Ministry's decisions. That is, not even the governing bodies are autonomous.

An excessive dependence of the collective bodies on the member states' Foreign Ministries can have a delaying or paralyzing effect on the decision-making process of the Organization, particularly if Ministries do not have adequate human resources to follow closely the evolution of issues in the OAS and are thus unable to formulate positions and communicate instructions fluidly. This can occur especially during considerations of non-emergency issues at the regular meetings of the Permanent Council, when Ambassadors address them without direct instructions from their Foreign Ministries at home. In these cases, the diplomatic decision-making is overly cautious, slow and frequently based on the lowest common denominator (as in many other multilateral intergovernmental organizations). However, in times of crisis or urgent matters (like a coup d'état), those Ministries obviously pay due attention to OAS deliberations, Ambassadors always act on instructions, and decision-making is swift and lasts whatever time it takes to reach consensus on a resolution. Only occasionally will an Ambassador intervene in debates and vote on serious consequential issues without consultation or instructions from the Foreign Ministry, at the risk of being de-authorized and even fired.[1] Both cases nevertheless are indicative of the governing collective body's lack of broad autonomy. This institutional dependency is a frequent source of OAS ineffectiveness or inaction.

The Secretary General

The limited autonomy of the Organization is also reflected in the responsibilities and roles assigned to the General Secretariat through the OAS Charter and the IADC. While this is a central and permanent organ of the Organization, its powers are limited by the Charter and members' mandates. The Secretary General is elected for a period of five years by a simple majority of member states and can be re-elected for one additional term.

Originally, member states sought to limit the powers of the General Secretariat and are, to this day, very cautious about ceding their sovereignty and giving "interventionist" supranational powers to the office. The extent and effectiveness of its formal allowed powers, however, depend on the Secretary General's informal leadership ability to maximize his considerable administrative powers to manage and shape the internal bureaucracy and on his diplomatic skills to negotiate with member states' Ambassadors and build consensus around his initiatives.[2] The interplay between his formally assigned powers and his informal ones is in constant flux and is a source of frequent conflict and tension between the General Secretariat and the governing bodies.

A superficial understanding of this complex relationship will commonly lead to the misconception and presumption that the OAS it is an independent, autonomous organization, controlled or directed at will by the Secretary General, who may then be unrealistically expected to make decisions or take actions that are not within his competence/jurisdiction.

Nevertheless, since the 1985 Charter modifications and the signing of the IADC in 2001, the power of the Secretary General has expanded with new and broader political and diplomatic responsibilities, particularly in the area of democracy promotion. The principal functions of the Office of the Secretary General now include carrying out the duties entrusted to it by these new instruments and by mandates from the General Assembly and other governing bodies' resolutions. These involve, among others: being the legal representative of the Organization and, informally, its spokesperson; participating "with voice but without vote in all meetings of the Organization;" bringing to the attention of the governing bodies "any matter which in his opinion might threaten the peace and security of the hemisphere, or the development of the member states;" promoting cooperation among them; preparing and proposing a program-budget for the Organization and, once approved by the General Assembly, executing it; presenting an annual report; and providing a host of administrative and support service to the governing bodies.[3]

Also, according to the IADC, the Secretary General, "in the event of an unconstitutional alteration of the constitutional regime that seriously impairs the democratic order in a member state," may convene a meeting of the Permanent Council in order "to undertake a collective assessment of the situation" (Art. 20); may organize EOMs and provide technical assistance "for strengthening and developing their electoral institutions upon request from a member state" (Art. 23), and may "carry out programs and activities designed to promote democratic principles and practices and strengthen a democratic culture in the hemisphere" (Art. 26).

In terms of the latter attributes, within the general mandate to promote democracy and with the Secretary General's approval, the Secretariat for Political Affairs has certain leeway (as the UPD had had earlier) to promote, suggest and execute technical assistance programs to strengthen democratic institutions and the democratic political culture in member states. Indeed, programs like those examined previously to promote democratic values and strengthen democratic institutions, can take on a limited life of their own, particularly if they are carried out in consultation and coordination with relevant and politically well-connected institutions, so that the Foreign Ministry of a nation will not object to their implementation. Within such a parameters, those programs do have a degree of autonomy, and can amount to a relatively independent contribution to promoting democracy.

Likewise, although prudence and tradition requires that the Secretary General consult and inform member states regularly before proceeding, the new attributes allow, if not oblige him, for example, to act with greater autonomy to respond without delay to threats to the democratic order. Within this framework, the last three Secretaries General have convened immediately the Permanent Council in cases of a threat to the democratic order or its actual interruption in a member state. Their actions activated rapid collective responses in defense of democracy in the cases Haiti (1991), Peru (1992), Venezuela (1992), Guatemala (1993) Paraguay (1996), Bolivia (2008), Honduras (2009) and Ecuador (2010), as analyzed in Chapters 5 and 6.[4]

As we have also seen, in 2000 Secretary General Gaviria made a personal effort to "save" President Bucarám from being ousted by an irregular act of the Ecuadorian legislature, to no avail and to his own public humiliation by opposition forces and the national press. He also made a personal effort in 2004 in Venezuela to mediate between then President Chávez and the political opposition. While he did get both parties to agree to a recall referendum, the effort, which lasted almost a year, in the end failed to reconcile the parties or diminish the political confrontation and polarization between the *chavistas* and the opposition. In fact, both sides became dissatisfied and quite critical of his mission's performance. The opposition was disappointed by the recall results and by Gaviria's refusal to disqualify it as fraud, while Chávez thought that his mission favored the opposition and interfered in the country's internal affairs.[5]

In many ways, Chávez' dissatisfaction with Gaviria's performance parallels the *chavistas'* negative view of Secretary General Insulza's conduct vis-à-vis Venezuela in recent years. Presidents Chávez and Maduro, and the Venezuelan Ambassador to the OAS, have publicly chided and insulted Insulza for his comments (albeit always timid) on violations of press freedoms, military participation in politics or students' protests. The *chavista* regime vetoed Insulza's attempts to visit Venezuela during the student strikes and demonstrations in front of the OAS offices in Caracas (April 2011), and has refused to invite OAS/EOMs since 2006.

More recently, Maduro's government and the *chavista* alliance at the OAS rejected as "interventionist" Insulza's call—in support of Panama's proposal—for an open discussion of the Venezuelan situation in the Permanent Council, *à propos* of the political crisis resulting from new student demonstrations throughout the country (February 2014).[6] Additionally, Maduro's Government disregarded the Secretary General's suggestion that the OAS facilitate a dialogue between the government and the opposition—which the government had promised to initiate.[7] Instead, Maduro invited UNASUR to enable the dialogue (now discontinued), precluding the OAS from any role in the process. For all intents and purpose, the *chavista* regime and its coalition at the OAS have not simply checked the Secretary General's autonomy but effectively also marginalized the Organization from exercising its mandate to promote democracy in Venezuela.

On the other hand, Secretary General Insulza has not chosen to use his authority (albeit limited) to actively promote democracy in Venezuela. While supporting the Panamanian initiative at the PC/OAS, he misleadingly and gratuitously commented afterwards that the "OAS will not intervene in Venezuela," as, in his view, conditions in that country did not merit the Democratic Charter's application.[8] His was an unnecessary comment since the majority of member states had already refused to even discuss in a public session the Venezuelan situation or allow Venezuelan National Assembly's member, María Corina Machado, to speak in the Permanent Council from the Panamanian chair, let alone send a fact-finding or dialogue- promoting diplomatic mission. He is correct to say that the OAS would not "intervene," but only in so far as the present hemispheric correlation of forces in favor of the *chavista* alliance would not permit it.

During his period in office (2005–2015), Insulza, while occasionally receiving opposition figures and students leaders, has never attempted to bring the issue of Venezuela's eroding democracy for a collective discussion in the Permanent Council as the Democratic Charter allows him to do. Nor has he raised the issue publicly in the media, using the "power of the pulpit." The limitations and impediments imposed on the Secretary General's role by an increasingly authoritarian, intolerant and "rejectionist" *chavista* regime, should not, nevertheless, prevent him, strictly speaking, from resorting to his authorized "powers." Since the regime has unconstitutionally altered the democratic order, the Secretary General can indeed convene a meeting of the Permanent Council "to undertake a collective assessment of the situation," or at least to bring it to the attention of the governing bodies.

Realistically, however, given the existing diplomatic majority of the *chavista* coalition in the OAS, such initiative is unlikely to prosper, as it would not even get sufficient votes to be included in the agenda of the OAS Permanent Council. The *chavista* regime and its allies would scorn the move. Nevertheless it would certainly get media and public attention and at least demonstrate to democrats in Venezuela and the hemisphere the Secretary's democratic conviction and political courage to uphold the Inter-American Democratic Charter.[9] A collective action by the OAS in defense of democracy (e.g., with a resolution calling attention to the alteration) would not be "interventionist", as it falls under the collective responsibility and commitment to defend democracy agreed upon in IADC by all member states, including Venezuela.

But the above shows, regretfully, that given the Secretary General's limited powers and dependence on the will of the member states and the correlation of forces among them, it is useless to ask him to activate the IADC by himself, or to unilaterally criticize hemispheric transgressors and their violations of the Charter, without the consensus of the member states and/or the consent of the countries involved. It also shows that an ideologically-fragmented OAS, lacking the leadership to generate the consensus needed to promote and protect democracy, is limited in its ability to effectively prevent its erosion, particularly when it takes place behind the veil of fraudulent democracies and non-interventionism (Perina, "Hemisferio Fragmentado" 2014) (Perina, "Ganadores y Perdedores en la OEA" 2014).

Nevertheless, as we have seen, member states and the Secretary General have certain autonomy in invoking the IADC to collectively assess "the unconstitutional alterations" of the democratic order in a member state. But in cases where the alteration of the constitutional regime is less self-evident than a coup and takes place in the form of a gradual process of institutional degradation (a coup in slow motion), member states and the Secretary General are reluctant to call for a collective assessment of the situation. The reluctance results not only from the lack of a clear definition of what exactly is an "alteration" of the democratic order, but also from the certainty that those who attempt such a move will be chastised as interventionist, if not as lackeys of U.S. "imperialism." In those cases, the Secretary General cannot even visit the country without the consent of the government involved.

Thus, in the broad context of the tension between the principle of non-intervention and the democracy principle, these institutional limitations represent a weakness of the Organization that at times has the effect of paralyzing it in its democracy-promoting role. Critics should take note of the limiting institutional reality.

Management and Leadership Deficiencies and Shortcomings

As shown in Chapter 7, technical assistance programs are useful instruments for democracy promotion, and at the OAS they played a significant role. However, as presently carried out by the Secretariat for Political Affairs (formerly the UPD), democracy promotion programs face serious internal shortcomings that need to be addressed, if they are to regain their prominence in promoting democracy, beyond electoral observation and assistance. [10]

OAS democracy promotion programs, in general, lack adequate human and financial resources to perform their tasks and are frankly limited to "safe" subjects that do not raise eyebrows among member states. While important in themselves, they do not directly address issues concerning key democratic institutions and processes such political parties and legislatures, decentralization and local governance, or the promotion of democratic values and practices and the development of new democratic leadership. These subjects and their "technical/political" cooperation activities had a substantive presence in the programmatic agenda of the UPD (well recognized in many member states), but were downgraded and/or eliminated and substituted with more "political" activities after 2005—to the point of dropping the word democracy from the title of the new Secretariat for Political Affairs (SPA). This was a minor but significant message (intentional or not) to the detriment of the Organization's democracy promotion role.

These weaknesses are not isolated, but in fact are related to a generalized malaise in administrative and management matters plaguing the wider General Secretariat: The Organization has too many mandates from the member states and, as a result, the General Secretariat manages a diverse if somewhat esoteric portfolio of programs and projects of technical cooperation in its Secretariat for Integral Development.

Integral development is a program area where the Organization has been working for years, and it is a field that can and does include mandates or requests for cooperation in almost any issue related to socioeconomic development. [11] Its inclusion as a pillar in the new Strategic Vision for the OAS once more indicates the member states' incapacity or lack of political will to agree to reduce or prioritize their mandates and related technical assistance programs–so that they can be adjusted to the Organization's limited budgetary resources and true priorities, which should be democracy, human rights and security and peace. The OAS does not have the technical expertise, human resources or the budgetary means to provide adequate technical cooperation services in so many areas of socioeconomic development; these would be best provided by the Inter-American Development Bank (IDB), the Andean Development Corporation (CAF), the Caribbean Development Bank (CDB) or the World Bank. Persistent inclusion of integral development also ignores the Secretary General's recommendation to reduce mandates and programs or to increase the member states' quotas to finance them. The Secretary General has frequently suggested concentrating OAS activities on what it can do best and where it can really make a difference (Secretary General of the OAS April 2013, 12). Thus, programs for democracy and human rights which should be the Organization's priorities and for which it does have comparative advantage and the potential to make significant contributions, do not have sufficient financial and human resources assigned to them. For the Organization to be proactive and lead a significant and sustained hemispheric cooperative effort in these areas, it must have clear and concise priorities with specific objectives and methodologies, sufficient human and financial resources and fully committed leadership.

Today, the OAS seems to be in a permanent budget-deficit mode, with constant threats of or actual personnel reductions because of unpaid quotas or diminishing voluntary financial contributions by member states or observer countries. But the problem is more profound.

According to a recent study, the Strategic Plan for Management and Modernization, whose stated purpose was to improve efficiency, transparency and accountability in the Organization, the General Secretariat is immersed in a serious administrative/management and leadership quagmire that requires solutions and modernization. Among other things, it points to a General Secretariat that is too fragmented and without adequate communication and coordination among its various offices, mainly as a result of poor leadership and the lack of "single corporate agenda." It reveals the existence of an archaic cumbersome Results-Based Management (RBM) system for "technical" cooperation programs that is "more a hindrance than a help" and that provides "little incentive for officers to use it." The report proposes sixty-eight recommendations to modernize the OAS, which speaks volumes about the current shortcomings and weaknesses of the Organization.[12] Among other things, it calls for "sweeping changes to the way the Secretariat works," including in its "management culture," "the way decisions are made" and "funds allocated," and in "the nature of staff work." It recommends modernizing the communications and technology platform for administrative and budgetary processes and for management of "technical" cooperation programs, so that transactions "become simpler, quicker and more accurate." Finally, it suggests that these shortcomings should be addressed in a coordinated manner between the General Secretariat and the Permanent Council and as part of a jointly agreed Strategic Vision for the Organization (Murray September 2014).[13]

As indicated earlier, the report concurs with the critical assessment and recommendations made in July 2013 by the 113th U.S. Congress.[14] This unusual and incisive Act of Congress followed another harsh assessment made by the Democratic Senators Robert Menéndez and John Kerry and Republican Senators Richard Lugar and Marco Rubio. The critical bipartisan letter sent to the Chair of Permanent Council faulted the Secretary General for budgetary and personnel mismanagement, which, in their view, has demoralized "the Organization's most precious asset, its experienced and talented human capital."[15]

The Secretariat's deficiencies and mismanagement of financial, administrative and personnel matters have discredited it and have generated low morale among the staff, as well as mistrust and criticism among member states' diplomats. OAS staff members, diplomats and external observers have perceived Secretary General Insulza's management style as detached, wavering and "politicized," and as detrimental to the Organization. Equally damaging to it were his frequent "flirtations" with his presidential (October-November 2008) or senatorial candidacy in Chile, which to many indicated a weak commitment to the Organization.[16] These bureaucratic deficiencies do disrupt planning and implementation of programs of cooperation, and generate job insecurity, discontent, poor motivation and non-commitment amongst the staff.

Critics have also questioned the Secretary General's timorous pro-democracy leadership or lack of it. As evidence of his lack of conviction and commitment to the Democratic Charter they point, for example, to his pro-Cuban stance, his deference to Chávez and his regime, and his apparent indifference to violations of human rights in Cuba and democratic principles in Nicaragua, Bolivia, Ecuador and Venezuela. Similarly, staff members have pointed to his lack of interest in and support for or outright elimination of substantive "technical" cooperation programs (except for electoral observation) for democracy promotion that were the backbone of the UPD. In recent years, human rights activists have also been dismayed by his apparent attempts, under pressure by Brazil, Bolivia, Ecuador, Venezuela and others, to undermine and weaken the role of the Inter-American Human Rights Commission.

Not So New Strategic Vision

Perhaps another indication of the declining commitment of some of Latin American member states to promote and defend democracy through the Organization is the disappointingly meager results of the recent special session of the General Assembly held at OAS Headquarters to approve a new Strategic Vision for the Organization. The Assembly adopted strategic guidelines and objectives for the four substantive pillars that member states chose as priorities: 1) Democracy, 2) Human Rights, 2) Integral Development and 4) Multidimensional Security, which are supposed to guide the formulation of the 2015–16 OAS program-budget (Asamblea General Extraordinaria de la OEA, September 4, 2014). [17] However, the new priorities of the Organization are in fact not new areas at all: the Organization has been working on them for the past several years.

On the subject of democracy, after more than two years of debate and negotiations in the Permanent Council, the member states could only agree on the lowest common denominator, a disjointed, not very innovative, timid statement about contributing to the "strengthening of democracy and the consolidation of the rule of law," and about helping to "enhance public administration," to "modernize and strengthen electoral institutions," and to "consolidate a democratic culture"–all of which are supposed to be the strategic objectives for the democracy pillar. This component of the "Vision," however, does not contain any indication as to how its guidelines and objectives are to be achieved. Most surprisingly, the "Strategic Vision" for this fundamental pillar ignores pertinent suggestions made by Secretary General Insulza on strengthening the Inter-American Democratic Charter and the role of the OAS in promoting democracy and preventing the breakdown of the democratic order. It also ignores the several suggestions made by the Permanent Council in its report on the Dialogue about the Effectiveness of the Application of the Inter-American Democratic Charter, some of which are included in this book's recommendations in the final Chapter (Secretary General of the OAS May 2010) (Consejo Permanente de la OEA 14 de diciembre 2011).

The Dominance of the Executive Branch

The executive branch of government has always been the dominant player in inter-state relations and in multilateral intergovernmental organizations. Their representatives (e.g., Foreign Ministers, Ambassadors) have always been the ones who have gathered together to negotiate, draft and sign the treaties or conventions that create multilateral institutions. In most democratic states, the legislative branch of government often has the role of ratifying them. As such, and with the exception of the European Union, which has a relatively independent and relevant European parliament, the OAS is an exclusive club of representatives from the executive branch of the member states' governments. Only the executive branch has the right to be represented and heard in the governing bodies of the Organization.

The dominance of the executive branch over the other branches of government in OAS affairs constitutes another tension and limitation that constrains the OAS role in promoting and preserving representative democracy. Despite the fact that all member states are representative democracies and that they have established that one of the fundamental elements of republican representative democracy is the principle of separation, equality, independence and balance of power among the different branches of government (Art. 3), only the executive branch of each state has the right to be represented and heard at the governing bodies of the Organization. As discussed in Chapter 6 the executive branch is the only branch that can request or authorize a request for assistance from the OAS in cases of political or electoral crises that threaten the democratic order. The same principle applies to electoral observations, which cannot be deployed by the Secretary General without an invitation from the executive branch. Such imbalance in favor of the executive branch provokes a somewhat awkward if not obsolete situation that contradicts the very essence of democracy and of what member states want to accomplish with the Organization.

In cases of political crisis, where the executive branch is violating the Democratic Charter and its own Constitution, the OAS governing bodies cannot dispatch a good-offices political/diplomatic mission, nor can the Secretary General visit the member state without its executive branch's approval. Neither can they consult other branches of governments—in an attempt to facilitate a dialogue or a public assessment of the situation at the Permanent Council that could prevent the breakdown of the democratic order—without the consent of the executive branch. Furthermore, if the Secretary General were to be asked by opposition forces or other branches to "intervene" in the situation, he would likely invoke the principle of non-intervention to avoid a confrontation with and criticism by the Government in question.

However, the reverse is, of course business as usual: Whenever the executive branch, the President specifically, feels threatened by other branches of government or the political opposition in whatever institutional form, this branch can invoke the IADC and request OAS assistance, as we have seen in the cases of Paraguay (1996), Nicaragua (2004), Ecuador (2005–2006), Bolivia (2008) and Guatemala (2009). The President would likely receive assistance immediately, even if it is clear that the executive branch itself is the transgressor, as we have seen in the cases of Bolivia in 2008, Nicaragua in 2008 and Honduras in 2009. Note here, however, that Secretaries General, in cases of political-institutional crises, will always respond diligently to a request for assistance or "intervention" by the President of a country, but not necessarily to a request from representatives from another branches of government or from the media or other sectors of the society (students, for example) when they perceive their rights as being violated or the democratic order as being altered by the executive branch.

Paradoxically, however, *after* a coup d'état has taken place, extensive efforts will be made to include all stakeholders in negotiating a path to restore democracy. The governing bodies always will call on all relevant actors to respect the rule of law, the democratic institutions and the observance of human rights. They will then proceed to send a diplomatic/good offices mission, which will try to persuade the transgressors to restore the deposed Government and, failing that, will convoke all relevant political actors in efforts or generate a process of dialogue and negotiations that may eventually lead to the restoration of the democratic order—usually by calling elections in the short run.

This un-democratic reality within the Organization, as in any intergovernmental organization, does reveal the serious limitations that member states and the Secretary General face in attempting to solve or manage political crises caused by the executive branch, before the collapse of democratic order. In other words, the exclusive predominance of the executive branch essentially limits the OAS, its members and its Secretary General from adequately and effectively carrying out the mandate to promote and protect democracy, particularly in preventing its erosion or its breakdown when the executive branch is the transgressor—as in Honduras in 2009. This exclusiveness generates political and diplomatic tensions and institutional paralysis, especially when it is the executive branch that violates the principles of democratic governance and the Democratic Charter. Other branches of government (the legislative or judicial powers, for example), individual legislators, or state/provincial governors (as in a federal system) from the political opposition, or pertinent nongovernmental organizations such as human rights or freedom of the press advocates, cannot appeal or have official or formal access to the OAS collective organs without the consent of the executive branch. Nor can they request technical/political assistance or electoral observation, without the official approval of their respective governments.

In effect, even in situations of clear and deteriorating political crisis threatening the democratic order in a member state, neither the collective bodies of the Organization nor the Secretary General have the political autonomy to be proactive and engage relevant and legitimate political actors, in order to facilitate a dialogue among all stakeholders that might contribute to a peaceful, civic and democratic solution to such crisis. This elemental, non-interventionist exercise of good offices cannot be pursued without the approval of the executive branch of the member state concerned. Because of this limitation, it can be argued that the failure of the OAS (the Permanent Council or the Secretary General) officially to respond or even listen to denunciations by legitimate, relevant opposition political actors of presidential abuse of power and deliberate alteration of the constitutional democratic order contributed to its collapse in Ecuador in 2005 and in Honduras in 2009, and most certainly it has not averted its deterioration in Venezuela and/or Nicaragua.[18]

INSTITUTIONAL OBLIGATIONS AND NON-COMPLIANCE

It is, of course, incumbent upon OAS member states to respect the Organization's binding Charter, including its norms, purposes, duties and rights, and in some cases the sanctions and obligations derived from its application. Not complying with agreed to norms and obligations generates friction and tension between member states and limits the Organization's effectiveness.

The OAS Charter is an international treaty designed to regulate and channel the international conduct of its member states to guarantee an inter-American order of peace and security. The maintenance of this order today depends on the member states' compliance with their commitment to exercise and promote democracy. Within this framework, OAS members, through the governing bodies, also make collective decisions that are transmitted in the form of resolutions, which may recommend courses of action that the members are expected to respect and execute. Although these OAS resolutions do not, strictly speaking, have the legal binding status of a treaty (with its due ratification process), they do constitute a formal commitment and obligation by the official representatives of the member states and thus must be equally observed and fulfilled. Such is the case with the General Assembly resolution adopting the Inter-American Democratic Charter (IADC).

But then, what happens if member states fail to abide by the norms, principles and obligations of the OAS constituent Charter (e.g., the principle of non-intervention)? Or if they fail to respect the IADC and the collective commitment to exercise democracy and observe human rights? Or if they do not comply with the resolutions of the governing bodies?

The answer is that it depends. The consequences depend on the extent to which the other members of the democratic community feel threatened by the violation and are united and willing, and have the persuasive and coercive capacity, collectively or unilaterally, to enforce compliance with the provisions of the constituent Charter, the IADC or the decisions of the governing bodies.[19] This "realist" argument underscores an inherent OAS limitation: it does not possess the legal authority or capacity to enforce respect for its principles and provisions or, merely by enunciating them, to prevent member states from using force in unilateral interventions or from violating their commitment to exercise democracy.

Despite this room for "non-compliance" due to the OAS's limited ability to enforce its decisions, extreme situations of violation of the core principles of non intervention and democracy in a member state, if deemed by others to pose a clear and present threat to democracy and to the peace and security of the democratic community, will likely trigger the application of even coercive measures from a group of concerned states or unilaterally from a powerful state. As we have seen, in the cases of violation of the non-intervention

principle by the Castro and Trujillo Governments in the early sixties, a majority of member states can take forceful collective actions, such as suspension from the Organization that will have a significant impact on the viola-
tor.[20]

The Principle of Non-intervention vs.
the Collective Commitment to Democracy

The principle of non-intervention is intimately linked with other traditional
principles of inter-American relations and international law, such as absolute
sovereignty, juridical equality of states, and territorial integrity. Latin
American countries have sought to institutionalize respect for those principles since their independence and through the evolution of the inter-
American system. The Calvo (1868) and Drago (1902) doctrines first expressed them with the essential purpose to restrain or contain, at least juridi-
cally, military interventions and occupations carried out by some European
powers in various independent republics, and by the U.S. government during
the first three decades of the twentieth century (in the context of the Monroe
Doctrine and the Roosevelt Corollary). After decades of "negotiations" between Latin American countries and the U.S., the principle of non-intervention became definitively institutionalized with the signing of the treaty
founding the OAS. As part of international law, it has become the only
"protection" for small and weak countries from aggression, occupation or
even annexation; it is the only principle that "guarantees" their security and
integrity.

The principle, however, has become an ambiguous and all-encompassing
term, one which can be used or misused (Furguson, 1970). It is supposed to
preclude not only the most extreme form of interventionism (military aggression and occupation), but also a wide range of collective or individual acts by
nation-states, such as the fomenting of military coups or subversive guerrillas
in a member state, the non-recognition of new governments, the imposition
of embargoes and economic, trade and financial sanctions, the display of
coercive diplomacy or diplomatic threats, or the support of opposition forces
or NGOs working on democracy promotion, or even the proposal of electoral
observation or *in situ* investigation of human and political rights violations.
Undoubtedly, in today's world, hacking national communications and information systems (databases) would also be considered interventionism.

The OAS Charter seeks to prevent interventionism by asserting that international law and order requires the "respect of the personality, sovereignty
and independence of States," and by establishing several broad provisions on
the rights and duties of member states, including, among others, that "every
State has the right to choose, without external interference, its political, economic and social system and to organize itself in the way best suited to it,

and has the duty to abstain from intervening in the affairs of another State" (Art. 3, b); that "the political existence of the State is independent of recognition by other States" (Art. 13); that "no State has the right to intervene directly or indirectly, for any reason whatever, in the internal or external affairs of any other State (Art 19); that "no State may use or encourage the use of coercive measures" (Art. 20); and that "the territory of a State is inviolable" and "may not be the object, even temporarily, of military occupation or of other measures of force...on any grounds whatever." (Art. 21). There is, however, a fundamental exception: "measures adopted for the maintenance of peace and security...do not constitute a violation of Articles 19 and 21." (Art. 23).

As seen in Chapter 3, during the first four decades of the Organization, which coincided with the Cold War, member states invoked the non-intervention principle against leftists (Castro's Cuba) or right wing dictatorships (Trujillo's Dominican Republic) in the Caribbean, which were violating the principle of non-intervention by interfering in other members' affairs and threatening their security and that of the region itself. When collective sanctions against dictatorial regimes, adopted to stop their aggression or intervention in member states' affairs, proved insufficient or ineffective, successive U.S. Governments have unilaterally taken coercive "interventionist" measures, as they did against Castro in Cuba (naval blockade, support for anti-Castro forces, and a continuing embargo), or against pro-Castro revolutionaries in the Dominican Republic in 1965. In any case, collective or unilateral measures were taken in the hypersensitive context of the strategic confrontation during the Cold War and, paradoxically, they constituted a form of "interventionism" to stop subversive, aggressive interventionism from both leftist and rightist dictatorial regimes, and were taken out of a collective concern for democracy, security and peace in the hemisphere. However, when dictators like Trujillo or Somoza invoked the principle of non-intervention and the Rio Treaty, member states decided that the principle of non-intervention did not apply because the requesting states were non-democratic and well-known repressive dictatorships (Slater 1967, 86–91).

But how does the principle of non-intervention today limit the OAS role of promoting democracy? In many ways, the promotion and defense of representative democracy is a new transnational collective value and commitment that appears to be in contradiction with the principle of non-intervention. The tension is apparent when it is invoked and misused by dictators and authoritarian regimes to cover up violations of human rights and/or political misdeeds that erode the democratic order, or even to stop efforts to endow the OAS with a greater role in promoting and defending democracy. In these cases upholding the non-intervention principle appears misplaced and retrograde. In the last few years, for example, the principle has been used (and misused) by the *chavista* regime to hinder the IACHR's attempt to investigate human rights or freedom of the press violations, or prevent the Secretary General from facilitating a dialogue in the ongoing political crisis in Venezuela. It has also been misused to deny the deployment of EOMs to Venezuela (and Nicaragua on one occasion), and to reject an attempt by Panama to discuss in an open session of the Permanent Council the Venezuelan political situation following student demonstrations of February 2014.

The foregoing "anti-interventionist" actions by increasingly authoritarian regimes contravene the collective commitment to defense and promotion of democracy established in the Democratic Charter. For them now, the international promotion and protection of democracy implies a kind of "interventionism" in the internal affairs of member states. It represents a threat to their authoritarian regimes, and they unabashedly use the non-intervention principle to counter it. More generally, it also poses a significant challenge to the all-encompassing traditional conception of interventionism.

In today's hemisphere, collectively promoting and defending democracy cannot be construed as interventionism, particularly when it has been established as a collective responsibility and when democracy has been recognized as a people's right and as a government's obligation to promote and exercise. The effective exercise of representative democracy is no longer a question of exclusive domestic jurisdiction of any OAS member state, it is an *inter-mestic* and indivisible issue that concerns the entire hemispheric democratic community. Nor can violation of the commitment to promote and exercise democracy or observe human rights be excused or ignored under the traditional principle of the absolute sovereignty of states–particularly when member states have formally agreed to defend, promote, and exercise it effectively.[21]

Moreover, as seen previously, in recent years, the principle of non-intervention has lost some of its absolute force and has gradually receded in the face of the inexorable reality of globalization, interdependence, transnationalism and the process of integration itself. Despite this progress, however, authoritarian regimes have perversely used it to cover up violations of human rights and freedoms and the erosion of democratic institutions, to the point of hindering or even paralyzing collective efforts at the OAS to promote and protect democracy and human rights.

Violations of the Non-intervention Principle

Member states and the Organization also face fundamental limitations in enforcing compliance of the OAS Charter's provisions by the "realism" principle. Essentially, this denotes their incapacity to prevent the superpower in their midst (the U.S.) from violating the principle of non-intervention when it intervenes militarily once it perceives an imminent threat to its national interests or security.

Even though the principle of non-intervention was developed and established to constrain or prevent European powers and the U.S. from intervening militarily or from employing coercive measures in Latin America, there have been cases in which the U.S. unilaterally violated the principle with impunity, particularly in the context of the struggle against communism during the Cold War, and when no multilateral consensus could be achieve for collective action within the Organization. Particular instances include the Central Intelligence Agency (CIA) support for the overthrow of the leftist governments of Jacobo Arbenz in Guatemala in 1954 and of Salvador Allende in Chile in 1973; the military and logistical support for exile anti-Castro forces in Cuba (Bay of Pigs, 1961), the naval blockade of Cuba of 1963 (after it was suspended from the OAS), the beginning in 1964 of the economic embargo against the Cuban regime that continues today; the invasion of Grenada in the Caribbean to prevent communist Cuba's takeover of the island in 1983; and the military and logistic support for the Contras, the Nicaraguan rebels that tried to oust the *Sandinista* Government led by Daniel Ortega in the 1980s.

The 1989 U.S. invasion of Panama to oust General Manuel Noriega, a tyrannical dictator in control of the country since 1983, merits special attention. It is, after all, the last U.S. military intervention in the hemisphere, carried out on the grounds that the General's regime was violating fundamental political and human rights, and was threatening the security of the Canal and of the subregion with his drug trafficking activities. The intervention took place after General Noriega annulled the presidential elections of May 1989 and engaged in a brutal public repression of the opposition forces that had triumphed at the ballots. In view of this, Venezuela called an emergency Meeting of Consultation of Ministers of Foreign Affairs to discuss the situation. The conclave took place in Washington, D.C. and held Noriega responsible for the physical aggression perpetrated against the opposition candidates and for human rights violations, and called for a transfer of power to be facilitated by a Mediation Commission (Meeting of Consultation of Ministers of Foreign Affairs May 17, 1989). The collective "action" of OAS members, however, proved to be ineffective or insufficient to obtain the resignation of General Noriega and essentially led to President George Bush's decision to carry out the military intervention on December 29, 1989. The Permanent Council condemned the intervention and called for the withdrawal of U.S. troops. In response, the U.S. Secretary of State James Baker expressed his regret over the OAS statement and noted the Organization's failure to support political and economic sanctions against Panama prior to the intervention, which could have avoided military action.

Thus, the collective failure to act forcefully and in timely fashion against a dictator that was violating human rights and destroying the democratic order in Panama, in addition to threatening the security and peace of the

Canal and the region, was the inevitable precursor of the U.S. unilateral intervention. In the face of OAS members' incapacity to react together and forcefully against Noriega, they could do no more than criticize or condemn, collectively and individually, the behavior of the superpower. Realism here trumped the principle of non-intervention. [22]

Essentially, what the foregoing interventions reveal is the practical limitations that "realism" imposes on the principle of non-intervention, for obvious reasons: No country or alliance of member states has the economic ad military power to confront and stop the United States from intervening or not complying with the principle of non-intervention, and any economic sanctions against it would have no major effect, except for being counterproductive to those imposing it.

As noted earlier, the crude reality is that countries that have the necessary power, especially superpowers, will do whatever they deem necessary, including the use of force to eliminate what their governments perceive as a threat to their vital national interests, without consideration for the non-intervention principle. From a "realist" perspective, this is inevitable, even though analysts, international officials or governments consider it illegal, illegitimate, unfair, and contrary to the most elemental principles of a peaceful and "democratic" international coexistence.

Other countries in the hemisphere have also used their economic or geopolitical power to interfere in the affairs of allies and neighbors. Venezuela, for example, under the *chavista* regime used leverage from its seemingly limitless oil resources to intervene in the both internal and external affairs of its Panamanian and Colombian neighbors. It has also used this power to meddle in the internal affairs of its ALBA allies, supporting their governments and undermining the opposition in election times, and to pressure them to vote against any attempt in the OAS to question or challenge the Venezuelan political situation, as occurred in when Panama challenged Venezuela in the Permanent Council. The regime has also intervened in the domestic affairs of Paraguay in a failed effort to prevent President Lugo's congressional destitution in 2011. In addition, there have been press and official Colombian reports that the regime has provided logistical and military support to the guerrilla insurgent forces in Colombia (FARC), by allowing them to camp safely inside Venezuelan territory and carry on their drug trafficking to finance their operations and obtain arms with the complicity of the Venezuelan armed forces.

On the other hand, as we saw in the previous Chapter, from a "realist" perspective, "interventions" are likely and almost inevitable when democracy, security and peace are imminently threatened, as demonstrated by the Colombian incursion into Ecuador in pursuit of the FARC. And this will take place despite the outrage that may be expressed by academics, analysts, international or governmental officials. Security and democracy will trump the principle of non-intervention and absolute sovereignty in cases of extreme situations that present a clear and imminent danger to the security and peaceful existence of a democratic state or the region. Violations of the democratic order and of the non-intervention principle by a *non-democratic* regime will not be tolerated and will trigger the application of coercive economic/financial and commercial sanctions and/or military intervention from a group of concerned states or unilaterally from a powerful individual state, to eliminate what is perceived as a the threat to the their collective vital national interests, and to preserve or restore democracy. This will inevitably generate tensions and friction with those states anachronistically cling to the principles of absolute non-intervention and state sovereignty.

Violation of the Democracy Principle

The "democracy principle" refers to the collective commitment to exercise, promote, preserve and defend representative democracy and the observance of human rights as agreed freely by member states in the constituent Charter, the Inter-American Democratic Charter and the American Convention on Human Rights. As previously noted, violations of human rights and of the democratic order do generate a strong collective and individual reaction by the democratic community in defense of democracy, eliciting strong and unprecedented condemnations and collective sanctions to restore democracy where it has been violated or overthrown. The first path-breaking case was the 1979 decision of the Seventeenth OAS Meeting of Consultation of Foreign Ministers to condemn the Somoza regime in Nicaragua for its violations of human rights and to call for its replacement by a democratic one, which delegitimized the Somoza regime and accelerated its demise (Acevedo and Grossman 1996, 138).

Additionally, as we have seen in previous chapters, after member states amended the OAS Charter in 1985 to include representative democracy as one of its main purposes, they rejected unambiguously the violations of the democratic order by a military coup in Haiti (1991), to the extent of imposing severe economic sanctions against the country and calling upon the United Nations Security Council to authorized the use force to remove General Cédras' *de facto* Government.[23] Similarly, member states refused to accept auto-coups in Peru (1992) and Guatemala (1993) and an attempted military coup in Paraguay (1996), condemning the events and employing diplomatic pressures and the threat of economic, financial and commercial sanctions to successfully restore the democratic order. More recently, the OAS also condemned the 2009 coup in Honduras and suspended its illegal Government from the Organization until after elections restored the democratic order.

However, as we have also seen in Chapter 7 in the past few years, there has been a slow but persistent retreat from this commitment in the OAS by a few authoritarian/populist regimes. In doing so, these states are violating their commitments and obligations to democracy and human rights and are bent on limiting and/or obstructing the Organization's role in both areas.

The most flagrant transgressor for the past ten years or so has been the *chavista* regime in Venezuela, which has rigged elections, prohibited electoral monitoring, illegally modified the Constitution, manipulated the legislative and judicial systems to arrange the election of Maduro and remain in power, restricted press freedom and persecuted, jailed and tortured political opponents. The regime has violated the American Convention on Human Rights as well as the Democratic Charter. But so far, it has been able to avoid the democratic community's sanctions or even criticism of its multiple and blatant transgressions. It has basically bought its immunity with discretionary dispensation of its oil and with aggressive threats to those who oppose or criticize its eroding of the democratic order in Venezuela. In this case, economic realism (oil) trumps the democracy principle.

Other cases include the *Sandinista* regime, with Daniel Ortega's attempts to perpetuate himself in power. His regime has also manipulated the legislative, judicial and electoral systems to illegally amend the Constitution so that he can be elected interminably, and has rejected or restricted independent electoral observation. Or the Evo Morales' plurinational and nationalistic anti-imperialist revolution, which has also manipulated the legislative, judicial and electoral systems to willfully misinterpret the new Constitution so as to permit Morales' reelection, while persecuting the opposition politically and judicially. And finally in Ecuador, where President Correa has also harassed the independent media and the political opposition, and has sought changes in the Constitution so that he too can be re-elected indefinitely,[24] a possibility which the Ecuadorian Supreme Court has recently approved.

Nevertheless, these violators of the democracy principle have not yet turned into tyrannical, aggressive, "interventionist" regimes that would imminently threaten the security or the peace of their neighbors and the region. But if they were to do so, one would expect that, under the doctrine of "collective democratic security for democracy" advanced here, the hemispheric democratic community, collectively or individually, would react forcefully, with sanctions and/or coercive measures, to avert or revert the erosion and breakdown of the democratic order where it is taking place. The historical precedents of dictatorial regimes like those of Trujillo, Castro, Somoza, Ortega (in the 1980s), Noriega and others are a reminder of this possibility. Member states themselves have established in the OAS Charter and the IADC that the exercise and prevalence of democracy in all members guarantees the security and peace of the hemisphere.

In short, in today's increasingly interdependent and inter-mestic hemisphere, there is some room for non-compliance with some of the fundamental norms, principles and provisions of OAS Charter and the Democratic Charter—mainly because of the limitations these instruments pose, because of member states' reluctance to enforce their decisions, or because of their inability to achieve consensus on measures to apply sanctions for non-compliance.

But if the violations are deemed to be grave and threat to the peace and security of the region, it is likely, as we have seen, that member states, collectively or individually, will take the necessary actions to meet those violations with sanctions which may go as far as to exclude and isolate the transgressors from the Organization and the inter-American democratic community, or to the use of force to oust the usurpers and secure a return to democracy where it was overthrown, or simply defeat and eliminate militarily the threat. That is, the democratic nation-states of the hemisphere perceive regional peace and their own security as depending on the security, stability, and continuity of each democracy of the region. Internal threats aimed at interrupting or destroying democracy in a member state can pose a threat to every democracy of the hemisphere. If a non-democratic government is perceived as an real and immediate threat to national or regional security, and legal/diplomatic measures are not a sufficient deterrent, or are not effective in correcting the deviation from a democratic order, countries with the political will and military means will take action, unilaterally and militarily, if deemed necessary, to restore democracy. The examples of U.S. unilateral military intervention against the *Sandinista* communist dictatorship in Nicaragua in the 1980s and in Panama in 1989 are cases in point. The latter was perhaps the last vestige of unilateral interventionism that provoked and hastened discussions within the OAS about possible mechanisms for the collective defense and promotion of democracy. Moreover, as in the case of Colombia, a government will even "intervene" militarily in a neighbor member state if an insurgent military force bent on destroying its democracy uses territory of its neighbors as sanctuary for its operations, as did the FARC in Ecuador and Venezuela.

CONCLUSION

Thus, the tensions between the principle of non-intervention and the democracy principle, and the related ones between institutional obligations and non-compliance and between institutional dependency and autonomy, plus the frictions and strains produced by the dominant role of the executive branch in OAS affairs and the reigning divisions resulting from ideological differences, do limit, if not paralyze the Organization's ability to exercise its role of promoting and defending democracy. This is compounded by the *chavista* regime and its allies' resistance to have their political performance evaluated in terms of their compliance with the IADC norms, which were established freely by their own representatives not long ago, when consensus on the democracy principle predominated in the Americas. In resisting collective assessment and reneging on the IADC, they abusively and wrongly invoke the principle of non-intervention and anachronistically adduce interventionist or imperialist intentions by the U.S. Government and its "lackeys." But by doing so, in effect, they engage in a concerted and strategic attempt to paralyze and marginalize the U.S., Canada and other responsible democracies from playing a significant role in democracy issues in Latin America. However, if a violation of the democratic principle is perceived as an imminent threat to the peace and security of the region, member states, collectively and individually will likely react with coercive sanctions, including military intervention, under the doctrine of collective security for democracy.

It is therefore imperative that analysis and criticism of OAS performance in democracy promotion and its defense adequately examine and understand the complexities involving the tensions and structural limitations that condition and constraint the behavior of its governing bodies or its Secretary General. Critics from academia, the press or the political world would do well to broaden and deepen their analysis and, in certain cases, should redirect their criticism and demands to the very source of the problem: the foreign policy establishment of their very own states. A deeper analysis and understanding of the nature of the OAS would help critics to focus their demands and be more realistic about their expectations and suggestions for strengthening and revitalizing its role in promoting and preserving democracy in the hemisphere.

NOTES

1. For example, in early 2013, the Government of Panama, under pressure from the Government of Venezuela, removed its Ambassador to the OAS, Guillermo Cochez, because he made statements critical of the irregular presidential transition in Venezuela after the death of Hugo Chávez, and for claiming (correctly) that Chávez had been deceased before the Venezuelan Government announced his death publicly.

2. Many Permanent Council Ambassadors still think the Secretary General has too much autonomy in administrative affairs, particularly in hiring advisors and consultants.

3. See Chapter XVI of the OAS Charter, as amended in 1993.

4. The last three Secretaries have been João Clemente Baena Soares (1984–1994), César Gaviria (1994–2004) and José Miguel Insulza (2005–2010). The role of the Secretaries General, Ambassadors and Foreign Ministries in carving out the new OAS role of promoting and defending democracy deserves a separate and much more detailed and profound analysis than can be offered here. It would also be worthwhile, for example, to detail the role played by the Ambassadors of Argentina (Juan Pablo Lohlé and Hernán Patiño Mayer), Brazil (Bernardo Pericás Neto), Canada (Jean-Paul Hubert), Chile (Heraldo Muñoz), Colombia (Julio Londoño), Saint Lucia (Joseph Edmunds), United States (Luigi Einaudi), Venezuela (Guido Grooscors), Uruguay (Didier Opertti) and others in designing and approving Resolution 1080 and the Washington Protocol. With respect to the importance of individual leadership in the dynamics of international cooperation, see Moravcsik (1999) and Young (1991).

5. Both the opposition and Gaviria's team were convinced that Chavez would lose the referendum. His prolonged, unusual and unnecessary absence from headquarters was the subject of private criticism within OAS diplomatic circles and its bureaucracy.

6. Panama intended to have a Venezuelan opposition leader, María Corina Machado, speak to the Council about the situation in her country, but was also voted down. Also, as mentioned earlier (Note 38, Chapter 6), neither the United States nor the Canadian delegations to the OAS could even convince the Caribbean group to vote in favor of the meeting being open to the public and the media, let alone to let the opposition leader speak at the Council.

7. http://m.eluniversal.com/nacional-y-politica/protestas-en-venezuela/140222/insulza-sugiere-una-participacion-de-actores-externos-en-venezuela

8. http://www.martinoticias.com/content/segun-insulza-en-venezuela-no-hay-condiciones-para-carta-de-oea/.

9. Private rumors and press account had it that Insulza's timid comments on the *chavista* regime's violations of the IADC or his refusal to comment on them at all, alleging his lack of authority to intervene in the internal affairs of Venezuela, were due to his fears of Chávez's vicious and insulting public reactions and to his reluctance to alienate the socialist and communist members of the leftist political coalition (*Concertación*), which he hoped to lead as its presidential candidate in the election of 2009. Incidentally, in his efforts to become its candidate, in 2008 Insulza occupied much of his OAS time negotiating and "campaigning" for his candidacy with the Socialist party (he even had a candidate's webpage), but eventually withdrew from it as he could not obtain assurance of his candidacy without going through the coalition's primary. Many in the coalition hoped he would resign as Secretary General to participate fully in the primary process; but in OAS diplomatic circles and in the Latin American and Chilean press he was widely criticized and questioned for surreptitiously pursuing his candidacy while acting as Secretary General of the OAS—behavior considered unethical and incompatible with his OAS responsibilities.

10. The current SPA is organized in three departments: 1) the Department of Electoral Cooperation and Observation (DECO), dedicated to electoral observation and assistance, which has remained as one of the strongest and most effective programmatic areas; 2) the Department for Effective Management, assigned to provide technical cooperation related to the strengthening of public administration (executive branch ministries), involving areas such as civil registry, access to information, transparency and e-government; and 3) the Department of Sustainable Democracy and Special Missions, responsible for providing political analysis for the Secretary General and developing methodologies for supporting the Organization's Special Missions related to the promotion of national dialogue, mediation and conflict management and to peaceful settlement of disputes between member states. http://www.oas.org/en/spa/. The General Secretariat has other offices that are involved in democracy promotion activities, such as the Secretariat for Legal Affairs, and its Department of Legal Cooperation, which carries out a technical cooperation program to promote and assist member states in the implementation of the Inter-American Convention against Corruption, mainly through a peer review follow-up mechanism (MESICIC, for its Spanish acronym). http://www.oas.org/juridico/english/Fight-Cur.html. And, of course, it houses the autonomous Inter-American Commission on Human Rights, with its wide-ranging and renowned activities promoting and protecting human rights in the hemisphere. http://www.oas.org/en/topics/human_rights.asp.

11. See for example the multitude of projects in its Departments of Economic and Social Development, Sustainable Development and Human Development/Education/Employment. Currently, this Secretariat manages close to forty-five programs/projects for a total of approximately US$80 million, mostly from voluntary contributions from various donor countries, members or not. Current programs/projects include subjects as diverse as social protection and inclusion to reduce poverty and inequality, tourism development, micro enterprise development, competitiveness, natural and human science, technology development, trade development, social responsibility, water resource management, forest ecosystem management, agricultural development, satellite systems development for earth observation, urban environment management, renewable energy, energy efficiency and climate, biofuels, capacity building for sustainable energy, closed loop cycle production methods, disaster risk reduction, flood alert, disaster management, migratory species information system, biodiversity management, coral

reef management, public participation in sustainable development management, strengthening planning for pathways to prosperity, capacity building for sustainable use of natural resources, graduate scholarships, scholarship for technical training, labor administration, education in science, technology, mathematics and engineering, curriculum development for undergraduate studies, education and new technologies, virtual education. http://www.oas.org/en/sedi/prd/projects.asp. In addition, the Organization carries out activities related to ports, women, children and youth issues, migration and refugees. The inevitable question is whether the Organization is really the place for these activities, without prejudice to their merit and value, and whether OAS work on them can really make a difference or add any value to them. For more variety yet, see programs/projects (760) financed by FEMCIDI (Special Multilateral Fund of the Inter-American Council for Integral Development since 1998. http://www.apps.oas.org/projects/default.aspx. In addition the Organization finances ancillary activities that could or should be funded by private contributions from foundations or from voluntary contributions from member states: these includes the Art Museum, the Pan American Development Foundation, the Columbus Memorial Library, the Young Americas Business Trust and the Trust for the Americas (Secretary General of the OAS April 2013). Finally, it is interesting to note that the voluntary funds that these programs obtain, plus the 11% indirect cost recovery (ICR) charged to the donors, are used, of course, to fund posts for numerous staff members who manage the programs but also for administrative staff for the whole Secretariat. Given this revenue source, one wonders if there is within the Secretariat a real desire to reduce "development" projects, which, as argued above, do not correspond to the true priorities of the Organization.

12. The report was prepared by an external Canadian consultant. But it is interesting, and puzzling, to note, given its damaging findings, that the Secretary General himself assumed responsibility for this report, and presented it to the Permanent Council for its deliberations on the 2015–16 program-budget of the Organization.

13. The report specifically recommends the strengthening of the Project Evaluation Committee (CEP), which evaluates and approves technical assistance programs and projects. National or regional (multilateral) programs/projects are in effect one of the most important instruments the Organization has to provide services and cooperation to its members. They correspond to its very nature; their programing and execution constitute a major and substantive part of its activities. The report notes as a critique that the CEP approves projects without funding, but that is not its real problem, as indeed projects should be approved before officers can fundraise for them. A more serious issue is that, while the report correctly critiques the current RBM system used in technical assistance project as incomplete (p. 10), it ignores the fact that the whole process of project evaluation and approval by the CEP can be (and has been) applied in a rigid or discretionary manner to favor one or another project or area, based on donors' particular interests or on bureaucratic politics considerations by its members, who are not always politically impartial or simply knowledgeable enough about the project's formulation and execution process or the substance/discipline involved in it. Another problem is that the evaluation forms required to be filled out by project managers include identifying a complex set of "measurable" objectives, inputs, outputs, activities, costs and outcomes and requiring detailed information usually not readily available or even relevant, and which would be more appropriate for large multimillion dollar infrastructure projects to be financed by a development bank, than for a modest, democracy promotion project on strengthening legislative institutions. This, along with the time and effort needed to compile the required information from the partner institutions in the member states, plus the multiple internal approval stages the project has to go through before reaching the CEP, is indeed a discouraging prospect for officers intent on executing projects in response to the member states' requests. The Committee and its evaluation forms presume (pretentiously) an understanding (doubtful) of the nature and complexity of promoting democracy from an international organization (including project formulation and implementation in the field nonetheless) and of the outcomes that such projects should seek. The ultimate outcome of a democracy promotion project from an international organization perspective, in theory, should aim at changes in the political culture (attitudes and behavior), but these are not measurable in any meaningful way even over the medium term, let

alone in the time span of a project (See discussion on a theory of democracy promotion in Chapter 7).

14. See the full Act in http://www.foreign.senate.gov/publications/download/oas-bill-as-pased-by-the-house.

15. Interestingly enough, some of the reforms proposed by the Act and the letter from the U.S. Congress concur with those made by the Secretary General in his document presented to the Permanent Council in December 2011, as he himself pointed out in his response to the U.S. Senators (Secretary General 21 November 2012). See also: http://internacional.elpais.com/internacional/2013/09/27/actualidad/1380301382_115633.html The writer's personal experience can attest to the validity of the assertions made by the three insiders' reports concerning the administrative, personnel and leadership deficiencies.

16. The low morale among the staff of the Secretariat is not only the result of perverse personnel policies, but also the product of job insecurity and uncertain prospects for career growth, as posts are increasingly funded by voluntary funds, which by definition are not permanent. Thus, the young or newly hired professionals (with short contracts and uncompetitive salaries) have limited commitment to the Organization and its goals, consider it just a temporary job, and the best leave the Organization as soon as they can.

17. Interestingly enough, not one Foreign Minister was present at the special session of the General Assembly. Additionally, as of late, some of the member states have not assigned Ambassadors to the Permanent Council.

18. See details in Chapter 6.

19. On the issue of whether decisions of the Organ of Consultation in application of the Rio Treaty are compulsory, see the enlightening discussion in García Amador (1981, 838–841).

20. See also the discussion on the U.S. intervention in Panama to oust General Noriega below and the Colombian incursion into Ecuador in pursuit of the FARC in Chapter 9.

21. See Franck, "The Emerging Right to Democratic Governance" (1992), and his argument that the self-determination of peoples or popular sovereignty is a right that governments must accord the people who live under their authority, and that to the extent that this right to democracy advances, the traditional sovereignty of states will diminish, since states will gradually cede sovereignty in exchange for legitimacy and membership in the community of democratic nations (Franck, "The Democratic Entitlement" 1994, 1–5). See also Vio-Grossi (1998), Acevedo and Grossman (1996) and Muñoz (1996).

22. Secretary General Baena Soares noted the frustration and inability of the OAS Mission to achieve change (Baena Soares 1994, 38). See Larman Wilson (1989).

23. See Vio Grossi, (1998, 113). According to T. Franck, the decision of the U.N. Security Council established a precedent by permitting the use of force, on the grounds that violations of human rights and the right to democracy constituted a threat to the peace of the region. (Franck,"The Democratic Entitlement" 1994, 9).

24. On the obligation of a member state to govern democratically, Thomas Franck argues that states acquire that obligation upon associating themselves voluntarily and that it is the price they must pay for belonging to a democratic community (e.g. OAS, MERCOSUR). This is an obligation to recognize the rights of its citizens to be governed democratically, or if it fails to do so, to face sanctions by the international community. See Franck, "The Democratic Entitlement" (1994, 3). Similarly, Farer also suggests that one way of binding member states would be through national legislation that authorizes and obliges the executive branch to comply with sanctions imposed against violators of democracy and human rights. To this end, Farer proposed that the UPD/OAS design and promote model legislation on the issue (1996, 22).

Chapter Eleven

The Challenging
Hemispheric Horizon

Despite the strengths of the new OAS norms and instruments to promote and defend democracy and the considerable progress made in applying them, the Organization and the Inter-American Democratic Regime (IADR) still face the institutional tensions and weakness discussed earlier, as well as some considerable contextual challenges on the horizon posed by the remaining authoritarian pseudo-democracies and the ideologically fragmented geo-politics of the hemisphere.

AUTHORITARIAN PSEUDO-DEMOCRACIES

The inter-American community of democracies that makes up the IADR contains democracies that are imperfect democracies, or pseudo-democracies. Despite the façade of periodic elections, countries like Argentina, Bolivia, Ecuador, Nicaragua and Venezuela still betray remnants of an authoritarian political culture that still predominates in them to differing degrees. Rulers of these countries pretend or claim to be democratic because they win periodic elections, but elections alone do not make a democracy whole; neither does a modicum of socioeconomic progress. Elected governments must also govern democratically—otherwise democracy stagnates.

The pseudo-democracy model essentially results from a lingering authoritarian political culture. As discussed in Chapter 6, this political order includes the predominance of *illiberal* democratic values and practices in the leadership and in an electorally significant portion of the citizenry. The model is characterized by authoritarian, charismatic, caudillo-run governments, which employ populist/clientelistic "progressive" social policies that produce electoral majorities that in turn allow them to get re-reelected, in some cases by distorted if not fraudulent elections, as in Venezuela, Bolivia and Nicaragua, and to remain in power indefinitely. These governments, and others like those of Argentina and Ecuador, perhaps less oppressive, not only violate their own democratic constitutions, but also violate the Inter-American Democratic Charter.

The rulers of these regimes have a tight, all-pervasive control of the state and the polity. The regimes they have created are marked by limited respect for the rule of law, rampant corruption and impunity, weak or non-existent separation of powers, hyper-presidencies, and restrictions on individual liberties and human rights. Political parties are fragmented and weak, parliaments are acquiescent and merely rubber-stamp the decisions of the hyper-presidencies. Judges and courts are not neutral, electoral authorities are manipulated, the independent media are disdained, muzzled and threatened, and opposition politicians are persecuted and jailed, as are independent business leaders. All of this characterizes today's Latin American incomplete, illiberal pseudo-democracies (Weyland 2013) (Mainwaring and Perez-Liñan 2013, 258–62) (Arnson and de la Torre 2014).

Until the 1980s, military leaders did not hesitate to overthrow a government when, in alliance with opposition civilians, they perceived their nation-state as being threatened. They staged coups for many reasons, including political instability resulting from leftist subversive activities, labor and student unrest, political demonstrations and violence, economic chaos, government mismanagement and corruption, leftist electoral victories, leftist governments' attempts to impose a socialist or communist socioeconomic model, and violations of human and political rights, among others (Nun 1967) (Perina 1983) (Putnam 1976) (Lowenthal 1976). Most military governments were almost automatically recognized by OAS member states because of their anti-communist, anti-Castro stance, and because of their adherence to the principle of non-intervention. Today, however, governments change because of elections or constitutional democratic procedures, and rulers resulting from a coup d'état are no longer accepted and may be suspended from the OAS and isolated from the IADR. With few exceptions, the armed forces remain in their barracks and are respectful of civilian, democratic and constitutional rule. [1]

However, the fact that the military are not seizing power and running nations, and that they generally seem to understand the futility of using force to take over a government, does not mean that they are no longer influential actors in their countries' political processes. There have been cases in the twenty-first century when they have interfered with, if not interrupted, the democratic order or participated with civilians in its breakdown, as in Ecuador (2000), Venezuela (2002) and Honduras (2009), ignoring, willfully or not, the hemispheric commitment to democracy and the Democratic Charter.

And there is of course the overwhelming, corruption-filled, perverse presence of the Venezuelan armed forces in Maduro's *chavista* regime, probably the sustaining pillar of its fragile existence. This persistent military presence marks its lingering influence and underscores the need for the hemisphere's democratic forces to be vigilant and determined to use and strengthen the inter-American collective norms and instruments that promote and protect democracy.[2]

THE LINGERING ABUSE
OF THE NON-INTERVENTION PRINCIPLE

The principle of non-intervention is anachronistic and unwarranted in today's world, because of the ascendancy of the democracy principle and a common commitment to collective democratic security. Nevertheless, it is still perversely misused, mostly for internal reasons, by today's pseudo-democracies to prevent external monitoring and denunciation of violations of political freedoms, human rights and the rule of law, or to justify increasing repressive internal measures. These regimes will inevitably invoke the principle of non-intervention to dissuade other member states' governments from attempting to invoke the Inter-American Democratic Charter for a collective assessment of their political situation. Most governments, including the U.S., are reluctant to criticize a transgressor or call for a collective assessment of a deteriorating democratic situation, as the Inter-American Charter would allow. They fear being branded as interventionist or as lackeys of U.S. imperialism. But not only that, a government that is criticized would likely break diplomatic and commercial relations with those who dare propose such an "interventionist" and "aggressive" motion, as happened recently between Venezuela and Panama.

The indiscriminate and unwarranted (mis)use of the principle of non-intervention prevents the OAS and the democratic community from exercising fully their collective obligation to promote and defense democracy. However, to repeat, if the threat to or the violation of the democracy principle is perceived as an imminent threat to the security of other democracies in the hemisphere, member states that have the political will and military capacity will likely ignore the principle and intervene militarily, to extirpate the threat.

THE DECLINING COMMITMENT TO DEMOCRACY
AND HEMISPHERIC FRAGMENTATION

The remaining authoritarian regimes and their abuse of the non-intervention principle has also had the effect of breaking down the hemispheric democratic consensus and the cohesiveness of the Organization and the Inter-American Democratic Regime, and this in turn generates tension in the hemisphere and, for all intents and purposes, can paralyze the Organization and render it irrelevant as a protector of democracy—at least in the eyes of the democrats of the hemisphere. The OAS and its Democratic Charter are fully operative only when and if there is a democratic congruence in political regimes, and a firm consensus and collective commitment to defend and strengthen democracy in the hemisphere.

The authoritarian pseudo-democratic populist regimes have undermined and violated the democratic values, practices and institutions that are enshrined in their own constitutions and in the IADC, and have retreated from their commitment to promote and defend democracy. Together, they have constituted a "leftist" Latin American and Caribbean block, spearheaded by Chávez while he was alive and his ALBA followers, and encouraged by Brazil and Argentina, led by their anti-U.S. "leftist progressive" leaders, Lula and Dilma Rousseff and the Kirchner couple. They have challenged U.S. influence in Latin America and, collectively or individually, have attempted to reduce the role of the OAS, and thereby the role of the U.S. and Canada in protecting human rights, mediating political crises (Venezuela), deploying electoral observations (Nicaragua, Venezuela), or even discussing the Venezuelan crisis publicly in the Permanent Council. These developments have led to the current ideological geo-political/diplomatic divisions or fragmentation that afflicts the hemisphere and therefore the OAS. The enthusiastic, unanimous collective commitment to democracy of the turn of the century (roughly from the early 1980s to 2005) no longer exists or is dormant. Fragmentation reigns and constitutes a major impediment to obtaining the consensus that is necessary for the OAS to perform its role effectively.

Fragmentation and/or lack of consensus prevents the Permanent Council or the Secretary General from publicly discussing or collectively assessing clear and unconstitutional alterations of the democratic order and violations of the Inter-American Democratic Charter taking place in various member states. The repression of demonstrators and persecution and jailing of political opponents, the curtailing of press freedoms, the violation of human rights and the manipulations of judicial and electoral institutions to permit indefinite reelection that are taking place in Venezuela and to a lesser extent in Bolivia, Ecuador and Nicaragua, do not seem to elicit sufficient consensus for anyone to invoke the Democratic Charter or to convoke the Permanent Council, as permitted by the Charter itself.[3] The absence of consensus on these matters frequently leads to interminable debates in the governing bodies that generate ill will and tension among its members, and that eventually conclude with innocuous decisions based on the lowest common denominator that all but paralyzes the Organization, or simply marginalizes it from having any significant role to play in the promotion and protection of democracy.

This trend was evident at the OAS General Assembly in Honduras (2009), where the "populist" countries (the *chavista* alliance) insisted on allowing Cuba's unconditional return to the OAS, and, later, on its participation in the Cartagena Presidential Summit of 2011. However, after lifting the 1962 suspension, member states agreed to Cuba's reintegration to the system only if its government complies with OAS purposes and principles, including the Democratic Charter—an unlikely event in the near future.

Another indication of this disturbing move away from the commitment to democracy is the refusal of the Venezuelan and Nicaraguan Governments to invite the OAS to monitor their elections (though Nicaragua reluctantly and belatedly invited the Organization and the European Union to observe the 2011 elections). More disturbing, however, are the Brazilian, Bolivian, Venezuelan and Ecuadorian Governments' aggressively unfriendly reaction to the decisions of the Inter-American Human Rights Court and Commission to protect the human rights of individuals, political opponents and indigenous groups in those countries, or in some cases redress violations committed by those states. Argentina, Colombia and others, incomprehensibly, agreed. Furthermore, those countries have led surreptitious efforts to limit and weaken the Human Rights Commission, and have initiated a process to examine its role, scope and financing to supposedly "strengthen" it, when in fact their intention was to weaken it. Venezuela has gone as far as to denounce and withdraw from the Inter-American Convention on Human Rights. However, the special session of the General Assembly convened to "strengthen" the Inter-American Human Rights System (March 2013) was unable to reach consensus on the reforms proposed by those countries.

Simultaneously, the "populists" or *chavista* alliance moved to create the Union of South American Nations (UNASUR, *Unión de Naciones Suramericanas*) and the Community of Latin American and Caribbean States (CELAC, *Comunidad de Estados Latinoamericanos y del Caribe*), as subregional organizations for political cooperation and eventual integration. It is no secret, however, that these organizations intend to challenge the authority and legitimacy of the OAS, and limit its presence and that of the United States and Canada in the affairs of the subregions. This was attempted, without success, during the political events in Paraguay in June 2012, when President Lugo was summarily impeached and removed from office by the Paraguayan Congress, much to the dismay of the Governments of Argentina, Brazil and Venezuela. They immediately suspended the new Paraguayan Government from the subregional organizations, but could not achieve consensus at the OAS to do the same. A few months later, in a most revealing, ironic and paradoxical decision, the CELAC members, all of which have signed the Democratic Charter and the "democratic clauses" of the subregional organizations, selected Raúl Castro, the Cuban dictator, as its President.

Today, the "populists", with the tacit acquiescence of the more liberal democracies, were able to obtain practically unanimous Latin American support in favor of Cuba's inclusion in the April 2015 Summit of the Americas, which the U.S. and Canada opposed until recently because the Castro Government has not complied with OAS principles and norms on democracy and has not shown any interest in returning to the Organization. Cuba's non-movement towards democracy and the U.S. embargo against the island are together the two most divisive issues between the U.S. and Canada on one hand, and Latin America and the Caribbean on the other. One disturbing feature of this Latin American posture is its indifference to the Castro dictatorship and its violations of human rights for more than forty years.

The result has been the emergence of two distinct opposing camps in the hemisphere. The fragmented map also includes a moderate block of democracies that have formed the so-called Atlantic Alliance (Chile, Peru, Colombia, Mexico) that occasionally plays both sides of the field, depending on the issues and circumstances. This fragmentation has essentially prevented hemispheric consensus on crucial issues of democracy promotion and defense. The lack of consensus has undermined the collective commitment to democracy, and transgressors find it easier to invoke the non-intervention principle to prevent the OAS and its members from utilizing its instruments and executing its mandates to promote and protect democracy or even discuss publicly issues related to democratic transgressions in member states.

THE U.S. ESTRANGEMENT FROM LATIN AMERICA

Parallel to the new "good neighbor" pro-democracy (and free trade) stance towards Latin America discussed in Chapter 9, in recent years diplomatic and academic observers have also seen an apparent distancing of the U.S. from Latin America. In their view, U.S. policy towards Latin America has been marked by a sort of indifference to the erosion of liberal democracy and violations of human and political rights in some member states and a disinterest in addressing these issues within the Organization.[4] This reality is expressed in the very choice of "lightweight" Ambassadors to represent the U.S. in the Permanent Council in recent years (the last "heavyweight" being Ambassador Luigi Einaudi, 1989–1993), as well as in the incredible U.S. diplomatic incapacity or lack of effort to influence collective decisions in the governing bodies of the Organization. Examples include the U.S. delegation's powerlessness to get approval for its proposal at the General Assembly in 2005 to establish an OAS democracy monitoring mechanism (not to speak of its failure to obtain consensus to open up a process for a free trade agreement at the Presidential Summit in Argentina that year), and its minor but telling incapacity to convince the Council's majority to approve its suggestion that the SG/OAS visit Venezuela to observe and report back on the political crisis engulfing the country, or even to allow an open and public session to discuss the Venezuelan situation (2014), as proposed by Panama. Worse yet is the U.S. delegation's passivity and reluctance to invoke the Democratic Charter and convoke the Permanent Council to carry out "collective assessment" of situations that threaten the democratic order in a member state and violate the Democratic Charter, as in Venezuela.[5] This absence of leadership, resulting in an apparent loss of influence within the Organization and the region in general, is particular disturbing because the U.S. is the strongest democracy in the OAS, and its active leadership is indispensable to keep it vibrant and effective in its role to promote and defend democracy.

There are several probable reasons for this "disengagement." One certainly is the U.S. foreign policy concentration on the war efforts in Iraq and Afghanistan and the war on terrorism after September 11, 2001. The War on Terror marks a U.S. foreign policy game changer, as the U.S. Government has since dedicated most of its attention to diplomatic negotiations and military operations (covert and overt) throughout the Middle East, the Persian Gulf and Africa, in pursuit of al-Qaeda and now the Islamist State terrorists, with corresponding high costs in terms of money and blood. Other preoccupations include the U.S. concern over the "Arab Spring," and its increasingly tense, conflictive relations with China over its expansion in Pacific, and with Russia over its annexation of Crimea and its threats to Ukraine's territorial integrity. These security concerns around the globe have distracted the world power from Latin America, a relatively peaceful if increasingly challenging region.

Another reason for the distancing between Latin America and the U.S. since the beginning of the twenty-first century is the surge of Brazil, and Argentina to a lesser extent. Both, led by their "leftist progressive," autonomy-seeking leaders (Lula and Dilma Rousseff in Brazil and the Kirchner couple in Argentina), have enjoyed until recently substantive and rapid economic growth, which has given them the confidence to form a "revolutionary" coalition with the *chavista* regime, leader of the ALBA alliance, to challenge U.S. influence in Latin America and at the OAS.[6] This anti-U.S. grouping would obstruct any U.S. attempt in the OAS (if there were such an attempt) to obtain the necessary consensus for a collective assessment of the erosion of democracy or the violation of human rights in a member state like Venezuela, the most contemptible transgressor. Such a U.S. move would certainly be rejected with disdain as interventionist and imperialistic. Since 2005, this leftist "alliance" has blocked U.S. initiatives to strengthen the role and autonomy of the OAS to promote democracy and protect human rights, has thwarted the U.S. push for a hemispheric free trade zone, and has frequently chastised it for its embargo against Cuba and its opposition to Cuba's participation in the OAS and in Presidential Summits. This anti-U.S. stance has tended to alienate the U.S. even further from the OAS, to the point that, in the eyes of U.S. policy makers, congressional leaders, the media, and academic experts, the Organization has become practically useless and irrelevant not only for the promotion and protection of democracy but also for U.S. foreign policy.[7]

This apparent "estrangement" of the U.S. from Latin America paradoxically contradicts the persistent strident claims of the leaders of the anti-U.S. coalition (Presidents Correa, Chávez/Maduro, Morales, Ortega, Lula/Rousseff and the Kirchner couple) that the U.S. Government pursues, through the OAS or unilaterally, a policy of imperialism or interventionism in Latin America. They still prefer, anachronistically, to frame U.S. policy towards the region in the context of the Cold War. But the fact is that the U.S. no longer acts like an imperious hegemon, does not overtly dominate relations with Latin America, nor does it dictate administrative policies or diplomatic outcomes within the OAS, as it might have done in the past or as some would still like to portray. Their accusations of U.S. conspiracies are obsolete and unwarranted, and are manufactured for domestic consumption.

The reality is that it is improbable that the U.S. today would engage in covert activities to overthrow unfriendly governments or that it would carry out a military intervention against a member state, unless, of course, there emerges an unquestionable and imminent threat to the security of the region and to itself. It is also a reality that the U.S. today presents a less arrogant or interventionist posture towards Latin America, one that emphasizes partnership, cooperation, multilateralism and commitment to promote and defend democracy. And this in itself, paradoxically again, may be a positive development that, if understood correctly by Latin American leaders, could bolster U.S.-Latin American relations that were once marred by U.S. military intervention, occupation, and by constant interference in the internal and external affairs of Latin American countries. This new, less imposing role of the U.S. could also strengthen the OAS as the only and vital forum for political dialogue and cooperation in the hemisphere (Kerry 2013) (Perina 2013). However, it would be naive, of course, to think that the U.S. Government is totally withdrawing from Latin America and does not try to influence events in the region or does not carry out intelligence and covert activities to promote and protect its political, economic and security interests, as any country will if it has the resources and power to do so (Tokatlian 2013).

THE CUBAN CHALLENGE

The U.S. estrangement from Latin America and the fragmentation of the hemisphere, which have somewhat inhibited and hindered the OAS from performing its role of promoting and defending democracy, may be coming to an end as a result of the new rapprochement between the Castro regime and the Obama administration, which has been celebrated throughout the Americas. The reestablishment of diplomatic relations between the United States and Cuba on December 17, 2014 represents a symbolic victory for a demand long held by majority of Latin American Governments (including, of course, the Cuban Government), intellectuals, the progressive/liberal "Latin Americanists" in political and academic sectors in the U.S., and the new Cuban generation living in the U.S.

The resumption of relations is a culmination of demands and pressures that started perhaps in 1973, when the OAS General Assembly approved a declaration calling for the end of the isolation of Cuba and acceptance of "ideological pluralism" as the basis for hemispheric solidarity. Subsequently, in 1975, the Sixteenth Meeting of Consultation of Foreign Ministers lifted the 1964 sanctions (diplomatic, travel and transportation, commercial, financial) against Cuba and declared that all member states were free to determine their individual relations with Cuba. They did so, and most normalized their relations with the island (Orrego-Vicuña 1977, 121) (Puig 1986, 163) (Garcia Amador 1981, 861) (General Secretariat of the OAS 1973). That year also, the Commission on United States-Latin American Relations, chaired by Ambassador Sol Linowitz and composed of prominent Latin Americanists from the U.S. business, diplomatic and academic world, called for an end to the U.S. embargo against Cuba (Commission on United States-Latin American Relations, The Linowitz Report 1975). Yet, not until thirty-five years later, in Honduras in 2009, did the U.S. finally acquiesce to an OAS General Assembly resolution abrogating the 1962 suspension of Cuba from the activities of the inter-American system. However, readmission was preconditioned on the Cuban regime's acceptance of the Organization's principles and purposes related to democracy. To no one's surprise, however, the regime has not yet announced its intention to abide by this precondition in order to return to the Organization.

By 2014, Latin American Governments from the ALBA coalition and supported by Argentina and Brazil reaffirmed their demand that the Cuban Government participate in the Seventh Summit of the Americas to be held in Panama City in April 2015. This was despite the fact the Summits have a "democracy clause," which essentially limits participation in Summits to democratic Governments. Under pressure from Latin America and domestic sectors in favor of an opening to Cuba, and to avoid the risk of further estrangement from Latin America, the Obama administration (like most Latin American Governments) chose to ignore this fact and agreed to participate.

For Latin Americans, the resumption of relations ends an anachronistic, failed and offensive U.S. stand. It removes the last vestige of the Cold War in the Americas and an era of presumptuous, arrogant U.S. dominance of the hemisphere. It eliminates a bone of contention that has plagued U.S.-Latin American relations for several decades, and opens the way for a new and improved hemispheric relationship. It could signify the beginning of a new U.S.-Latin American rapprochement.

The Panama Summit of April 2015 will probably reveal to some extent the future nature of this new relationship. One can only hope that it will start a new era of greater mutual understanding that would contribute to the reaffirmation and strengthening of the historical hemispheric guiding principles of solidarity and partnership for a peaceful, secured and prosperous continent, grounded on the common values of sovereignty, freedom, equality, social justice and democracy. Why could the Americas not enjoy a relationship of equals and enlightened self-interest, as exists, for example, between the United States and Europe, or with Canada and Mexico within NAFTA?

Improved relations between Latin America and the United States would likely help strengthen the OAS as the only inter-American forum and instrument responsible for hemispheric cooperation to guard and promote those principles and common values. Until recently, the ALBA coalition has attempted to ignore and marginalize the OAS from hemispheric political/democratic affairs because of the Organization's supposed submission to the traditional U.S. hegemonic policies and dictates to maintain Cuba's suspension —an inaccurate assessment of the U.S. stance of the last twenty-five years or so, or simply an ignorant or ill-intentioned distortion of a new reality. [8]

However, this negative attitude towards the U.S. and the OAS appears to have fragmented and relented recently, as the Bolivian delegation, backed by El Salvador, Ecuador, Nicaragua and Venezuela, was unable to obtain the OAS Permanent Council's majority to call for an end of the embargo and thus derail a consensus declaration expressing satisfaction with the Cuban-United States reestablishment of relations and its support for complete normalization of relations in the future. [9]

So, it is appropriate to celebrate the end of this Cold War anachronism and the beginning of a new era in U.S.-Cuban and Latin American relations. But it is also an occasion to call on all democracies of the hemisphere to pressure the Castro regime to liberalize its economy and its anachronistic, authoritarian repressive communist political regime. They should request that the Castro regime accept the 2009 OAS lifting of its suspension and the preconditions for its return to the OAS, and that it sign and comply with the principles and purposes of the OAS Charter and Inter-American Democratic

Charter of 2001, both of which are a collective commitment to the promotion, defense and exercise of representative democracy.

In 1973, Latin American countries succeeded in establishing the democratic principle of "ideological pluralism" for inter-American relations. Will they now call on the obsolete Castro regime to democratize and accept "ideological pluralism" domestically? If so, this will be yet the most resounding victory for Latin American democracy.

CONCLUSION

The emergence of authoritarian caudillo-led populist pseudo-democracies at the beginning of the twenty-first century has halted if not reversed the progress of democracy in Latin America. It has also fragmented the region and has debilitated the consensus and cohesiveness of the hemisphere in terms of its commitment to democracy and support for the OAS. This is in marked contrast to the consensus and cohesiveness existing in the 1980s and 1990s, and as a result, we are witnessing now an OAS that is less active and effective in the promotion and defense of democracy.

Given this reality, one could be pessimistic and conclude that democracy in Latin America is merely an illusion. This book, however, maintains that democracy is what the peoples of the Americas have always aspired to, sought and fought for, and that it is what they support and prefer as a system of government, as *Latinobarómetro* indicates. It also sustains that the democratic deficiencies and shortcomings of the pseudo-democracies in Latin America do not necessarily mean that democracy has failed in the region; rather, it means that it still requires greater domestic and regional effort to consolidate. Those democracies are not completely failed as yet. Their Governments' authoritarian populist economic polices may eventually prove too much for the new middle class and even for the seduced electorate, who may indeed vote the authoritarians out—if free and fair democratic elections are allowed. The final test for the consolidation of democracy is whether the authoritarians will accept defeat at the polls—a question that will require a watchful eye and electoral observations to assure their validity.

The survival, consolidation and thriving of democracies in the hemisphere depends on the willingness and capacity of their national leaders to govern democratically, maintain and deepen a democratic political culture, and be responsive to the socioeconomic needs and aspirations of their citizens by carrying out sensible economic policies that generate economic prosperity with social justice. Only economic policies that encourage private investment and the development of a market economy will generate the wealth that will permit the implementation of progressive social policies to reduce poverty and increase social justice and equality, and that will, in turn, elicit greater citizenry trust and confidence in democracy as the preferred system of government.

The weaknesses and shortcomings of some of the hemisphere's evolving and consolidating democracies does suggest, however, the need for strengthening and revitalizing the OAS as an instrument of solidarity and cooperation to support member states in their own efforts to nourish, consolidate and protect democracy when its existence is threatened and/or to prevent its breakdown by all necessary and possible means. But inevitably, the revitalization of the OAS depends on the cohesiveness and consolidation of the democratic community, that is, the IADR, which in turn will depend on the degree of commitment from each member to representative liberal democracy, its exercise and defense, and on the degree of cohesiveness among them. Commitment and consensus guarantee cohesiveness.

Needed in this effort is the political/diplomatic leadership of the well-established democracies as well as outspoken democratic hemispheric leaders, including the Secretary General of the OAS, with an inter-American democratic vision and the capacity to negotiate, build consensus and mobilize the member states and their citizenry around it. This would counter the vitriolic and strident, charismatic, media-savvy authoritarian *caudillos* that have appeared in recent years with a populist and anti-imperialist (U.S.) message, claiming to represent and be working for the great majority of Latin Americans.

The inter-American democratic community, using OAS norms and instruments, must remain attentive and committed to protecting democracy and to guaranteeing that the progress made in building and consolidating democracy is not reversed, and that there is no return to non-democratic or *de facto* governance in the hemisphere. What to do is the subject of the next and final chapter.

NOTES

1. In Guatemala (1993), Paraguay (1996) and Ecuador (1997), the high command of the armed forces kept their distance by supporting the constitutional process and did not yield to the temptation to stage coups d'état. In Argentina during the 1980s, the military accepted the trials of military officers that governed Argentina in the 1970s, although some minor segments of the military still revolted against President Alfonsín. In Venezuela in 1992, senior officers rejected an attempted coup led by Colonel Chávez and then respected President Pérez' trial; in 2002, they returned President Chávez to power and today they are the backbone of the *chavista* regime. In Brazil in 1992, the armed forces also respected the trial and constitutional removal of President Collor de Melo. In Chile, they accepted the detention of General Pinochet in England in 2000, as well as accusations leveled against the members of the military for human rights violations during the military government.

2. Perhaps an additional way of strengthening the mechanisms for the protection of democracy is for member states to consider, through the OAS, the exclusion or suspension of armed forces from inter-American military cooperation agreements, such as military conferences, the

Inter-American Defense Board and joint exercises when those armed forces have been involved in an attempted coup d'état or have seized power by force.

3. Concerning violations of political and human rights and deterioration of the democratic order see, see *Fundación Nueva Democracia, Observatorio de Derechos Humanos* (2013), Freedom House (2013), Inter-American Commission on Human Rights (2009), Paez (April 2012) and Weyland (2013). See also devastating reports on the human rights situation in Venezuela in the 2013 and 2014 annual reports of the IACHR, in http://www.oas.org/en/iachr/docs/annual/2013/docs-en/AnnualReport-Chap4-Intro-A.pdf. Also see the reports of the IACHR freedom of expression rapporteurship at http://www.oas.org/en/iachr/expression/docs/reports/annual/2014_04_22_%20IA_2013_ENG%20_FINALweb.pdf. See also the U.N. High Commissioner for Human Rights, asking the Venezuelan government to release from jail political opposition leader, Leopoldo Lopez: http://www.ohchr.org/SP/NewsEvents/Pages/DisplayNews.aspx?NewsID=15187&LangID=S. Inexplicably and regretfully, Secretary General Insulza has not commented publicly on the fabricated charges against López or his illegal imprisonment, and has not appealed the Venezuelan Government for his release.

4. One U.S. diplomat, responding to this commonly held view in academic circles, recently suggested that this misperception of U.S. distancing from Latin America may in fact be attributed to the U.S. media, which does not adequately cover U.S. relations with its southern neighbors.

5. Recently, however, at the same time that the U.S. Government was reestablishing diplomatic relations with Castro's Cuba, it was imposing new visa restrictions on officials of the Venezuelan Government accused of human rights violations and drug trafficking.

6. Both countries in the last couple of years (2012–2014), however, have experienced a considerable slowdown in their economic growth as a result of the global recession and the subsequent reduction in demand and prices of their commodities exports, coupled with protectionist and nationalist/statist economic policies.

7. On recent patterns of U.S.-Latin American relations, see Amaral (2011), Russell (2011), Lowenthal (2011) and Hakim (2014).

8. Historically, the U.S. has exercised its hegemony through the hemisphere to prevent real or perceived external threats: First, during the 19th century, within the framework of the Monroe Doctrine and Roosevelt Corollary, to prevent the return of European colonial powers to re-occupy fragile Latin American countries after their independence; second, during the first half of the 20th century, to prevent the Nazi-fascist expansion and penetration of the Americas; and finally, during most of the second half of the twentieth century, to prevent Sino-Soviet communist aggression and penetration, particularly through their proxy, the Castro regime. Throughout, U.S. allies were oligarchical republics, dictatorships and even democracies–whichever best served its purpose. However, since the beginning of the 1990s, this openly interventionist, hegemonic practice in the Americas, driven by the U.S. obsession to protect its economic and security/strategic interests, is no longer patently operative in U.S. foreign policy towards Latin America. This will remain so until a new extra-continental challenge (perhaps China, Islamic terrorism or cyber terrorism) or a radical continental anti-democratic strategic challenge emerges to threaten the *pax democratica* in the hemisphere.

9. In view of their failure, the five countries joined the consensus and the Council approved the Declaration by acclamation. However, Bolivia stated in a footnote that it rejects "the economic and financial embargo against the Republic of Cuba and demands its immediate suspension as a measure to contribute to the normalization of diplomatic relations, and we reject any unilateral sanction against the sovereign states of the Americas." Venezuela, also in a footnote, condemned "the international practice of imposing unilateral sanctions against sovereign states," and demanded "an end to member states' enforcement of laws that have extraterritorial effects that affect the sovereignty of other states and the legitimate interests of entities and individuals under their jurisdiction as well as free trade and investment." Similarly, the Nicaragua delegation stated that its Government "believes that the historic announcement made by the Presidents of the Republic of Cuba and of the United States of America on December 17, 2014 marks the beginning of a new state of affairs that will allow the end of the economic, commercial, and financial blockade imposed by the Government of the United States on the Republic of Cuba," called "for the continuation of the process toward the full normalization of

relations between the two countries," and rejected "the imposition of unilateral sanctions on the Bolivarian Republic of Venezuela and on other countries of the world." (Permanent Council of the OAS 2014).

Chapter Twelve

Suggestions for Revitalization

INTRODUCTION

The preceding Chapters identified several challenges facing the OAS collective bodies and its General Secretariat, as well as the norms, instruments and programs that member states created and applied to promote and defend democracy in the hemisphere. It is time now to suggest ways to address the threats, limitations, weaknesses or deficiencies those challenges pose, in an effort to strengthen and improve the Organization's effectiveness in performing its new and unique role of promoting and protecting democracy. This Chapter is also intended to contribute to the revitalization of the OAS as the central hemispheric multilateral institution of and for inter-American cooperation. In today's world, cooperation is a requirement for a peaceful, secured, prosperous and democratic hemisphere.

The suggestions for change are directed to the policy-making bodies of the Organization, mainly the Permanent Council and the General Assembly, and to the Secretary General, whose office has considerable administrative authority as well as important but limited "political" powers. The suggestions concern the General Secretariat as a whole and specifically the activities of its Secretariat for Political Affairs in the area of democracy promotion, Electoral Observation Missions (EOMs) and the Inter-American Democratic Charter (IADC).

Some of these recommendations can be applied without amending the OAS Charter or the IADC; others will require changes to both. The General Assembly can make partial changes to the latter, which is not a treaty but a General Assembly resolution, through future specific resolutions. In any case, any changes will require prolonged, complex and arduous negotiations, compromise and consensus building, as well as effective leadership from the Secretary General and certain member states. [1]

SUBSTANTIVE PRIORITIES AND A NEW METHODOLOGY

As discussed in Chapter 10, member states recently approved strategic objectives for four strategic pillars—Democracy, Human Rights, Integral Development and Multidimensional Security—as part of their Strategic Vision for the Organization, and instructed the Permanent Council to develop it further by preparing a "comprehensive strategic plan to accomplish those objectives." [2] But the new priorities are not so new and the strategic objectives for three of the four pillars, Integral Development, Multidimensional Security, and Democracy, are all-inclusive, not prioritized, and ill defined. The following suggestions seek to enrich the dialogue for strengthening and reinvigorating the OAS by recommending the consolidation and concentration of the Organization's substantive areas and methodologies on what are considered to be the most relevant and realistic priorities for today's OAS and the hemisphere.

Integral Development

The member states should eliminate the Integral Development pillar, and concentrate on the Democracy, Multidimensional Security and Human Rights pillars.

As defined in Chapter VII of the OAS Charter, [3] integral development includes almost any issue related to socioeconomic development. But the OAS simply does not have the human and financial resources to address all those issues. Other inter-American institutions, including the IDB, CAF, CDB or the World Bank are better equipped to tackle them. That is why the governing bodies should terminate this program area, which is currently implemented by the Executive Secretariat for Integral Development (SEDI) and the Inter-American Agency for Cooperation and Development with oversight by the Inter-American Council for Integral Development (CIDI). Eliminating this area, however, will require amending the OAS Charter, inasmuch as both SEDI and CIDI are OAS organs whose purposes and functions are specified in the OAS Charter. [4] In the meantime, the Secretary General, with the approval of the General Assembly, should begin to negotiate a gradual transfer of programs and activities currently within the purview of CIDI and SEDI to inter-American institutions with more realistic prospects and better capabilities for implementing them.

The elimination of SEDI, IACD, and CIDI, if implemented, would reduce the General Secretariat's bureaucracies and thereby free up human and financial resources in order to strengthen the Human Rights, Democracy and

Multilateral Security pillars, which cover issues and activities in which the OAS still has a comparative advantage relative to other international organizations, member states acting unilaterally, and NGOs.

However, it is highly unlikely that the member states will in the foreseeable future decide to eliminate the Integral Development pillar from the Organization's strategic agenda and amend the OAS Charter accordingly: The area remains a high priority for most Caribbean and some Central American member states. So the next best alternative is to adopt a new technical cooperation methodology. Ideally, the new methodology would eliminate "direct bilateral technical assistance" between the OAS and a national government and would concentrate exclusively on regional multilateral programs, projects or activities, be they training programs, workshops, horizontal technical assistance missions, web pages, data bases, research and publications and so forth. SEDI, through a new office of regional multilateral programing and coordination, would provide planning, fundraising, general coordination, evaluation and selection of activities for fundraising. Subsequently, the Secretariat and member states involved would officially "present" these selected activities for funding and implementation to partner regional institutions, such as the IDB, CAF, CDB, the World Bank, or development agencies from member states or observer countries. These technical cooperation programs would have the purpose of promoting and supporting, inter alia: i) high-level political dialogue among sectoral ministries, ii) exchange of information, knowledge and successful experiences, iii) horizontal technical cooperation, and iv) a clearing house for information and databases on best practices related to development issues. [5]

Multidimensional Security

The concept of security, by its very nature, is multidimensional. Nonetheless, in the Organization's current Strategic Vision, the concept remains abstract, unclear, and confused. Thus, it is ripe for refinement. It is misguided and unrealistic for the OAS to establish strategic objectives that link peace and security to a potpourri of multidimensional causes like social justice and integration, education, integral development, and other vague factors, particularly when the Organization is not equipped to deal with them in any effective manner. The Organization should limit its strategic objectives for multidimensional security to those supporting the strengthening of the capacity of government institutions to address the concrete and immediate threats to domestic public safety and regional peace and security, such as drug trafficking, organized crime, terrorism and cyber-attacks. Those objectives should give priority to regional multinational projects, with exceptions for bilateral cooperation in cases of national emergencies resulting from real and present threats to public safety, peace, and democratic security in a member state. In an ideal world, with unlimited human and financial resources, the Organization, in partnership with national and sub-regional institutions, could work on long-term regional or national preventive measures that might help mitigate the multidimensional causes of drug use, violence, crime and terrorism, like poverty, unemployment, social exclusion, deficient, mediocre education, school dropout and others. But even then it would have to clearly define its role.

The Democracy Pillar

The strategic objectives for democracy promotion require clarification and expansion. Currently, they are too limited. Those objectives should include an agenda for the Secretariat for Political Affairs that focuses on programs and activities for to strengthen political parties, legislatures, decentralization and local governance, and the independent media, plus the promotion of democratic values and practices in the educational system and through the training of young political leaders.[6] Those are all areas that had been part of the mandate of the Unit for the Promotion of Democracy (UPD) prior to its dissolution in the 2005 reorganization of the General Secretariat and the creation of the Secretariat for Political Affairs (SPA). Regrettably, they were downgraded and deemphasized in the reprogramming of the Secretariat's agenda that followed. They should be restored. Democracy is much more than well-organized, free and fair elections, and democratic governance requires the predominance of and respect for democratic institutions, values and practices. The strategic objective of this pillar, beyond the obvious and general objective of promoting and protecting of democracy, should simply be to support: (a) the strengthening of democratic institutions (not just public administration and electoral institutions), and (b) the promotion of democratic values and practices, in accordance with the Inter-American Democratic Charter, including, of course, probity and transparency in governmental affairs. Moreover, in recognition of the salience of the Democratic Pillar, the Secretary General and member states should change the name of the Secretariat for Political Affairs to the "Secretariat for Political and Democratic Affairs" (SPDA).

How may the Organization achieve these broader objectives? A regional multilateral approach should be employed primarily, coupled with national projects when "technical assistance" is needed and requested to strengthen and consolidate the republican and institutional democratic order of a member state—particularly when it is threatened by internal erosion or decay.

In this new framework, the SPDA would be a catalyst for cooperation amongst member states around the current and new programmatic areas identified above. In that capacity, the SPDA would cooperate technically and politically with pertinent institutions from member states to design, fundraise, and execute programs, projects and activities of a regional/multinational and national nature. These may include high-level political fora to stimulate dialogue amongst, for example, heads of legislatures, leaders of local government and municipal associations, political party leaders, electoral authorities and others, so that they could identify common challenges and strategies for cooperation to address them. They could also include technical meetings for the exchange of information, knowledge and experience on strengthening democratic institutions; "technical/political" horizontal cooperation and assistance; training programs for young political and societal leaders on democratic values and practices and techniques of political management; and a virtual clearing house for information and data bases on best practices related to institution building.[7] They could also include technical assistance for teaching, research and publications, which would support and encourage relevant academic centers and young scholars in their efforts to generate expertise and new endogenous knowledge, particularly through empirical and comparative research, publications, web sites on crucial subjects such as democratic values and practices, institutions, and leadership and their role in consolidating democracy. Research and better knowledge and understanding is also needed on the relevance and effectiveness of technical assistance instruments used in democracy promotion; the nature and extent of the changes they seek and how to measure them; the challenges and obstacles they face to achieve those changes; ways to refine those instruments in order to obtain the desired changes; and the nature and effectiveness of evaluation methodologies. Arguably, these types of programs and activities of democracy promotion offer indeed the best long-term prospects for preventing democratic decay and breakdown.

Democracy promotion would be greatly enhanced if the promoters' community (donors, academics, diplomats, government officials, legislators, and practitioners) would support and finance long-term technical assistance programs for democracy promotion like the ones suggested here. The knowledge and expertise gained and disseminated through these efforts would be invaluable for the international community engaged in democracy promotion.

THE GENERAL SECRETARIAT

The Secretary General

The leadership functions of the Secretary General, both those specified under the OAS Charter[8] and those acquired by way of custom and practice under international law, dictate that the person who occupies that position be knowledgeable about the inter-American system and its history, and of the OAS role in it. Thus, member states should elect to that position only those persons who demonstrate an adequate understanding of and an unwavering commitment to the Organization's role in the promotion and protection of democracy and human rights, which are essential for the peace, security, and development of the hemisphere.[9]

Those who occupy the position of Secretary General must have a clear understanding of the non-interventionist limits placed on the position by member states, but must also have the political courage to defend democracy, human rights, and the instruments the member states have created for their promotion and protection. The SG/OAS must be fearless and resolute in countering any attempts, by countries with increasing authoritarian traits, to impede OAS involvement in the solution or even analysis of political situations that threaten human rights and the democratic order, to avoid electoral observations, or even to weaken the Inter-American Commission on Human Rights, as Bolivia, Ecuador and Venezuela have attempted to do in the recent past.

As for the administration of the General Secretariat, the principal responsibility of the Secretary General under the Charter,[10] he or she must possess the leadership and determination to implement needed changes. Today there is a felt need to adjust and modernize the Organization's bureaucracy to address its real priorities, which involves dealing with serious and urgent internal financial and management issues and reassessing its human capital (oftentimes undervalued and misused), whose commitment to the Organization has deteriorated in recent years. He/she must be determined to assign human capital in accordance with the priorities and programmatic necessities of the Organization, and not on the basis of cronyism or political accommodation. The Secretary General must implement a transparent and merit-based personnel policy that balances expertise (institutional memory) with varied and fresh perspectives, in addition to proper gender and geographical representation. The recommendations of the Plan for Management Modernization of the OAS are quite pertinent for this crucial task.[11] Accordingly, the Secretary General should not recruit and appoint staff members based on their political ideology; nor should he or she appoint staff who have little knowledge of or commitment to the OAS and the inter-American system, its values and institutions. Nonetheless, those persons appointed by the Secretary General to high-level advisory and administrative positions, including the Chief of Staff, must be capable of managing urgent and delicate diplomatic, financial, and administrative issues and interacting productively with the Ambassadors of the member states in the Permanent Council, whose consensus is necessary for resolving them.

A Secretary General cannot successfully fulfill his/her leadership responsibilities to the Organization simply by presenting a proposal for a "new vision." Rather, the task requires that he or she follow up on such a proposal by constantly persuading, pressuring, negotiating and building consensus with the member states–the difficult but essential tasks of leadership. As the spokesperson for the Organization, the Secretary General must have the necessary communications skills, not only in his or her native language but also in English—to project or "sell" the Organization adequately in diplomatic, media, academic and fundraising circles.

So as to minimize the possibility that reelection concerns may temper a Secretary General's zeal and disposition to take the courageous and difficult decisions that leadership often requires, member states should seriously consider amending the OAS Charter to limit each Secretary General to a single six-year term, with no possibility of reelection. [12] Also, under the applicable conflict of interest rules, [13] member states should be quick to sanction any Secretary General who campaigns for office in his home country or for a position in any other international organization. Regrettably, member states have been reluctant to act on this in the recent past.

In sum, the Secretary General must be a leader with the ability to present a renewed vision and mission for the OAS, focused on its priorities, and with the necessary communications and negotiating skills to generate the (currently elusive) consensus that is needed for its renovation and revitalization. He or she should also be an inspirational leader not only to the member states but to the staff as well. This type of leader does not have to be a former Foreign Minister or former President: Ambassador Baena Soares of Brazil was a very successful Secretary General (1984-1994). But a record of successful stewardship of high office in a member state or other international organization requiring political, diplomatic, and administrative expertise and leadership, is an important indicator of potential for the position.

The Assistant Secretary General

Member states should consider amending the OAS Charter to eliminate the post of Assistant Secretary General. [14] The office was created to promote a regional balance at the helm of the Organization.

The Assistant Secretary General (ASG/OAS) is independently elected for a renewable term of five years. The formal responsibilities of the position include supporting the organization and preparation of the meetings and activities of the Permanent Council and the General Assembly, and acting as the Secretary of the Permanent Council (not minor or irrelevant functions in the complex OAS diplomatic bureaucracy). Also, under the Charter, the ASG serves as acting Secretary General when the Secretary General is unable to perform his/her functions. He or she may perform additional functions, as assigned by the Secretary General. Because the ASG is elected by the General Assembly in a separate election, he or she may have a political constituency and political commitments different from those of the Secretary General.

While the Secretary General at his discretion delegates to the ASG responsibilities and activities that are supposed to be executed in consultation and coordination with the SG's office, those activities are usually conditioned by the personal agenda and/or personality of the person holding the ASG position and frequently end up producing (unspoken but widely-known) friction, tensions and estrangement from the SG/OAS staff. This institutional situation may prejudice coordination and implementation of Secretariat services and the political initiatives of the Secretary General. As others have recommended in the past, an OAS Charter amendment abolishing the office of the ASG/OAS would eliminate that potential. The functions currently performed by the ASG could be performed by a Secretariat for Meetings and Conferences directly responsible to the Secretary General or indirectly through his or her Chief of Staff. The savings realized by eliminating the office of ASG could be reassigned to the program priorities established under the pillars.

Another option, as suggested by the Plan for Management Modernization of the OAS, would be to have the AGS/OAS elected jointly with the Secretary General to assure a common agenda and teamwork. The office, in addition to its formal functions, should also be responsible for the general administrative and financial matters of the Organization and report to the Secretary General.[15]

Programming, Evaluation and Fundraising

The Secretary General should eliminate the current Project Evaluation Committee (CEP) and the Department within the Secretariat for Administration that supports it. The Secretariat that develops a project is the entity most capable of evaluating a project's successes and failures. That is where the expertise and political rationale for the project resides, not in the CEP. The Secretariat should develop evaluation forms/questionnaires concerned more with the programming objective of the project than with the wording and the measurability of the information requested and provided. Forms should be simple and require the identification of few, clear and concise objectives and limited, realistic, relevant and strategic expected outcomes. These changes are likely to result in more meaningful evaluations for donors, project developers, and project administrators, as well as a more efficient evaluation process.

If the Secretary General does not eliminate the CEP, he/she should consider limiting its functions to the following: designing a standard format for presentation/evaluation, to make sure that the project objectives are congruent with the strategic objectives of the Organization's pillars; receiving the approved projects from the different Secretariats, and constructing a data base of all projects approved for fundraising as well as of their implementation status, for biannual reporting to the SG and to the Permanent Council, and finally, designing, coordinating, and monitoring with the pertinent Secretariats or Departments a flexible fundraising strategy that avoids duplication and favoritism based on cronyism or political accommodation. The successful implementation of this latter function will require the strong political/ diplomatic engagement from the Secretary General or his Chief of Staff.

THE INTER-AMERICAN DEMOCRATIC CHARTER (IADC)

The weaknesses and shortcomings of the IADC, identified in Chapter 6, provide the basis for some suggestions as to how to strengthen it as a more useful and effective instrument for promoting and defending representative democracy in the hemisphere. The first option for strengthening the IADC is to apply its provisions to the fullest extent; the other is to amend it.

The Challenge of Applying the IADC to the Fullest without Amending It

As already discussed, the IADC contains provisions to provide an early warning of democratic decay and the adoption of measures to prevent an institutional breakdown or otherwise arrest it. As further explained in the following recommendations, there are ways in which those provisions can be applied more effectively without the need to amend the IADC.

Recommendation No. 1

The timely invocation of Article 20 would provide the early warning necessary to prevent an institutional breakdown. Article 20 provides that in "the event that an unconstitutional alteration of the constitutional regime…any member state or the Secretary General may request the immediate convocation of the Permanent Council to undertake a collective assessment of the situation." This clearly and unequivocally empowers the Secretary General and/or any member state to convene the Council when events in another member state indicate that an unconstitutional alteration is underway. The meeting and ensuing collective analysis would elucidate the situation. Given the ambivalence of the term and the probable lack of consensus among member states about the real nature of the political situation, such a move would be controversial, but Article 20 establishes a firm legal basis for the Secretary General or any member state to call for a collective assessment of the situation in the Permanent Council, without the consent, necessarily, of the government affected.

Action pursuant to Article 20 may be necessary in cases in which it is the executive branch of a member state that may be causing the alteration of the democratic order. The president may be concentrating and abusing his or her power, or assuming that just because he/she won an election and has a legislative majority, he/she can violate the rule of law and the separation and independence of powers, or limit freedom of the press and association, manipulate electoral processes, or persecute the opposition. In such cases, a collective analysis would certainly clarify the situation for all the stakeholders in the Organization, would serve as an early warning, and would provide the basis and rationale for fostering and initiating a process of dialogue, negotiation and consensus building amongst the institutional or political contenders—which could very well prevent an eventual institutional rupture.

Action under Article 20 does not necessarily constitute intervention in the internal affairs of the member state affected because all member states have committed themselves to promote and defend democracy and all have agreed voluntarily to respect the provisions of the IADC. On the other hand, a collective assessment would be necessary, if not imperative, in those cases in which the threat to democracy in one member state is likely to become a threat to its neighbors' democracy. One would think, hypothetically, that if a guerrilla group were about to overthrow a democratically elected government in a member state, its neighbors would not stand idly by because of the non-intervention principle. They would, in effect, see it as a threat to their own democracy and to the democratic community in general, and would react collectively in ways that might even include a military response to prevent the collapse of the neighbor's democratic government.

Recommendation No. 2

The collective assessment by the OAS of a critical political situation in a member state would greatly benefit from including representatives of the legislative branch in the assessment process. This would be quite useful and pertinent particularly when and if it is the executive branch itself that is violating the democratic institutional order, by, for example, suppressing the political opposition in the legislature or violating its constitutional prerogatives and independence to make unconstitutional changes and thus generating a political crisis that threatens the democratic order. In this circumstance, while representing a member state is the exclusive attribute of the executive branch, relevant opposition legislative leaders and other significant stakeholders should/could be included as discussants or witnesses in informal meetings related to the collective assessment of the situation. This could help elucidate for member states what is usually a complex, fast-moving and unclear political situation and could provide the occasion and venue for the members to facilitate a peaceful and timely resolution of the crisis and thus prevent an institutional collapse.

Similarly, the Organization should seek to involve national legislatures and their representatives in its activities, as the UPD did in its programming between 1994-2005 (Chapter 7). It is after all, the legislative branch that in most countries ratifies international agreements (including treaties, conventions) reached by representatives of the executive branch, and that approves the national budget, which normally contains payments or contributions to the Organization. The Organization should in effect reach out to national (at least) and regional legislative institutions to engage them in activities that would promote a better knowledge and understanding of the Democratic Charter, and even to encourage them to incorporate it into their own bodies of laws. For example, the SPDA could assist legislatures in developing and drafting legislation that would make it an obligation for citizens, governmental institutions and leaders to respect the IADC, as well as their right to have recourse to it, invoke it, or ask for it to be applied whenever they feel that their political rights have been violated or that there has been a pervasive erosion or alteration of the democratic order. It could also propose constitutional reforms to include the IADC in their national Constitutions as some countries have done with the Inter-American Convention on Human Rights.[16] Finally, their knowledge and support of the Charter will be vital in the event the decision is taken by the Organization to transform the IACD into a multilateral treaty, as proposed below.

Recommendation No. 3

The Secretary General and member states should, as a basis for initiating action under Article 20 of the IADC, utilize those reports of the Human Rights Commission (IACHR) that identify significant departures from democratic constitutional practices in the member states. To do so, the Secretary General or a member state would coordinate with the IACHR, and without contravening the Commission's independence, refer to its reports or that of the Freedom of the Press Rapporteur to express concern in cases of violations of political rights or fundamental freedoms, which in themselves may have constituted or may have resulted from "an alteration of the constitutional regime." Indeed, Article 91(f) of the OAS Charter confers upon the Permanent Council responsibility to "consider the Commission's reports...and present to the General Assembly any observations and recommendations it deems necessary." Over the years, the Commission's reports have recognized, as does the IADC and the American Convention on Human Rights,[17] the integral relationship between human rights and democracy, and have not refrained from indicating those instances where failure to observe those rights have placed democracy in peril.[18]

Because of their independence, the IACHR reports and the reports of its special Rapporteurs can be very useful instruments for promoting a public

debate on presumed or corroborated violations of political rights and democratic institutions, values and practices–a debate which may be an early
warning of democratic erosion and possible interruption of the democratic
order. Further, appropriate utilization of the Commission's reports would
strengthen its role in protecting human and political rights in the hemisphere.

Recommendation No. 4

The General Secretariat should further institutionalize and strengthen its political observation missions and use of its good offices, both as a tool for
preventing the breakdown of the democratic order and for restoring it once it
has broken down.

When a government requests the assistance of the Organization under
Articles 17 or 18 of the IADC after concluding that its institutional order is
being threatened by an emerging political crisis, normally the Permanent
Council or a special session of the General Assembly will instruct the Secretary General to send a political/diplomatic mission to analyze the situation
and to offer its good offices to help preserve the democratic order and then
report back.[19] Similarly, in those instances in which a coup topples a constitutional democratic regime, the Council or the Assembly will, pursuant to
Article 20 of the IADC, order a political/diplomatic mission in an effort to
negotiate the restoration of the democratic order.[20]

The main role of these political/diplomatic missions is to promote and
facilitate a process of political dialogue, negotiation and consensus building
amongst the contending forces, and then to observe compliance with the
accords they have reached to preserve or restore the democratic order. Because of its critical role, this type of mission should be prepared to remain in
the country long enough to generate confidence amongst the political forces;
it should be led by an SG/OAS representative who is politically savvy and
well versed in the nature and history of the inter-American system and the
Democratic Charter; and it should be well staffed with experts in negotiation
and mediation. Recent missions of this type have not met all of these requirements, as exemplified by the SG/OAS mission sent to support former Honduran President Zelaya's effort in 2009 to hold a referendum that the legislature
considered unconstitutional.

Recommendation No. 5

The Organization should develop and implement adequately financed technical cooperation programs designed to promote democratic values and practices, and the strengthening of political institutions and democratic governance, as proposed in Articles 26 and 27 of the IACD. To that end, the
Secretary General should reinstate the former (eliminated) UPD medium and

long-term democracy programs for strengthening and modernizing legislatures, political parties and local governments, for promoting democratic values and practices through the educational system, and for training young political leaders. All branches of a democratic government, not just the executive branch, plus the independent media and pertinent nongovernmental organizations should be able to benefit from OAS democracy promotion programs. There is no logical reason or institutional/formal restriction within the OAS to limit democracy promotion assistance to the executive branch and its ministries or agencies.

Recommendation No. 6

The SPDA should report regularly to the Permanent Council on its democracy promotion activities, as the UPD used to do quarterly. The Permanent Council should review the reports, and, if needed, provide political guidelines to improve and or expand the activities. This would afford member states periodic information and better understanding of OAS democracy promotion activities, which would, in turn, likely translate into the political/ diplomatic and financial support these activities require to be successful.

Recommendation No. 7

The General Secretariat, in consultation with the Permanent Council, could also improve the usefulness and effectiveness of the IADC by promoting a greater knowledge and better understanding of its nature and functions within the member states. Thus, the SPDA should assist academic institutions (graduate and undergraduate schools of political science, international relations and international law) and diplomatic academies in offering courses on the IADC, the relationship between the IADC and other inter-American legal instruments pertaining to human rights and democracy,[21] and the role of the OAS in promoting and protecting democracy and human rights. This type of course or subject is inexcusably absent from most of these institutions in the Americas.

The Challenge of IADC Reform

The other possible way of strengthening the usefulness and effectiveness of the IADC is by reforming it. As one would expect, this is a more complicated task and perhaps unattainable in the present state of inter-American relations. As indicated before, member states can, in principle, amend specific provisions of the IADC by means of General Assembly resolutions, and can do so without amending the entire IADC, which might open a Pandora's box in that pseudo-democracies might use the occasion to change the nature of the Charter and reduce or limit its reach and scope. Nevertheless, there exist a few possible reforms which appear necessary to improve the Organization's capacity to prevent alterations to the democratic institutional order, and which the governing bodies should consider.

Recommended Reform No. 1

The first recommended reform would be to improve the definitions of essential terms for triggering action under Articles 20 and 21 of the IADC. Member states should consider introducing language into the IADC that clarifies the difference, if any, between "an unconstitutional *alteration* of the constitutional regime" on the one hand, and an "unconstitutional *interruption* of the democratic order" on the other. The former may trigger action to evaluate the situation under Article 20 of the IADC; the latter may trigger a decision of the General Assembly to suspend a member state under Article 21. But according to Article 19 of the IACD, both pose an "insurmountable obstacle" to participation in the OAS political bodies. A definition of these concepts that pinpoints the kinds of events and occurrences that each would constitute would aid member states and the Secretary General in identifying when action under Articles 20 and 21 is appropriate. It would also facilitate the ability of the Secretary General or member states to convoke the Permanent Council for a collective assessment of the situation, which may in turn serve as an early warning and the basis for preventive actions against interruptions of the democratic order.[22]

Recommended Reform No. 2

The second recommended reform would be to formally include the judiciary and the legislature of affected member states in the warning and evaluation process. The member states should amend the Charter to include a process (formal or informal) whereby representatives of the legislature and/or judiciary of a country, whose executive authorities have produced an unconstitutional alteration or interruption in the democratic order, may testify and provide information to the pertinent OAS political bodies, regardless of objections from the executive branch. Their perspectives on the political situation may be different from that of the executive branch and may be useful if not necessary for an effective collective decision.

The member states should also amend Article 17 of the IADC so as to permit members of the legislature and judiciary to request, without the consent of the executive branch, a visit by the Secretary General or Permanent Council to observe *in situ* the political situation in their country. The reports of such visits would include the results of interviews with representatives of the legislative and judicial branches, and would be a component of the collective assessment of the situation. The participation and voice of pertinent representatives of the legislative and judiciary of a country whose constitutional democracy is in peril would enrich the member states' understanding of the situation and would provide the inputs and the basis for a well-substantiated collective decision in response. Their greater involvement in the promotion and protection of democracy would strengthen the Charter and would democratize the inter-American system. The Organization's 2009 experience in Honduras makes a very good case for greater legislative and judicial participation in the early warning and the collective assessment processes under the IADC. If the Secretary General and Permanent Council had at that time engaged the legislative and judicial branches—which vehemently opposed President Zelaya's proposed referendum to change the constitution's no re-election provision—in an attempt to mediate a process of negotiation and consensus building to solve the budding political crisis, the June coup d'état that deposed the President might have been averted.

The above leads to further considerations concerning the limitations caused by the exclusive predominance of the executive branch in intergovernmental organizations (IGOs) such as the OAS (or MERCOSUR and UNASUR), whose members are representative democracies and adhere to the "democracy clause." Arguably, their continued relevance in promoting democracy or preventing its breakdown will depend on their own capacity to democratize themselves. This means that, in order for these IGOs to play any significant moderating and mediating role in a political crisis threatening the continuity of the democratic order in a member state caused by the undemocratic conduct of a president, their formal or informal deliberations must include consultation with other branches of government, opposition leaders and relevant nongovernmental organizations, *before* the crisis ends in the total breakdown of the democratic order. In cases of national political crises (which usually involve confrontation among branches of government), the voice of those other branches in international organizations would guarantee the observance of democratic principles in the member state and would strengthen their capacity to prevent institutional rupture. It would also enhance the role of an international organization like the OAS as a "democratic" forum that can promote and facilitate dialogue and negotiations between contending parties. To that effect, member states' executive branches (governments) should forsake their reluctance to abandon or even diminish their exclusive privilege and monopoly of international organizations.

Recommended Reform No. 3

A third recommendation for reform is creation of an entity to observe, evaluate, and report on IADC compliance. Member states should amend the IADC to create such an entity. One option would be to create a Commission similar to the Inter-American Human Rights Commission, composed of five to seven experts elected by the member states. Its primary function would be to observe, with appropriate and rigorous methodology, member state compliance with the Charter. As an alternative, a mutual or peer evaluation mechanism, similar to the one utilized to assess implementation of the Inter-American Convention against Corruption, could be established.[23] In either case, the entity so established would present periodic reports to the Permanent Council on the state of democracy in the hemisphere, and could advise or provide political/technical assistance, in collaboration with the General Secretariat, to any branch of government that requests cooperation to strengthen democratic institutions.

ELECTORAL OBSERVATION MISSIONS (EOMS)

Because of the centrality of elections and the crucial role they play in the origins, renovation and consolidation of a democracy, and because Electoral Observation Missions are such a prominent component of the OAS toolbox for promoting democracy, they merit special attention and specific recommendations here. The purpose of the following recommendations is to suggest ways to reinforce the effectiveness and relevance of EOMs in promoting and defending democracy. Member states and/or the Secretary General may adopt some of the recommendations without reforming the IADC; other recommendations may require that it be amended.

Recommendations on EOMs That Would Not Require Amendment of the IADC

Recommendation No. 1

Both the governing bodies and the Secretary General should consider establishing an independent permanent fund for EOMs, to insure proper planning and organization and to avoid delays and possible financial/political dependence on certain donors.

Recommendation No. 2

The Secretary General should insure the professionalism, independence and impartiality of EOMs by not appointing sitting OAS Ambassadors as Chiefs of Mission, and by not appearing to be partial or biased towards the government. The best insurance against claims of bias and incompetence is to staff the missions, including the position of Chief, with regular OAS international civil servants and experienced professionals from the elections commissions of the member states.

Recommendation No. 3

The Secretary General should instruct the SPDA to follow up effectively on EOMs' technical recommendations from previous missions, and to strengthen technical assistance for long-term electoral institution building efforts that would contribute to the integrity, transparency, reliability and credibility of the electoral process.

Recommendation No. 4

The SG/OAS should establish the principle that observers of general and presidential elections should be present in country at least two months before election day, particularly in contentious and vulnerable electoral processes, so that the Mission can properly evaluate whether the recommendations of previous EOMs have been implemented, assess the conditions and compliance with the instituted norms, and if necessary help correct deficiencies or irregularities.

Recommendation No. 5

In situations of political polarization that threaten the integrity of the electoral process and/or the democratic order, and before accepting an invitation to observe, the Secretary General, in consultation with the Permanent Council, should invite the stakeholders to a meeting with the Permanent Council to discuss and agree on the rules of the electoral game, with enough time to implement an agreement. It is not enough for the Secretary General to be properly informed of a serious situation in a country; member states must also be informed by all of the parties concerned. After all, the Permanent Council should be a democratic forum for dialogue and negotiations. The Secretary General must have the political courage and independence to bring to the attention of the Permanent Council under IADC Article 20 and Article 110 of the OAS Charter "an unconstitutional alteration that seriously impairs the democratic order in a member state."[24] The Permanent Council can then assess the situation and decide on a collective response to a threat to free and fair elections. Furthermore, by inviting the stakeholders to participate in such meetings when initial signs of possible deviations from democratic practices in a member state´s electoral processes are brought to its attention, the Permanent Council may help avert the rupture of the democratic order in that state.

Recommendation No. 6

Before accepting an invitation to mount an EOM in a state that already shows initial signs of deviating from democratic norms in its electoral procedures, the Secretary General, with the consent of the Permanent Council, should condition acceptance of the invitation to the requesting member state's agreement to permit and receive a Political Observation and Mediation Mission (POMM). Its purpose would be to meet with stakeholders and helping solve a political/electoral crisis that may threaten the democratic order or the integrity of the election. The Mission should include experts in negotiation and consensus building to facilitate agreement on issues that must be resolved before the electoral process begins in earnest. A well-conceptualized and staffed POMM is just one other tool the Organization may rely upon to assist in preventing the kind of breakdown of the democratic order that occurred in Honduras in 2009. Its report to the Permanent Council should be the basis for a collective decision on whether to accept an invitation to establish an EOM and/or take other preventive measures under the IADC.

Recommendation No. 7

For situations in which an EOM encounters serious and significant irregularities that threaten to invalidate the electoral process, and which the Government or the electoral authorities refuse to redress, the governing bodies and the Secretary General should consider establishing the principle of withdrawal. In such a case, the EOM may cancel its observation and leave the country, as it did in Peru in 2000. The same would apply in cases where an EOM is obstructed or is prevented from performing its functions, or if the government or electoral authorities violate the agreement on procedures for observation, or if those authorities do not fully comply with electoral norms and fail to accept the Mission's suggestions. In these cases, the EOM will inform the government of its intention to withdraw and advise the Secretary General to recall the Mission and so inform the Permanent Council.

Recommendation No. 8

The Secretary General should be selective in accepting invitations to observe elections, and be prepared to reject such invitations when the request arrives too late to mount an effective EOM and/or when the electoral process is clearly biased in favor of the government, is marred by constitutional irregularities, violates democratic and values and practices, and/or is challenged by the opposition, as it perceives serious violations and a lack of integrity and impartiality in the electoral process. If an EOM is invited too late and is unable to comment or help correct serious deficiencies in the electoral process, it becomes irrelevant. An irrelevant EOM devalues its usefulness as a collective instrument to strengthen democracy.

Recommendation No. 9

Similarly, the SG/OAS should resist the temptation to observe every scheduled election, no matter its significance. Not all elections require observation. Automatic acceptance of invitations vitiates the relevance of EOMs.

Recommendation No. 10

The Secretary General should consider reestablishing the practice of being present on at least the last two or three days of an EOM that is observing Presidential elections, as other Secretaries General have done. This enhances the prestige of the EOM.

Recommendation No. 11

The Secretary General should continue developing and refining appropriate methodology and manuals for monitoring of "new" issues, such as electoral technology, the role of the media, campaign financing and use of the state resources, and should include data analysis from their application in final reports. These measures would facilitate standardization and comparative analysis, and would enhance the professionalization and credibility of EOMs.

Recommendation No. 12

The Permanent Council or the General Assembly should use EOM reports for the collective assessment of the state of democracy in the member states, and, in pertinent cases, as an early warning instrument to analyze situations that may require collective action to prevent serious alterations or the very breakdown of the democratic order. These collective political bodies are the only ones that can actually take multilateral preventive action.

Recommendation No. 13

The Secretary General should reestablish the practice of having an EOM issue pre-Election Day reports on the electoral process. Final reports should be published in a timely fashion soon after the election, not months afterwards, as has recently been the case.

Recommendations on the EOMs
That Would Require Amendment of the IADC

Recommendation No. 1

Member states should amend the IADC to establish the principle of "automatic invitation"—in other words, the Secretary General should have the authority to send an EOM to any member state—whether or not it has requested an EOM—when the Secretary General, in consultation with the Permanent Council, concludes that the conditions in that member state so require. In essence, this means that under an amended IADC, the Organization would have a standing invitation to observe any electoral process in a member state, and the member state in question would have the obligation to make every reasonable accommodation for the EOM consistent with the standards established in the IADC for effective EOMs.

Recommendation No. 2

Member states should amend the IADC to permit the Secretary General to consider requests for electoral observation not just from the executive branch of a member state, but also from the legislature, judiciary, or regional governmental authorities, political parties, the press, and NGOs. The amendment would authorize the Secretary General, upon consultation with the Permanent Council, to respond positively to a request if in the Secretary General's opinion, the conditions in the member country warrant the presence of an EOM, and it would obligate that member state to make every reasonable accommodation for the EOM consistent with the standards established in the IADC for effective EOMs.

A FINAL CAVEAT

The implementation of most of the above suggestions, with or without IADC reform, will require political will from the Secretary General, as well as consensus amongst the member states—which at this point in time seems improbable. The present absence of consensus within the Organization reflects the various political/ideological differences or divisions existing in the hemisphere—in marked contrast to the regime congruence of the 1980s and 1990s when the first inter-American instruments for the promotion and defense of democracy were designed, approved and applied, and in 2001 when the IADC was unanimously approved. These differences and divisions have fragmented the hemisphere and are the principal obstacles impeding a renewed commitment to collectively protect and defend representative democracy.

The necessary consensus will not likely be attained while pseudo-democratic regimes continue to invoke rhetorically and without real justification the proverbial but obsolete principle of non-intervention, in an effort to conceal violations of their own democratic constitutions, the IADC, the American Convention on Human Rights and the OAS Charter itself, as well as to prevent an even-handed collective public assessment of the democratic situation in their countries. The pretext is, of course, the defense of state sovereignty (not the sovereignty of citizens proclaimed in most democratic constitutions) against a supposed supranational encroachment by international organizations like the OAS, which leaders of pseudo-democracies consider, pejoratively and untenably, to be dominated or manipulated by the United States.

In the short term at least, this disturbing lack of consensus to protect democracy will persist unless there are significant political/electoral changes in countries like Argentina, Brazil, Ecuador, and Venezuela, and/or unless there emerges a coalition of truly (liberal) democratic regimes supported by a new Secretary General with leadership qualities, who together will have the political courage to invoke and use the IADC to challenge the pseudo-democracies, in an effort to prevent further deterioration of the democratic order in those countries as well as their estrangement from their commitment to the IADC. The effectiveness and relevance of the OAS, the IADC, and the other inter-American instruments intended for the recognition and protection of political rights depends on the state of inter-American relations. If there is consensus and cohesiveness amongst member states, they are useful and effective instruments; if there is division and fragmentation, they are not. Today, division and fragmentation reign. Thus, the OAS finds itself transiting through one of its periodic crisis of identity, compelling member states to engage recently in efforts to develop a new strategic vision—efforts that were, however, meek and insufficient.

However, as discussed in the previous Chapter, the recent rapprochement between the United States and Cuba (December 2014) may contribute to the development of a new era of improved inter-American relations, which may in turn help revitalize the OAS as the principal instrument for cooperation and solidarity in the hemisphere.

Nevertheless, hopefully, the suggestions and recommendations advanced here can serve as a starting point to generate a debate that will eventually lead to the revitalization and strengthening of the role of the OAS and the IADC in promoting and protecting democracy in the hemisphere. Otherwise, as the "*The Economist*" has put it, "the danger is that not just the Charter [i.e., the IADC] but the OAS itself will sink into irrelevance." [25]

NOTES

1. Ideally, it would be a step forward in the promotion and defense of democracy to try to convert the Democratic Charter into a formal treaty. It would imply opening a wide and much needed public debate about the Charter, its relevance and effectiveness, at both the inter-American and national levels. The discussion would involve the legislative branch of a member state in the ratification process, and the Charter would thus become a much better-known and valued instrument for the defense of democracy throughout Latin America. Furthermore, the Charter as a treaty could become a part of the legal constitutional framework of a member state, as the Argentine Constitution of 1994 permits with some international conventions (Article 75 includes the Inter-American Convention on Human Rights and others). As such, the Charter would constitute one more legal domestic safeguard against the breakdown of the democratic constitutional order, as well as a reinforcement of the national commitment to promote, exercise and defend democratic institutions, values and practices at the inter-American level. However, there are those who argue, that as a treaty, it would become a less flexible instrument and more difficult to modify as circumstances change, and it would be applicable only to those that ratify it.

2. See special session of the OAS General Assembly, September 4, 2014.

3. See OAS Charter, Articles 30–52, as well as Article 95.

4. See OAS Charter, Articles 53, 93–98, 117.

5. It is interesting to note that some of the Caribbean countries pay an absurdly small annual quota. As of 2012, the annual quota for Antigua and Barbuda, Belize, Dominica, Grenada, Guyana, Saint Kitts and Nevis, Saint Lucia, Saint Vincent and the Grenadines was US$17,900 each; for Bahamas, US$50,600; for Barbados, US$36,700; for Haiti, US$27,700; for Jamaica, US$75,900; for Suriname, US$27,700; and for Trinidad and Tobago, US$146,800.

6. They should be added to the current Secretariat for Political (and Democratic) Affairs' program areas, which prioritize work with public administrations (executive branch) and electoral observation and assistance. Additionally, this Secretariat should be responsible for the anti-corruption program currently being carried out by the Secretariat for Legal Affairs.

7. For a specific model of a technical assistance project in democracy promotion, see Chapter 7, where there is also a discussion of the limited, realistic outcomes that can or should be expected from this type of model.

8. See OAS Charter, Articles 109, 110, 113.

9. See OAS Charter, preambular paragraph 3, which states: "Convinced that representative democracy is an indispensable condition for the stability, peace, and development of the region."

10. See OAS Charter, Articles 109 and 113.

11. See Murray, September 2014.

12. In the absence of such an amendment to the Charter, in the meantime, the Secretary General should make a commitment to remain in the post for only one term of the current two possible terms of office.

13. Those rules are set out in the General Standards to Govern the Operations of the OAS General Secretariat ("General Standards"), which are approved by the General Assembly.

14. See OAS Charter, Articles 114–116.

15. Still another alternative, as suggested by the present Assistant Secretary General, Ambassador Albert Ramdin, in a November 2014 meeting with the author, would be the creation of four Assistant Secretariats, one for each of the Democracy, Integral Development and Multidimensional Security pillars, and one for administrative and financial matters, which, together with the Secretary General, would constitute an executive committee that would be responsible for the management of the Organization. The current functions of the Assistant Secretary General would be performed by a Secretariat under the Secretary General. In Ramdin's view, this should reduce personnel and administrative costs in the General Secretariat, as well as unnecessary political/bureaucratic frictions within it.

16. Tom Farer, former president of the Inter-American Commission on Human Rights, before the IADC was adopted, suggested that one way of binding member states to promote and defend democracy would be through national legislation that authorizes and obliges the

executive branch to comply with sanctions imposed against violators of democracy and human rights. To this end, he proposed that the UPD design and promote model legislation on the issue (Farer 1996, 22).

17. After all, many of the rights identified as human rights in the Convention are also political rights, the exercise of which is necessary for the existence of democracy. They include the following: Article 13, Freedom of thought and expression. Exceptions: (a) respect for rights or reputation of others; (b) protection of national security, public order, public health or morals; (c) punishment for incitement to racial violence. Article 14, Right of reply. Article 15, Right of assembly. Limitations: public order, health, morals, rights, and freedoms of others. Article 16, Freedom of association. Same limitations as those in Art. 15; not extended to Army and Police. Article 23, Right to participate in government, through (a) direct participation or through freely chosen representatives; (b) right to vote and be elected in genuine periodic elections, by universal suffrage and secret ballot; (c) equal access to public service. Limitations may be imposed due to age, nationality, language, residence, education, and criminal activities. Article 24, Equal protection. All are equal under the law. And Article 25, right to judicial protection. Adjudication; Enforcement. Similar political rights are recognized in the 1948 Inter-American Declaration of Human Rights, which is still in force and occasionally referenced by the Commission in its reports.

18. See, for example, reports on Honduras, 2009 and 2010; Venezuela, 2009; Bolivia, 2009; Peru, 2000, Haiti, 1991–1993, and Nicaragua, 1978. For the criteria used in determining whether human and political rights violations do occur in a member state, see the introduction to Chapter IV in the Commission's annual report. http://www.cidh.oas.org/annualrep/2010eng/TOC.htm. See also (Goldman 2009).

19. See for example the cases of Bolivia, 2005 and 2008; Ecuador, 2005; Nicaragua, 2005 and 2008; Guatemala, 2009; pre-coup Honduras, 2009.

20. See, for example the cases of Haiti in 1991; Peru in 1992; Guatemala in 1993, and Honduras after the coup in 2009.

21. These included, among others, the American Convention on Human Rights, the American Declaration of the Rights and Duties of Man, and the OAS Charter.

22. Secretary General Insulza suggested that the Permanent Council open up a discussion on clarifying the concept of "alteration of the democratic order and on the Organization providing access" to other political actors (Secretary General of the OAS May 2010) (OAS Permanent Council December 14, 2011).

23. Known by its Spanish acronym MESICIC (Mecanismo de Seguimiento e Implementación de la Convención Interamericana contra la Corrupción).

24. Think of the failure to do so in the cases of Nicaragua and Honduras.

25. http://www.economist.com/blogs/americasview/2011/01/inter-american_democratic_charter

Bibliography

Acevedo, Domingo, and Claudio Grossman. "The Organization of American States and the Protection of Democracy." In *Beyond Sovereignty. Collectively Defending Democracy in the Americas*, edited by Tom Farer. Baltimore, Maryland: The Johns Hopkins University Press, 1996.

Ad Hoc Meeting of Foreign Ministers. "Support for the Democratic Government of Haiti." *Resolution.* Washington, D.C.: Organization of American States, October 3, 1991.

Alice, Mauricio. *La Evaluación de la Eficacia de la OEA en las Crisis Democráticas en el Continente. Las Posiciones Argentinas.* Buenos Aires: Grupo Editor Latinoamericano, 2002.

Almond, Gabriel, and G. Bingham Powell. *Comparative Politics.* 2nd ed. Glenview, Illinois: Scott, Foresman and Co., 1978.

Almond, Gabriel, and Sidney Verba. *The Civic Culture Revisited.* Sage Publications, 1989.

Álvarez, Marcelo, Adriana Delgado, and Ronny Rodriguez. *El Poder Legislativo, Democracia e Integración.* Bogotá: Pontificia Universidad Javeriana, 2001.

Amadeo, Jo-Ann, and Adriana Cepeda. *Políticas Nacionales sobre Educación para una Ciudadanía Democrática en las Américas.* Departamento de Educación y Cultura, Programa Interamericano de Educación en Valores y Prácticas Democráticas, Organización de los Estados Americanos, 2008.

Amaral, Sergio. "U.S.-Latin American Relations over the Last Decade." In *A Decade of Change. Political, Economic, and Social Developments in Western Hemispheric Affairs.* Washington, D.C.: Inter-American Dialogue, 2011.

Aparicio, Jaime, and Rubén M. Perina. "Fortalecer el Sistema Interamericano de Derechos Humanos." *El Universal*, Septiembre 24, 2011.

———. "Amenazas a la Protección de los Derechos Humanos." *El Universal*, Octubre 15, 2011.

Arnson, Cynthia, and Carlos de la Torre. "Viva el Populismo? The Tense Future of Latin American Politics." *Foreign Affairs*, April 2014.

Asamblea General de la Organización de los Estados Americanos. "Reunión del Consejo Permanente con Representantes de los Poderes Legislativos de las Américas." *Resolución.* Organización de los Estados Americanos, Junio 2005.

Asamblea General Extraordinaria de la OEA. "Orientaciones y Objetivos de la Visión Estratégica de la OEA." Washington, D.C.: Organización de los Estados Americanos, 4 de septiembre 2014.

Astiz, Carlos A., ed. *Latin American International Politics.* Notre Dame: University of Notre Dame, 1969.

Atkins, G. Pope. *Latin America in the International Political System.* 2nd ed., revised and updated. Boulder, Colorado: Westview Press, 1989.

241

Axworthy, Lloyd. "A Model for Promoting Democracy in the Americas." *Canadian Foreign Policy* (Norman Patterson School of International Affairs, Carlton University) 10, no. 3 (Spring 2003).

Aznaréz, Juan Jesús. "La Vicepresidenta Ecuatoriana Sustituye a Bucarám con el Apoyo del Ejército." *El País Internacional*, February 10, 1997.

Baena Soares, João Clemente. *Síntesis de una Gestión (1984–1994)*. Washington, D.C.: General Secretariat of the OAS, 1994.

Bemis, Samuel F. *The Latin American Policy of the United States*. The Norton Library, 1967.

Berman, Sheri. "How Democracies Emerge: The Lessons from Europe." *Journal of Democracy* (The Johns Hopkins University) 18 (January 2007).

Brzezinski, Zbigniew. *Power and Principle*. Revised Edition. New York: Farrar Straus Giroux, 1985.

Bull, Hedley. *Anarchical Society: A Study of Order in World Politics*. New York: Columbia University Press, 1977.

Caballero, Esteban, and Alejandro Vial. *El Poder Legislativo en el Cono Sur*. Asunción: Centro de Estudios Democráticos, 1994.

Caetano, Gerardo, and Rubén M. Perina. *La Segunda Generación de Reformas Parlamentarias*. Montevideo: CLAEH Instituto Universitario, 2004.

———. *Democracia y Gerencia Política. Innovación en Valores, Instrumentos y Prácticas*. Montevideo: CLAEH Instituto Universitario, 2006.

———. *La Dimensión Parlamentaria en la Re-institucionalización del Mercosur*. Montevideo: CLAEH Instituto Universitario, 2000.

———. *La Encrucijada Política del Mercosur. Parlamentos y Nueva Institucionalidad para Mercosur Nuevo*. Montevideo: CLAEH Instituto Universitario, 2003.

———. *Mercosur y Parlamentos. El Rol de los Congresos en la Democracia y la Integración*. Montevideo: CLAEH Instituto Universitario, 2000.

Caminos, Hugo, and Roberto Lavalle. "New Departures in the Exercise of Inherent Powers by the UN and OAS Secretaries General: The Central American Situation." *American Journal of International Law*, April 1989.

Cardwell, Paul James. "Mapping out Democracy Promotion in the EU's External Relations." *European Foreign Affairs Review*, 2011: 21–40.

Carothers, Thomas. "Comments on a Quarter of Century of Promoting Democracy." *Journal of Democracy* (The Johns Hopkins Unviersity) 18 (October 2007).

———. *Confronting the Weakest Link. Aiding Political Parties in New Democracies*. Washington, D.C.: Carnegie Endowment for International Peace, 2006.

———. *Critical Mission. Essays on Democracy Promotion*. Washington, D.C.: Carnegie Endowment for International Peace, 2004.

———. "Democracy Policy Under Obama. Revitalization or Retreat?" Carnegie Endowment for International Peace, 2012.

———. *Revitalizing Democracy Assistance. The Challenge of USAID*. Washington, D.C.: Carnegie Endowment for International Peace, 2009.

———. "An Unwanted League." *The Washington Post*, May 28, 2008.

Center for Human Rights and Humanitarian Law. "The Future of the Inter-American System of Human Rights." *Human Rights Brief* (Washington College of Law, American University) 20, no. 2 (Winter 2013).

Cevasco Piedra, José. *El Congreso del Perú. Un Modelo de Modernización*. Lima: Congreso del Perú, 2000.

"Change and the Alliance for Progress." In *Latin America and the United States in the 1970's*, edited by Richard B Gray, 75–124. Itasca, Illinois: F.E. Peacock Publishers, Inc., 1971.

Cheema, G. Shabbir. *Building Democratic Institutions*. Bloomfield, Ct: Kumarian Press, 2005.

Child, Jack. *Conflict in Central America: Approaches to Peace and Security*. Palgrave MacMillan, 1986.

———. *Geopolitics and Conflict in South America*. New York: Praeger Publishers/Hoover Institution Press, 1985.

Clarke, Richard. *Against All Enemies. Inside America's War on Terror*. New York: Free Press, 2005.

Claude, Inis L. "The OAS, the UN and the United States." In *International Regionalism*, edited by Joseph S. Nye. Little, Brown and Company, 1968.

Close, David, ed. *Legislatures and the New Democracies in Latin America*. Lynne Rienner Publishers, 1995.

Cochez, Guillermo. "OEA: Mal por fuera peor por adentro." *El Universal*, Septiembre 30, 2011.

Collier, David, ed. *The New Authoritarianism in Latin America*. Princeton University Press, 1979.

Comisión Interamericana de Derechos Humanos. *Democracia y Derechos Humanos en Venezuela*. Organización de los Estados Americanos, Washington, D.C.: Comisión Interamericana de Derechos Humanos, 2009.

Comisión Internacional de Apoyo y Verificación. *La Desmovilización y Reinserción de la Resistencia Nicaraguense*. Washington, D.C.: Organización de los Estados Americanos, 1998.

Consalvi, Simon A, and Eduardo Fernández. "Propuestas para la Promoción de la Democracia en Venezuela y Latinoamérica." In *Promoción de la Democracia*. Caracas: Fundación Konrad Adenaur, 1996.

Consejo Interamericano Económico y Social. *El Desarrollo de América Latina y la Alianza para el Progreso*. Washington, D.C.: Secretaría General de la Organización de los Estados Americanos, 1973.

Consejo Permanente de la OEA. *Carta Democrática Interamericana. Documentos e Interpretaciones*. Washington, D.C.: Organización de los Estados Americanos, 2003.

———. "Convocatoria de la Reunión de Consulta de Ministros de Relaciones Exteriores y Nombramiento de una Comisión." *Resolución*. Washington,D.C.: Consejo Permanente, 5 de marzo, 2008.

———. *Informe final: Diálogo sobre la Eficacia de la Aplicación de la Carta Democrática Interamericana*. Washington, D.C.: Consejo Permanente de la OEA, 14 de diciembre 2011.

———. "Programa de Apoyo para la Promoción de la Democracia." *Resolución*. Washington, D.C. : Organizatión de los Estados Americanos, 1991.

———. "Respaldo a la Institucionalidad Democrática, al Diálogo y la Paz de Bolivia." *Resolución*. Washington, D.C.: Consejo Permanente de la OEA, May 3, 2008.

Cooper, Andrew, and Thomas Legler. "The OAS in Peru: a Model for the Future." *Journal of Democracy* (The Johns Hopkins University) 12, no. 4 (October 2001).

Coppedge, Michael. "Prospects for Democratic Governability Venezuela." *Journal of Latin American Studies* 36, no. 2 (1994).

Corporación Tiempo 2000. *Parlamento y Democracia. Las Asesorías Legislativas en América Latina*. Santiago: Corporación Tiempo 2000, 1998.

Corrales, Javier, and Richard Feinberg. "Regimes of Cooperation in the Western Hemisphere: Power Interest and Intellectual Traditions." *International Studies Quarterly* 43 (March 1999).

Costa, José María, and Oscar Ayala-Bogarin. *Operación Goedón: Los Secretos de un Golpe Frustrado*. Asunción: Editorial Don Bosco, 1996.

Council on Foreign Relations' Independent Task Force. *Threats to Democracy: Intervention and Response*. New York: Council on Foreign Relations, 2003.

Cox, Cristián, Rosario Jaramillo, and Fernando Reimers. *Education for Citizenship and Democracy in the Americas. An Agenda for Action*. Education Unit, State, Governance and Civil Society Division, Inter-American Development Bank, Inter-American Development Bank, 2005.

Dahl, Robert A. *Poliarchy. Participation and Opposition*. 5th ed. Yale University Press, 1975.

———. *On Democracy*. New Haven: Yale University Press, 1998.

Dahl, Robert, Ian Shapiro, and Jose Antonio Cheibub. *The Democracy Sourcebook*. Cambridge, Mass.: The MIT Press, 2003.

Darnolf, Steffan. "Assessing Electoral Fraud in New Democracies. A New Strategic Approach." Washington, D.C.: International Foundation for Electoral Systems, March 2011.

Darren, Hawkins, and Carolyn M. Shaw. "The OAS and Legalizing Norms of Democracy." In *Promoting Democracy in the Americas*, edited by Thomas Legler, Sharon F. Lean and Dexter Boniface. The Johns Hopkins University Press, 2007.

Davis, Harold E., and John and Peck, F. Taylor. *Latin American Diplomatic History. An Introduction.* Louisiana State University Press, 1967.

Dawson, Richard E, and Kenneth Prewitt. *Political Socialization.* Chicago: Little, Brown and Company, 1969.

De la Torre, Carlos. "Technocratic Populism in Ecuador." *Journal of Democracy* 24, no. 24 (July 2013).

De Young, Karen. "U.S. Seen as Weak Patron of Latin American Democracy." *The Washington Post*, April 16, 2002.

Departamento de Asuntos Democráticos y Políticos. *Seminario sobre Educación en Valores y Prácticas Democráticas en el Sistema Educativo Uruguayo.* Washington, D.C.: Departamento de Asuntos Democráticos y Políticos, SG/ OEA, 2004.

Deutsch, Karl, and et al. *Political Community and the North Atlantic Area. International Organization in the Light of Historical Experience.* Princeton University Press, 1968.

Di Palma, Giussepe. *To Craft Democracies.* University of California Press, 1990.

Di Tella, Torcuato. "Populism and Reform in Latin America." In *Obstacles to Change in Latin America*, edited by Claudio Veliz. London: Oxford University Press, 1965.

Diamond, Larry and Mark Plattner, ed. *The Global Resurgence of Democracy.* Baltimore: The Johns Hopkins University, 1992.

Diamond, Larry. "Comments on A Quarter of Century of Promoting Democracy." *Journal of Democracy* 18 (October 2007).

———. "Defining and Developing Democracy." In *Democracy Sourcebook*, edited by Robert Dahl, Ian Shapiro and José Antonio Cheibub, 32–34. Cambridge, Mass.: The MIT Press, 2003.

———. "The Democracy Rollback." *Foreign Affairs*, March/April 2008.

———. *The Spirit of Democracy.* New York: Times Books, 2008.

Diamond, Larry, Francis Fukuyama, Donald Horowitz, and Marc Plattner. "Reconsidering the Transition Paradigm: A Discussion." *Journal of Democracy* 25, no. 1 (January 2014).

Dobriansky, Paula J. "The Core of U. S. Foreign Policy." In *Critical Mission. Essays on Democracy Promotion*, edited by Thomas Carothers. Washington, D.C.: Carnegie Endowment for International Peace, 2004.

Drake, Paul W. *Between Tyranny and Anarchy. A History of Democracy in Latin America, 1800–2006.* Stanford University Press, 2009.

Duffield, John S. "Political Culture and State Behavior." *International Organization*, no. 4 (Autumn 1999).

Dundas, Carl W. *Dimensions of Free and Fair Elections: Frameworks, Integrity, Transparency, Attributes, Monitoring.* London: Commonwealth Secretariat, 1994.

Education Unit. *Education for Citizenship and Democracy in the Americas: An Agenda for Action.* Washington, D.C.: Inter-American Development Bank, 2005.

Electoral Accompaniment Mission in Nicaragua. *Final Report of the Mission of Electoral Accompaniment to Nicaragua for the General Elections held on November 6, 2011.* Secretariat for Political Affairs, Organization of American States, Washington, D.C.: Permanent Council of the OAS, 25 January 2011.

Elshtain, Jean Bethke. "A Quarter of a Century of Promoting Democracy." *Journal of Democracy* (The Johns Hopkins University) 18 (October 2007).

Etzioni, Amitai. *Modern Organizations.* Englewoods Cliffs, New Jersey: Prentice Hall, 1964.

European Democracy Foundation. *The EU approach to democracy promotion in External Relations.* Brussels, 2006.

Expert Verification Mission. *Final Report. Expert Verification Mission of the Vote Tabulation of the November 28, 2010 Presidential Election in the Republic of Haiti.* Secretary General of the OAS, Port-au-Prince, Haiti: Organization of American States, January 13, 2011.

Fagg, John E. *Latin America. A General History.* New York: The Macmillan Company, 1963.

Feng, Yi. *Democracy, Governance and Economic Performance.* MIT Press, 2003.

Finkel, Steven, and Anibal and Selligson, Mitchell Perez-Linan. *Effects of Foreign Assistance on Democracy Building: Results of a Cross-National Quantitative Study.* Final Report, U.S. Agency for International Development, Washington, D.C.: U.S. Agency for International Development, 2006, 6–9, 12, 30.

Finnemore, Martha, and Kathryn Sikkink. "International Norm Dynamics and Political Change." *International Organization* 54, no. 4 (1998).

Forsyte, David. "The United Nations, Democracy, and the Americas." In *Beyond Sovereignty*, edited by Tom Farer. The Johns Hopkins University, 1996.

Franck, Thomas. "The Democratic Entitlement." *University of Richmond Law Review*, 29 (1994).

———. "The Emerging Right to Democratic Governance." *American Journal of International Law*, January 1992: 49–91.

Freedom House. *Freedom in the World 2013. Democratic Breakthroughs in the Balance.* Freedom House.

Fukuyama, Francis. "The End of History?" *National Interest*, 1989.

———. "'Stateness' First." *Journal of Democracy* 16, no. 1 (January 2006).

———. "Identity, Immigration and Liberal Democracy." *Journal of Democracy* 17 (January 2006).

———. *State Building, Governance and World Order in the Twenty-First Century.* Ithaca: Cornell University Press, 2004.

———. "The Primacy of Culture." *The Journal of Democracy* January 1996.

———. *Trust.* New York: Free Press, 1995.

Fundación Nueva Democracia. Observatorio de Derechos Humanos. *Reporte Cronológico de Violaciones a los Derechos Humanos Sucedidas en Bolivia. Enero-Abril 2013.* Santa Cruz, Bolivia: Fundación Nueva Democracia, 2013.

Gaddis, John Lewis. *Surprise, Security and the American Experience.* Cambridge, Mass: Harvard University Press, 2004.

Galán, Instituto Luis Carlos, ed. *Compromiso Democrático.* Bogotá: Instituto Luis Carlos Galán para la Democracia and Secretaría Ejecutiva del Convenio Andrés Bello, 2000.

Gaubatz, Kurt Taylor. "Kant, Democracy and History." *Journal of Democracy*, no. 4 (October 1996).

Gaviria, César. *Desafíos para un Nuevo Futuro 1999–2004.* Washington, D.C.: General Secretariat of the OAS, 1999.

———. *Las Américas: Una Nueva Era. Selección de Discursos 1994–1996.* Washington, D.C.: General Secretariat of the OAS, 1996.

———. "Ecuador and other States try to muzzle human rights protection." *Washington Post*, March 19, 2013.

General Assembly of the OAS, special session. "Suspension of the Right of Honduras to Participate in the Organization of American States." *Resolution.* 2009.

———. "Declaration on Democracy in Venezuela." *Declaration.* Washington, D.C.: Organization of American States, 2002.

General Secretariat, Organization of American States. *The 2005–2006 Electoral Cycle in the Americas.* Department of Electoral Cooperation and Observation, Washington, D.C.: General Secretariat of the OAS, 2006.

———. *A Manual for OAS Electoral Observation Missions.* Department of Electoral Cooperation and Observation, Secretariat for Political Affairs, Organization of American States, Washington, D.C.: General Secretariat of the OAS, 2007.

———. *Inter-American Treaties and Conventions.* Treaties Series Number 16. Washington, D.C.: Department of Legal Affairs, OAS, 1972.

Gershman, Carl and Allen, Michael. "The Assault on Democracy Assistance." *Journal of Democracy* 17 (April 2006).

Gil, Federico. *Latin American-United States Relations.* Edited by Harcourt Brace Jovanovich. New York, 1971.

Goldman, Robert. "History and Action. The Inter-American Human Rights System and the Role of the Inter-American Commission on Human Rights." *Human Rights Quarterly* 31 (2009).

Graham, John. *La Crisis Electoral de 1994.* Santo Domingo: Fundación Cultural Dominicana, 2011.

Grosso, Beatriz, and Alejandra Svetas, eds. *El Poder Legislativo en la Democracia y la Integración.* Buenos Aires: UPD-OEA y Cámara de Diputados del Congreso de la República Argentina.

Haass, Richard. "The Unravelling. How to Respond to a Disordered World." *Foreign Affairs* 93, no. 6 (November/December 2014).

———. "U.S. Foreign Policy in an Nonpolar World." *Foreign Affairs* 87, no. 3 (May/June 2008).

Hakim, Peter. "The Future of Inter-American Relations." *Calgary Papers in Military and Strategic Studies*, January 2014.

———. "Democracy and U.S. Credibility." *The New York Times*, April 21, 2002.

Hakim, Peter, and Abraham Lowenthal. "Latin Americas's Fragile Democracies." In *The Global Resurgence of Democracy*, edited by Larry Diamond and Marc Plattner. Baltimore: The Johns Hopkins University Press, 1993.

Hamill, Hugh M., ed. *Dictatorship in Spanish America.* New York: Alfred A. Knopf, 1965.

Harrison, Lawrence E. *The Central Liberal Truth.* Oxford University Press, 2006.

———. "Waking from the Pan-American Dream." In *Foreign Policy on Latin America 1970–1980.* New York: Westview Press/Carnegie Endowment for International Peace, 1977.

Harrison, Lawrence E, and Samuel Huntington. *Culture Matters.* Basic Books, 2000.

Hawking, Darren, and Caroline M. Shaw. "The OAS and Legalizing Norms of Democracy." In *Promoting Democracy in the Americas*, edited by Thomas Legler, Sahorn F. Lean and Dexter S. Boniface. Baltimore: The Johns Hopkins University, 2007.

Herman, Robert, and Theodore Piccone. *Defending Democracy. A Global Survey of Foreign Policy 1992–2002.* Washington, D.C.: The Democracy Coalition Project, 2002.

Herz, Monica. *The Organization of American States (OAS).* New York: Routledge, 2011.

Hiatt, Fred. "Obama's foreign policy follows his new democracy rhetoric." *The Washington Post*, October 4, 2010.

Holden, Robert H., and Eric Zolov. *Latin America and the United States.* New York: Oxford University Press, 2011.

Horowitz, Donald. "Comparing Democratic Systems." *Journal of Democracy* 2 (Fall 1990).

Huntington, Samuel. *Political Order in Changing Societies.* New Haven: Yale University Press, 1968.

———. *The Third Wave. Democratization in the Late Twentieth Century.* Noman and London: University of Oklahoma Press, 1991.

International Institute for Democracy and Electoral Assistance. *Código de Conducta para una Observación Electoral Etica y Profesional.* IDEA, Stockholm, Suecia: IDEA, 1998.

Infante, Maria Teresa. "La solución pacífica de las controversias." In *Antecedentes, balance y perspectivas del Sistema Interamericano*, edited by Rodrigo Díaz Albónico. Santiago: Instituto de Estudios Internacionales, Universidad de Chile, 1977.

Inglehart, Ronald, and Christian Welzel. *Modernization, Cultural Change and Democracy.* Cambridge University Press, 2005.

Inter-American Commission on Human Rights. *Basic Documents Pertaining to Human Rights in the Inter-American System.* Washington, D.C.: General Secretariat of the OAS, 1992.

———. *A Hemispheric Agenda for the Defense of Freedom of Expression.* OEA/Ser.L/V/II CIDH/RELE/INF.4/09, Office of the Special Rapporteur for Freedom of Expression, Washington, D.C.: Organization of American States, 2010.

———. *Annual Report 2013.* April 2014.

Inter-American Development Bank (IDB). *Modernization of the State Strategy Document.* Washington, D.C.: Inter-American Development Bank, 2003.

———. *Democracies in Development.* Washington, D.C.: Inter-American Development Bank, 2002.

———. *Frame of Reference for Bank Action in State Programs and Civil Society.* Washington, D.C.: Inter-American Development Bank, 1996.

Jaguaribe, Helio. *Political Development: A General Theory and a Latin American Case Study.* New York: Harper & Row Publishers, 1973.

Jervis, Robert. "Security Regimes." In *International Regimes.* Ithaca: Cornell University Press, 1983.

Johnson, John J. *The Military in Politics in Latin America.* Stanford University Press, 1964.

Journal of Democracy. "Comparing the Arab Revolts." *Journal of Democracy* 22, no. 4 (October 2011).

Journal of Democracy. "Do New Democracies Support Democracy?" 22, no. 4 (October 2011).

Kagan, Robert. *The Return of History and the End of Dreams.* New York: Alfred Knopf, 2008.

Katz, Richard. *A Theory of Parties and Electoral Systems.* Baltimore: The Johns Hopkins Unversity Press, 1980.

Katzenstein, Peter, Robert O. Keohane and Stephen D. Krasner. "International Organization and the Study of World Politics." *International Organization* 52, 4 (Autumn 1998): 645–85.

Keohane, Robert. "International Institutions. Can Interdependence Work?" *Foreign Policy*, Spring 1998.

Keohane, Robert, and Joseph Nye. *Power and Interdependence.* Boston: Little, Brown, 1977.

Kerry, John. "Secretary of State Remarks on U.S. Policy in the Western Hemisphere at the OAS." Washington, D.C., November 18, 2013.

Kissinger, Henry. *World Order.* New York: Penguin Press, 2014.

Klein, Richard, and Patrick Merloe. "Building Confidence in the Voting Registration Process." National Democratic Institute for International Affairs, 2001.

Kohl, James and Litt, John. *Urban Guerrilla Warfare in Latin America.* Cambridge, Mass.: Massachussetts Institute of Technology, 1974.

Kornblith, Miriam. "Chavismo after Chávez?" *Journal of Democracy* 24, no. 3 (July 2013).

———. "Elections vs. Democracy." *Journal of Democracy*, January 2005.

Krasner, Stephen D., ed. *International Regimes.* Ithaca: Cornell University Press, 1989.

Kuhn, Thomas. *The Structure of Scientific Revolution.* Chicago: University of Chicago, 1996.

La Tribuna. "Congreso pide OEA retirar misión." junio 24, 2009.

Lagos, Marta. "Latin America's Smiling Mask." *The Journal of Democracy* (The Johns Hopkins University), July 1997.

Lanus, Juan Archibaldo. *De Chapultepec al Beagle. La Política Exterior Argentina: 1945–1980.* Buenos Aires: EMECE, 1984.

Latin American Advisor Newsletter. *How Well is the OAS Handling the Coup in Honduras.* Inter-American Dialogue, Washington,D.C.: Inter-American Dialogue, 2009.

Legler, Thomas. "Venezuela 2002–2004. The Chávez Challenge." In *Promoting Democracy in the Americas*, edited by Thomas Legler, Sharon F. Lean and Dexter S. Boliface. The Johns Hopkins University, 2007.

Lehoucq, Fabrice. "Bolivia's Constitutional Breakdown." *Journal of Democracy* 19, no. 4 (October 2008).

LeoGrande, William. *Our Own Backyard. The United States in Central America, 1977–1992.* University of North Carolina, 2000.

Levinson, Bradley A.U., and Juan G. Berumen. "Democratic Citizenship Education and the State in Latin America: A Critical Overview." *Revista Electrónica Iberoamericana sobre Calidad, Eficacia y Cambio en Educación* 5, no. 4 (2007).

Levitsky, Steven, and Lucan A. Way. "International Linkage and Democratization." *Journal of Democracy*, July 2005: 27–33.

Levitsky, Steven, and Maria Victoria Murillo. "Lessons from Latin America. Building Institutions on Weak Foundations." *Journal of Democracy*, April 2013.

Linz, Juan. "The Perils of Presidentialism." *Journal of Democracy* 2 (Winter 1990).

———. "The Virtues of Parliamentarism." *Journal of Democracy* 2 (Fall 1990).

Linz, Juan, and Alfred Stepan. "Toward Consolidated Democracies." *Journal of Democracy* 7, no. 2 (1996).

Linz, Juan, and Arturo Valenzuela, *The Failure of Presidential Democracy.* The Johns Hopkins University, 1994.

Lipset, Seymour. "The Centrality of Culture." *Journal of Democracy*, Fall 1990.

Lowenthal, Abraham, ed. *Armies and Politics in Latin America.* New York: Holms and Meier Publishers Inc., 1976.

———. "The Obama Adminstration and the Americas." In *Shifting The Balance. Obama and the Americas*, edited by Abraham Lowenthal, Theodore Piccone and Laurence Whitehead. Washington, D.C.: Brookings Institution Press, 2011.

López-Pintor, Rafael. "Assessing Electoral Fraud in New Democracies. A Basic Conceptual Framework." Washington, D.C.: International Foundation for Electoral Systems, December 2010.

Mainwaring, Scott, and Aníbal Pérez-Liñán. *Democracies and Dictatorships in Latin America. Emergence, Survival and Fall.* New York: Cambridge University Press, 2013.

———. "Democratic Breakdown and Survival." *Journal of Democracy* 24, no. 2 (April 2013).

Mainwaring, Scott, and Timothy R. Scully. "Democratic Governance in Latin America: Eleven Lessons from Recent Experience." In *Democratic Governance in Latin America*, edited by Scott Mainwaring and Timothy R. Scully. Stanford University Press, 2010.

Major, Flavie. "Canada: Democracy's New Champion?" In *Promoting Democracy in the Americas*, edited by Thomas Legler, Sharon F. Lean and Dexter Boniface. Baltimore: The Johns Hopkins University Press, 2007.

Mann, Thomas E, and Norman J. Ornstein. *The Broken Branch.* Oxford University Press, 2006.

Mansfield, Edward, and Jack Snyder. "Democratization and War." *Foreign Affairs*, May/June 1995.

Martinez, Juan and Javier Santiso. "Financial Markets and Politics: The Confidence Game in Latin American Emerging Markets." *International Political Science Review.* 24, no. 3 (2003): 336–395.

Mazzuca, Sebastián L. "Lessons from Latin America. The Rise of Rentier Populism." *Journal of Democracy*, April 2013.

McCoy, Jenniffer. "One Act in an Unfinished Drama." *Journal of Democracy*, January 2005.

McFaul, Michael, Stephen Sestanovich, and John J. Mearsheimer. "Faulty Powers. Who started the Ukraine Crisis." *Foreign Affairs* 93, no. 6 (November/December 2014).

McGregor Burns, James. *Leadership.* New York, New York: Harper and Row, 1978.

McMahon, Edward R. and Scott H. Baker. *Piecing a Democratic Quilt? Regional Organizations and Universal Norms.* Bloomfield, CT: Kumerian Press, 2006.

Mearsheimer, John J, and Stephen M. Walt. "An Unnecessary War." *Foreign Policy*, no. 134 (January/February 2003).

Meeting of Consultation of Ministers of Foreign Affairs. "Resolution of the Twenty-Fifth Meeting of Consultation of Ministers of Foreign Affairs." *Resolution.* Washington, D.C., 4 April 2008.

———. "Support for the Reestablishment of Democracy in Peru." *MRE/RES 1/92.* Washington, D.C.: General Secretariat of the Organization of American States, April 13, 1992.

———. *Twenty-First Meeting of Consultation of Ministers of Foreign Affairs on the Situation in Panama.* Organization of American States, Washington, D.C.: Organization of American States, 17 May 1989.

Meeting of Consultation of Ministers of Foreign Affairs serving as the Organ of Consultation in application of the Rio Treaty. *Final Act of the Eighth Meeting of Consultation of Ministers of Foreign Affairs.* Doc. 38, Organization of American States, Punta del Este, Uruguay: Organization of American States, 31 January 1962.

———. *Final Act of the Ninth Meeting of Consultation of Ministers of Foreign Affairs.* Doc. 48, Organization of American States, Organization of American States, 26 July 1964.

Mejía, Marco R., and Gabriel Restrepo. *Formación y Educación para la Democracia en Colombia.* Bogotá: UNESCO y Instituto para el Desarrollo de la Democracia Luis Carlos Galán, 1997.

Mejía, Oscar, Arlene Tickner, Ramón Villamizar, and Catalina Ortiza. "La Democratización de la Democracia: Deficiencias y Estrategias de Democratización de los Congresos de los Países de la Región Andina." *Documentos Ocasionales No 42.* Bogotá: Centro de Estudios Internacionales, Universidad de los Andes, abril-junio 1996.

MERCOSUR. *Protocolo de Ushuahia sobre Compromiso Democrático en el Mercosur, La República de Chile y de Bolivia.* July 1998.

Misión de Observación Electoral en el Perú. *Informe de la Misión de Observación en el Perú, 8 de abril 2001.* Unidad para la Promoción de la Democracia-UPD, Organización de los Estados Americanos, Washington, D.C.: Consejo Permanente de la OEA, 18 de marzo 2002.

Misión de Observación de la Organización de los Estados Americanos. *Misión de Observación de la Organización de los Estados Americanos. Proceso de Recolección, Verificación, Validación y Reparo de Firmas y Referendo. Venezuela 2003–2004.* Secretaría General, Organización de los Estados Americanos, Washington, D.C.: Unpublished report, 13 September 2004.

Misión de Observación Electoral de la OEA en Venezuela. *Informe Final de la Misión de Observación Electoral de la OEA sobre las Elecciones Presidenciales Celebradas en Venezuela el 3 de Diciembre de 2006.* Secretaría de Asuntos Políticos, Secretaría General de la OEA, Organización de los Estados Americanos, Washington, D.C.: Consejo Permanente de la OEA, 10 de septiembre de2008.

Misión de Observación Electoral de la OEA. *Informe de la Misión de Observación Electoral de la OEA. Elecciones Ordinarias Generales Presidenciales del 20 de mayo de 2012 en República Dominicana.* Secretaría de Asuntos Políticos, Secretaría General de la OEA, Organización de los Estados Americanos, Washington, D.C.: Consejo Permanente, 26 de septiembre 2013.

Misión de Observación Electoral de la Organización de los Estados Americanos al Referendo Revocatorio Presidencial en Venezuela. *Informe de Observación Electoral de la Organización de los Estados Americanos al Referendo Revocatorio Presidencial en Venezuela, del 15 de agosto de 2004.* Secretaría General, Organización de los Estados Americanos, Washington, D.C.: Consejo Permanente, 21 de septiembre de 2004.

Misión de Observación Electoral de la Unión Europea. *Informe Final. Elecciones Parlamentarias. Venezuela 2005.* Unión Europea, 2005.

Misión de Observación Electoral en el Perú. "Observación Electoral en Perú. Elecciones Generales, 9 de julio de 2000." Unidad para la Promoción de la Democracia-UPD. Secretaría General de la OEA, Organización de los Estados Americanos, Washington, D.C., 13 de diciembre de 2000.

Misión de Observación Electoral en Guatemala. *Informe Final de la Misión de Observación Electoral de la OEA sobre las Elecciones en Guatemala.* Unidad para la Promoción de la Democracia-UPD, Organización de los Estados Americanos, Washington, D.C.: Consejo Permanente de la OEA, 12 de abril de 1996.

Misión de Observación Electoral en Paraguay. "Observaciones Electorales en Paraguay, 1991–1993." Unidad para la Promoción de la Democracia. Secretaría General de la OEA, Organización de los Estados Americanos, Washington, D.C., 1996.

Misión de Observación Electoral en República Dominicana. "Observaciones Electorales en República Dominicana 1994–1996." Unidad para la Promoción de la Democracia. Secretaría General de la OEA, Organización de los Estados Americanos, Washington, D.C., 1997.

Misión de Observación Electoral en Venezuela. "Observación Electoral en la Republica Bolivariana de Venezuela, 30 de julio de 2000." Unidad para la Promoción de la Democracia. Secretaría General de la OEA, Organización de los Estados Americanos, Washington, D.C., 2001.

Misión de Observación Electoral, Venezuela 2005. "Elecciones Legislativas. Diciembre 2005." Documento Interno del la Misión, 2005.

Misión de Observación Electoral. Elecciones Legislativas en Venezuela de diciembre 2005. *Informe Final de la Misión de Observación Electoral de la OEA sobre las Elecciones Legislativas celebradas en Venezuela el 4 de diciembre de 2005.* Secretaría de Asuntos Políticos de la OEA. Secretaría General de la OEA, Organización de los Estados Americanos, Washington, D.C.: Consejo Permanente de la OEA, 26 abril 2006.

Misión de Observación. *Informe de la Misión de Observación Electoral a las Elecciones Ordinarias Generales Congresionales y Municipales en la República Dominicana Celebradas el 16 de mayo de 2006.* Subsecretaría de Asuntos Políticos, Secretaría General de la OEA, Washington, D.C.: Consejo Permanente de la OEA, 21 de noviembre de 2006.

Molineu, Harold. "The Inter-American System: Searching for a New Framwork." *Latin American Research Review* (University of New Mexico) 29, no. 1 (1994).

Moravcsik, Andrew. "A New Statecraft? Supranational Enterpreneurship and International Coorperation." *International Organization* 53, no. 2 (1999).

Munck, Gerardo L. "Systematizing Practice: Criteria and Method for Electoral Observation." In *The 2005–2006 Electoral Cycle in the Americas*, by the General Secretariat of the OAS. Washington, D.C.: General Secretariat of the OAS, 2005.

Mungiu-Pippidi, Alina. "The Transformative Power of Europe Revisited." *Journal of Democracy* 25, no. 1 (January 2014).

Muñoz, Hugo Alfonso. *Manual Centroamericano de Técnica Legislativa.* San José: UPD-OEA Y FOPREL, 2000.

Muñoz, Hugo Alfonso. *Manual Hemisférico de Técnica Legislativa y Negociación Política.* Washington, D.C.: UPD-OEA, 2003.

Navia, Patricio, and Ignacio Walker. "Political Institutions, Populism, and Democracy in Latin America." In *Democratic Governance in Latin America*. Stanford University Press, 2010.

National Democratic Institute for International Affairs (NDI). *Manual para la Observación Nacional de Elecciones.* Washington, D.C.: NDI, 1995.

———. *Ensuring the Integrity of International Election Monitoring Through Mutually Recognized Standards and Methodologies.* Washington, D.C., February 2002 .

———. *NDI' s Approach to Criteria for Characterizing Election Processes.* Washington, D.C: NDI, National Democratic Institute for International Affairs 2007.

Needler, Martin C. *Political Systems of Latin America.* 2nd ed. New York: Van Nostrand Reinhold Company, 1970.

Newfarmer, Richard, ed. *From Gunboats to Diplomacy. New U.S. Policies to Latin America.* The Johns Hopkins University Press, 1984.

Nohlen, Dieter, ed. *Elecciones y Sistemas de Partidos en América Latina.* San José: Instituto Interamericano de Derechos Humanos, 1993.

North, Douglas. *Institutions, Institutional Change and Economic Performance.* Cambridge University Press, 1990.

Novak, Fabián. "Defensa de la Democracia y Aplicación de la Resolución 1080 en el caso de Perú." In *Sistema Interamericano y Democracia*, edited by Arlene Tickner. Bogotá: Centro de Estudios Internacionales, Universidad de los Andes, 2000.

Novak, Michael. *The Spirit of Democratic Capitalism.* New York: Simon and Schuter, 1982.

Nun, José. "The Middle Class Military Coup." In *The Politics of Conformity in Latin America*, edited by Claudio Veliz. London: Oxford University Press, 1967.

Nye, J. S. *Peace in Parts. Integration and conflict in regional organization.* Boston: Little, Brown and Company, 1971.

Nye, Joseph S., ed. *International Regionalism.* Little, Brown and Company, 1968.

———. *The Future of Power.* New York: Public Affairs, 2011.

———. "The New National Interest." *Foreign Affairs*, July-August 1999.

Obando-Arbulú, Enrique. "Democracy and Hemispheric Security." *International Analysis*, April-September 1994.

O'Donnell, Guillermo. "Delegative Democracy." *Journal of Democracy* 5 (1994).

———. "Do Economists know Best?" *Journal of Democracy* 6, no. 1 (January 1995).

———. *El Estado Burocrático Autoritario.* Buenos Aires: Editorial de Belgrano, 1982.

———."Horizontal Accountability in New Democracies." *The Journal of Democracy* July 1998.

———. *Modernización y Autoritarismo.* Buenos Aires: Paidós Editorial, 1972.

———."The Perpetual Crisis of Democracy." *Journal of Democracy* 18 (January 2007).

O'Donnell, Guillermo, and Philippe Schmitter. *Transitions from Authoritarian Rule. Tentative Conclusions about Uncertain Democracies.* Baltimore: The Johns Hopkins University Press, 1986.

Office of Summit Follow-Up General Secretariat of the OAS. "Official Documents of the Summit of the Americas Process from Miami to Quebec City." Washington, D.C.: General Secretariat of the OAS, 2002.

Office of the Historian. Bureau of Public Affairs. Department of State. "International Observation of Elections in Latin America 1962–1982." Washington, D.C.: Unpublished Research Memorandum No. 1304, March 1982.

Oneal, John R., and Bruce Russett. "The Classical Liberals were Right: Democracy, Interdependence and Conflict, 1950–1985." *International Studies Quarterly*, no. 2 (June 1997).

Oppenheimer, Andrés. "Democracies Stay out of Ecuador Controversy." *The Miami Herald*, February 8, 1997.

Organization of American States. *Charter of the Organization of the American States.* Washington, D.C.: Organization of American States, 1993.

———. *Inter-American Democratic Charter.* Washington, D.C.: Organization of American States, 2001.

Ornstein, Norman, ed. *The Role of Legislatures in Western Democracies.* Washington, D.C.: American Enterprise Institute, 1986.

Orrego-Vicuña, Francisco. "El Sistema Interamericano de Seguridad Colectiva." In *Antecedentes, Balance y Perspectiva del Sistema Interamericano*, edited by Rodrigo Díaz Abónico. Santiago: Instituto de Estudios Internacionales, Universidad de Chile, 1977.

Ortiz, Oscar. "Revista Perspectiva." May 14, 2013. http://www.revistaperspectiva.com/blog/politica/ruptura-constitucional (accessed April 7, 2014).

Paez, Andrés. "Ecuador: La Justicia Sometida al Poder Político." Washington, D.C., April 2012.

Parlamento Andino. *Sistemas Electorales en los Países Andinos.* Bogotá: Parlamento Andino, 1998.

Parlamento y Presupuesto. La Tramitación Legislativa del Presupuesto en el Congreso Uruguayo. Montevideo: CLAEH Instituto Universitario, 1998.

Participación Ciudadana. *Balance del Proceso Electoral 2012.* Participación Ciudadana, Santo Domingo, República Dominicana: Participación Ciudadana , 2012.

Pastor, Robert. *Whirlpool: U.S. Foreign Policy toward Latin America and the Caribbean.* Princeton University Press, 1992.

Patrick, John J., and Robert S. Leming. *Principles and Practices of Democracy in the Education of Social Studies Teachers.* Vol. 1. ERIC Clearing House for Social Studies/Social Science Education, Indiana University, 2001.

Pane, Mark, Daniel Zovatto, Fernando Carrillo, and Andrés Allamand. *Democracies in Development in Latin America.* Washington, D.C.: Inter-American Development Bank and International Institute for Democracy and Electoral Assistance, 2002.

Peannock, J. Roland. *Democratic Political Theory.* Princeton University Press, 1977.

Peeler, John. *Building Democracy in Latin America.* 2nd ed. Edited by Lynne Rienner Publishers. Boulder, Colorado, 2004.

Permanent Council of the OAS. "Situation in Honduras." *Resolution.* Washington, D.C.: Organization of American States, 2009.

Perina, Rubén M. "OEA: La Creciente Irrelevancia de su Observación Electoral." *El Universal*, Junio 24, 2011.

———. "Elecciones Inválidas in Venezuela." *El Universal*, May 3, 2013.

———. "Gobernabilidad Democrática, Sistema de Pesos y Contrapesos y Poder Legislativo." In *Presidencialismo y Parlamentarismo en América Latina*, edited by César Arias and Beatriz Ramacciotti. Washington, D.C.: Center for Latin American Studies, Georgetown University and Departamento de Asuntos Democráticos y Políticos, OEA, 2005.

———. "Hacia Nuevas Funciones y Criterios para las Misiones de Observación Electoral de la OEA." Washington, D.C.: Unpublished internal document for the Department of Democratic and Political Affairs, June 2005.

———. "Informe Verbal Preliminar. Misión de Observación Electoral de la Secretaría General de la OEA. Elecciones Parlamentarias del 4 de diciembre de 2005 en la República Bolivariana de Venezuela." Oral report to the Permanent Council of the OAS, Secretaría General de la OEA, Washington, D.C., 1 de Febrero, 2006.

———. "Elecciones Impugnadas en Venezuela." *Diario Perfil*, 11 de mayo, 2013.

———. "The Inter-American Democratic Charter: An Assessment and Ways to Strengthen it." Edited by Latin American Initiative. Washington, D.C.: Brookings Intitution, 2012.

————. "The Role of the Organization of American States." In *Protecting Democracy: International Responses*, edited by Morton Halperin and Galic Mirna. New York, New York: Lexington Books and the Council on Foreign Relations, 2005.

————. "La nueva presencia argentina en el sistema internacional." In *La Argentina en el Mundo*: 1973–1987, edited by Rubén M. Perina and Roberto Russell Perina. Buenos Aires: Grupo Editor Latinoamericano, 1988.

————. "Los Desafíos de Kerry en la OEA." *Diario Perfil*, 11 de noviembre, 2013.

————. "El Fortalecimiento del Poder Legislativo. El Rol de la OEA." In *Congresos y Democracia en los Países de la Región Andina. Deficiencias y Estrategias*, edited by Arlene B. Tickner and Oscar Mejía Quintana. UPD/OEA y Centro de Estudios Internacionales de la Universidad de los Andes. Bogotá, Colombia, 1997.

————. "Hemisferio Fragmentado." *El País*, 14 de marzo, 2014.

————. "Ganadores y Perdedores en la OEA." *El Universal*, 28 de marzo, 2014.

————. "Sobre Elecciones y Observaciones Electorales de la OEA." *El Universal*, 7 de november, 2005.

————. "Gobernabilidad, Cultura Política y Liderazgo. Esbozo para una Teoría." In *Democracia y Gerencia Política. Innovación en Valores, Instrumentos y Prácticas*, edited by Gerardo Caetano and Rubén M. Perina. Montevideo: CLAEH Instituto Universitario, 2006.

————. "La Carta Democrática Interamericana." *Estudios Internacionales*, 2012.

————. *Los Militares en la Política: Onganía, Levingston y Lanusse*. Buenos Aires: Editorial Universidad de Belgrano, 1983.

————. "Sistemas Electorales y Estabilidad Política." *Ideas en Ciencias Sociales* (Universidad de Belgrano) 3, no. 6 (1984).

Petrova, Tsveta. "How Poland Promotes Democracy." *Journal of Democracy* 23, no. 2 (April 2012).

Pevehouse, Jon C. *Democracy from Above. Regional Organizations and Democratization*. Cambridge University Press, 2005.

Piccone, Theodore. "International Mechanisms for Protecting Democracy." In *Protecting Democracy. International Responses*, edited by Morton Halperin and Galic Mirna. Lexington Books, 2005.

————, ed. *Regime Change by the Book: Constitutional Tools to Preserve Democracy*. Washington, D.C.: Democracy Coalition Project, 2004.

————. "The Democracy Agenda in the Americas: The Case for Multilateral Action." In *Shifting the Balance. Obama and the Americas*, edited by Abraham F. Lowenthal, Theodore, F. Piccone and Laurence Whitehead. Washington, D.C.: Brookings Institution, 2011.

————. "The Multilateral Dimension." *Journal of Democracy* 22, no. 4 (October 2011).

Piccone, Theodore, and Richard Youngs. *Strategies for Democratic Change*. Washington, D.C.: Democracy Coalition Project, 2006.

Pizarro, Crisóstomo, and Eduardo Palma. *Niñez y Democracia*. Bogotá: Editorial Ariel/UNICEF, 1997.

Plattner, Marc. "From Liberalism to Liberal Democracy." *Journal of Democracy* 10 (July 1999).

Pran, Vladimir, and Patrick Merloe. "Monitoring Electronic Technologies in Electoral Processes." Washington, D.C.: National Democratic Institute for International Affairs, 2007.

Pressacco, Carlos, ed. *Democracia en el Mercosur. Instituciones y Cultura Política*. Universidad Alberto Hurtado, 2002.

Przeworski, Adam, Michael Alvarez, José Antonio Cheibub, and Fernando Limongi. *Democracy and Development*. Cambridge University Press, 2000.

Puig, Juan Carlos. *Evolución Histórica de la OEA: Las Tendencias Profundas*. Vols. IX, 32–34, in *La OEA en la Encrucijada*, edited by Instituto de Altos Estudios de América Latina. Caracas: Unversidad Simón Bolívar/Mundo Nuevo, Revista de Estudios Latinoamericanos, 1986.

Putnam, Robert. "Bowling Alone." *The Journal of Democracy* January 1996.

————. "Towards Explaining Military Intervention in Latin America." *World Politics*, October 1976.

Ray, James Lee. "The Democratic Path to Peace." *Journal of Democracy* (The John Hopkins University), no. 2 (April 1997).

Ray, James Lee, and Olga P. Reyes. "The Inter-American System, the OAS and the Future." *Revista Interamericana de Bibliografía* (Department of Cultural Affairs, OAS) XXXIX, no. 4 (1989).

Riquelme, Jorge G., ed. *Desafíos y Oportunidades para la Consolidación de Instituciones, Valores y Prácticas Democráticas en el Mercosur.* Asunción: Viceministerio de la Juventud. Ministerio de Educación y Cultura, 2000.

Rodriguez, Ronny, ed. *Ética Parlamentaria en Centro América y la República Dominicana.* San José: UPD-OEA y IIDH-CAPEL, 2001.

————, ed. *Experiencias de Modernización Legislativa en América Central y República Dominicana.* San José: UPD-OEA y IIDH-CAPEL, 1999.

————, ed. *Los Parlamentos de Centroamérica en la Lucha contra la Corrupción.* FOPREL-UPD, 2001.

————, ed. *Sistema de Elecciones Parlamentarias y su Relación con la Gobernabilidad Democrática en América Central y República Dominicana.* San José: UPD-OEA y IIDH-CAPEL, 2000.

Ronning, C. Neale., ed. *Intervention in Latin America.* New York: Alfred Knopf, 1970.

Russell, J. Dalton, Doh C. Shin, and Willy Jou. "Understanding Democracy: Data from Unlikely Places." *Journal of Democracy* 18 (October 2007).

Russell, Roberto. "The Development of Inter-American Relations in the Past Decade." In *A Decade of Change. Political, Economic and Social Developments in Western Hemisphere Affairs.* Inter-American Dialogue, 2011.

Santiso, Cartlos. "Retos y Desafios de la Reforma de la Ayuda Europea. Mejorando las Respuestas de la Unión Europea a las Crisis de Gobernabilidad y las Erosiones de la Democracia." *Revista Instituciones y Desarrollo* 11 (May 2002): 7–62.

Sartori, Giovani. *Que es la Democracia?* Bogotá: Altamir Ediciones, 1993.

Scheman, Ronald L. *Greater America. A New Partnership for the Americas in the Twenty-first Century.* New York: New York University Press, 2003.

————. *The Inter-American Dilemma. The Search for Inter-American Cooperation at the Centennial of the Inter-American System.* New York: Praeger, 1988.

————. "Rebuilding the OAS: A Program for its Second Century." *Revista Interamericana de Bibliografía* (Department of Cultural Affairs, OAS) XXXIX, no. 4 (1989).

————. *The Alliance for Progress. A Retrospective.* New York: Praeger, 1988.

Schemo, Diana. "Ecuadoran Crisis over Presidency Ends Peacefully." *The New York Times,* February 10, 1997.

Schumpeter, Joseph A. *Capitalism, Socialism and Democracy.* 3rd ed. New York: Harper and Row, 1975.

Second Ad Hoc Meeting of Ministers of Foreign Affairs. Minutes. Washington, D.C.: Organization of American States, June 7, 1993.

Secretaría General de la Décima Conferencia Interamericana. "Conferencias Internacionales Americanas." Washington, D.C.: Departamento Jurídico, Unión Panamericana, 1956.

————. "Conferencias Internacionales Americanas." Washington, D.C.: Carnegie Endowment for International Peace, 1943.

————. "Conferencias Internacionales Americanas, 1889–1936." Washington,D.C.: Carnegie Endowment for Internacional Peace, 1938.

Secretaría General de la OEA. "Informe Anual del Secretario General." Washington, D.C.: Organización de los Estados Americanos: 1991–2002.

————. *Instrumentos Básicos de la Organización de los Estados Americanos.* Washington, D.C.: Subsecretaría de Asuntos Jurídicos, OEA, 1981.

————. *Tratado Interamericano de Asistencia Recíproca (TIAR): Aplicaciones Volumen II 1960–1972.* Washington, D.C.: Secretaría General de la OEA, 1973.

Secretariat for Political Affairs, OAS. *Report of the Electoral Observation Mission in Venezuela. Parliamentary Elections 2005.* General Secretariat, Organization of American States, April 2006.

————. *Tenth Anniversary of the Inter-American Democratic Charter. A Hemispheric Commitment to Democracy.* Washington, D.C: Organization of American States, 2011.

Secretary General of the OAS. *Note from the Secretary General of the OAS to the Chair of the Permanent Council Concerning Comments and Observations of the United States Senate Committee on Foreign Relations in Regard to the Organization.* Organization of American States, Washington, D.C.: Permanent Council, 21 November 2012.

————. *OAS: Peace, Security, Democracy and Development.* General Secretariat, Organization of American States, Washington, D.C.: Organization of American States, 2012, 112.

————. *Promotion and Strengthening of Democracy: Follow-up to the Inter-American Democratic Charter.* Office of the Secretary General, Organization of American States (OAS), Washington, D.C.: OAS, May 2010.

————. *Strategic Vision of the OAS.* Report, Permanent Council of the OAS, Organization of American States, Washington, D.C.: Permanent Council of the OAS, April 2013.

Sen, Amartya. "Democracy as a Universal Value." *Journal of Democracy* 10 (July 1999).

————. *Development as Freedom.* New York: Anchor Books, 1999.

Shaw, Caroline M. "The United States: Rhetoric and Reality." In *Promoting Democracy in the Americas,* edited by Thomas Lengler, Sharon F. Lean and Dexter Boniface. Baltimore: The Johns Hopkins University, 2007.

————. *Cooperation, Conflict and Consensus in the Organization of American States.* New York: Palgrave Macmillan, 2004.

————. "Limits to Hegemonic Influence in the Organization of American States." *Latin American Politics and Society* 45, no. 3 (2003).

Shifter, Michael. "Crisis in Honduras." *Statement before the Committee on Foreign Affairs, Western Hemisphere Subcommittee.* Washington, D.C., July 2009.

————. "Democracy in Venezuela: Unsettling as Ever." *The Washington Post*, April 21, 2002.

Sikkink, Cathryn. "Nongovernmental Organizations, Democracy and Human Rights in Latin America." In *Beyond Sovereignty. Collectively Defending Democracy in the Americas.* Baltimore: The Johns Hopkins University Press, 1996.

Slater, Jerome. *The OAS and United States Foreign Policy.* Ohio State University Press, 1967.

Smith, Peter H. *Talons of the Eagles. Latin America, the United States and the World.* 3rd ed. New York: Oxford University Press, 2008.

Smith, Peter H. *Democracy in Latin America.* Oxford University Press, 2005.

Smith, Tony. "The Alliance for Progress: The 1960s." In *Exporting Democracy: The United States and Latin America,* edited by Abraham Lowenthal. Baltimore: The Johns Hopkins University, 1991.

Snyder, Glenn H. "Mearsheimer's Word: Offensive Realism and The Struggle for Security. A Review Essay on John J. Mearsheimer, The Tragedy of Great Powers. New York, W.W. Norton 2001." *International Security* 27, no. 1 (Summer 2002).

Soto Cárdenas, Alejandro. *La Influencia de la Independencia de los Estados Unidos en la Constitución de las Nacionales Latinoamericanas.* Washington, D.C.: Secretaría General de la Organización de los Estados Americanos, 1979.

Stepan, Alfred. *The Military in Politics.* Princeton University Press, 1971.

Stoetzer, Carlos. *The Organization of American States.* Westport, CT: Praeger, 1993.

Strange, Susan. "A Critique of Regime Analysis." In *International Regimes,* edited by Stephen Krasner. Ithaca: Cornell University Press, 1983.

Subcommittee on American Republics Affairs of the Committee on Foreign Relations. "Survey of the Alliance for Progress." *Compilation of Studies and Hearings.* Washington, D.C.: U.S. Government Printing Office, 1969.

Tesón, Fernando. "Changing Perceptions of Domestic Jurisdiction and Intervention." In *Beyond Sovereignty. Collectively Defending Demcracy in the Americas,* edited by Tom Farer. Baltimore: The Johns Hopkins University, 1996.

The Carter Center. *Criteria for Assessing Democratic Elections. Discussion Paper.* The Carter Center, Atlanta, Georgia: The Carter Center, 2007.

————. "Resumen Ejecutivo del Informe final (sobre Referendum Presidencial)." The Carter Center, 2004.

The Human Rights Foundation. *The Facts and The Law Behind the Democratic Crisis in Honduras, 2009.* The Human Rights Foundation, New York: The Human Rights Foundation, March 2010.

The Inter-American Dialogue. "Responding to the Hemisphere's Political Challenge. Report of the Inter-American Dialogue Task Force on the OAS." Inter-American Dialogue: Washington, D.C., 2006.

The New Republic. "The Best-Do-Nothing Congress Money Can Buy." *The New Republic,* April 7, 1997.

The Washington Post. "The State of the Union." January 24, 2007.

The World Bank. *Itinerary for the World Bank in Latin America and the Caribbean. What does Reform of the State Mean for the World Bank?* Washington, D.C.: The World Bank, 1996.

Tickner, Arlene, and Oscar Mejía Quintana. *Congresos y Democracia en los Paises de la Región Andina.* Bogotá: Ediciones Uniandes, Universidad de los Andes, 1997.

Tilly, Charles. *Democracy.* New York: Cambridge University Press, 2007.

Tokatlian, Juan. "Bye, Bye Monroe, Hello Troilo." *El País,* November 13, 2013.

Tomasek, Robert D. "The Organization of American States and Dispute Settlement from 1948 to 1981. An Assessment." *Inter-American Review of Bibliography* (Department of Cultural Affairs, OAS) XXXIX, no. 4 (1989): 461–476.

Torre, Juan Carlos. "Transformaciones de la Sociedad Argentina." In *Argentina 1910–2010,* edited by Roberto Russell. Buenos Aires: Taurus, 2010.

Unidad para la Promoción de la Democracia (UPD-OEA). *Manual de Relaciones Legislativas con la Prensa.* Washington, D.C.: UPD-OEA, 2003.

———. *La Crisis Institutional de 1996 en el Paraguay.* Organización de los Estados Americanos, Washington, D.C.: UPD-OEA, 1996.

———. "Manual para la Organización de Misiones de Observación Electoral." Washington, D.C.: UPD-OEA, 1998.

———. *Observaciones Electorales en el Perú. 9 de Abril del 2000.* Washington, D.C.: UPD-OEA , 2002, 172.

———. *Proyecto de Plan de Trabajo.* Unidad para la Promoción de la Democracia-UPD, Washington, D.C.: Consejo Permanente de la OEA, 13 January 2004.

———. *Programa de Apoyo a las Instituciones Legislativas (PAFIL).* Washington, D. C.: Unidad para la Promoción de la Democracia (UPD-OEA), 2004.

Unit for the Promotion of Democracy (UPD-OAS). *Report of the General Secretariat to the Permanent Council of the OAS on the Activities of the Unit for Promotion of Democracy-UPD.* Permanent Council of the OAS, Washington, D.C.: Permanent Council of the OAS, May 21, 1996.

United Nations. *UN Democracy Fund: A First Year Analysis.* New York: United Nations, 2006.

United Nations Development Program (UNDP). *Democracy in Latin America. Towards a Citizen's Democracy.* UNDP, New York: UNDP, 2004, 26–30.

———. *Human Development Report 2002. Deepening Democracy in a Fragmented World.* New York, 2002.

Vaky, Viron P., and Heraldo Muñoz. *The Future of the Organization of American States.* New York: Twentieth Century Fund, 1993.

Valencia, Laura. "Representatividad, Legitimidad y Credibilidad Parlamentaria." *Revista Mexicana de Ciencias Políticas y Sociales* (Universidad Nacional Autónoma de Mexico), no. 162 (1995).

Valenzuela, Arturo. "Latin American Presidencies Interrupted." In *Presidencialismo y Parlamentarismo en America Latina.* Washington, D.C.: Centro de Esudios Latinoamericanos, Georgetown University and Departamento de Asuntos Democráticos y Políticos, Organización de los Estados Americanos, 2005.

Valenzuela, Arturo. "The Coup that Didn't Happen." *Journal of Democracy* 8 (January 1997).

———. "Bush's Betrayal of Democracy." *The Washington Post,* April 16, 2002.

Vial, Alejandro, ed. *El Poder Legislativo y los Nuevos Desafíos de la Democracia en el Mercosur.* Asunción: Universidad Americana del Paraguay , 2001.

Vickey, Chad, ed. *Guidelines for Understanding, Adjudicating, and Resolving Disputes Elections.* International Foundation for Electoral Systems (IFES), 2011.

Villagrán, Francisco. *La Crisis Constitutional en Guatemala. La Respuesta de la OEA y de la Sociedad Civil en la Defensa de la Democracia.* Washington, D.C.: Institute of Peace, 1993.

von Meijenfeld, Roel. "Democracy Promotion in the new International Context." *Conference on Global Promotion of Democracy and Human Rights, Finnish Institute of International Affairs.* Helsinki, Finland, 2012.

Weyland, Kurt. "The Threat from the Populist Left." *Journal of Democracy* 24, no. 3 (July 2013).

Whitaker, Arthur P. *The Western Hemisphere Idea: Its Rise and Decline.* Ithaca: Cornell University Press, 1954.

Wilson, Larman C. "The OAS and Promoting and Resolving Disputes." *Revista Interamericana de Bibliografía* (Department of Cultural Affairs, OAS) XXXIX, no. 4 (1989).

Wolf, Jonas. "Challenges to Democracy Promotion: The Case of Bolivia." The Carnegie Endowment for International Peace, Washington, D.C., 2011.

Wolfowitz, Paul. *Good Governance and Development: A Time for Action.* Office of the President, World Bank, Washington, D.C.: World Bank, 2006.

Young, Oran. "Political Leadership and Regime Formation: On the Development of Institutions in International Society." *International Organization* 45, no. 3 (1991).

Youngs, Richard. "Trends in Democracy Assistance. What has Europe been doing?" *Journal of Democracy* 19 , no. 2 (April 2008): 160–169.

Zakaria, Fareed. *The Post American World.* New York: W.W. Norton and Co, 2008.

———. "The Rise of Illiberal Democracy." *Foreign Affairs* 76 (November/December 1997).

About the Author

Rubén M. Perina currently teaches a course on the OAS and democracy promotion at the George Washington University's Elliott School of International Affairs and has taught at Georgetown University. As a former high official of the OAS, between 1990 and 2010, he directed several democracy assistance programs and led electoral observations missions in Colombia, Dominican Republic, Guatemala, Paraguay and Venezuela. He has published several books and articles related to the subject, and he holds a Ph. D. in International Relations from the University of Pennsylvania. He is a native of Argentina and resides in Washington, D.C.